How to Grade
for Learning

For information:

Corwin Press
A Sage Publications Company
2455 Teller Road
Thousand Oaks, California 91320
www.corwinpress.com

Sage Publications Ltd.
1 Oliver's Yard
55 City Road
London EC1Y 1SP
United Kingdom

Sage Publications India Pvt. Ltd.
B-42, Panchsheel Enclave
New Delhi 110 017 India

Printed in the United States of America

ISBN 978-1-57517-816-5

This book is printed on acid-free paper.

07 08 09 10 9 8 7 6

How to Grade for Learning

Linking Grades to Standards

Second Edition

Ken O'Connor

Foreword by Rick Stiggins

CORWIN PRESS
A SAGE Publications Company
Thousand Oaks, California

Dedication

To my parents, the late Hugh and Lorraine O'Connor, who believed in me in a way that gave me the confidence to be a risk taker and a challenger of the status quo;

To my wife, Marilyn, and my children, Jeremy and Bronwyn, who have provided me with the ongoing support and encouragement that made it possible for me to write this book;

To the Scarborough Board of Education (Ontario, Canada), which was my wonderful professional "home" for more than twenty years. Unfortunately, it no longer exists as it was merged with five other school districts on January 1, 1998, to become the Toronto District School Board; and

To Nancy McMunn who, with selfless devotion, has provided such wonderful leadership to the cause of improving classroom assessment. Her energy and passion in the face of considerable personal difficulty are truly inspiring.

Contents

Foreword

Early in our daughter Krissy's third grade school year, she arrived home after school with a paper in her hand and a tear in her eye. She was carrying a "story" she had written. Her assignment was to write about something or someone that she cared about. She gave it to her mom and me with obvious trepidation.

As we read, we found the touching tale of the kitten named Kelly who came to be a part of our family briefly and then had to go home to the farm because of allergies and because she was just too aggressive. Krissy had wanted a kitten so badly and was so sad about losing her special new friend. The story clearly reflected the work of an emergent writer. As unsophisticated as it was, it captured the emotions of the event. It was quite touching. Krissy's six or seven sentences filled about two-thirds of the sheet of paper. In the space below the story at the bottom of the sheet, there appeared a very big, very red F. So naturally, my wife and I asked why Krissy had been assigned a failing grade.

Her reply triggered some very strong emotions within both of us when Krissy replied with a tear in her eye, "The teacher told us that we were to fill the page, and I didn't do that. And so she said I didn't follow directions and I failed. I don't think I'll ever be a good writer anyway . . . ." As our disappointed little writer walked off, my wife and I could only shake our heads in wonder and fury.

We both know and understand that all classroom teachers face immense classroom assessment, record keeping, and communication challenges. We empathized. First, they must establish rigorous but realistic achievement expectations for each student. Then, they must provide opportunities for students to learn to meet those expectations. Next, the teacher must transform those achievement targets into high-quality assessments, in order to determine the level of student success. Finally, the teacher must transform assessment results into accurate information for those who need access to it and communicate that information in a complete, timely, and understandable form to those users.

Each of these steps can be carried out using sound or unsound practices. If teachers use sound practices, students can prosper. If they use unsound practices, students suffer the consequences. In other words, if achievement expectations are inappropriate (e.g., too high or too low) for a student, the learning environment will be counterproductive. If assessments are of poor quality, inaccurate information and poor instructional decisions will follow. When communication procedures fail, students will have great difficulty succeeding academically.

Krissy's teacher made it part way through this gauntlet of challenges. She wanted her students to write well—an important achievement target. She obviously provided her students with opportunities to write because Krissy had written her story. The assessment could have been of high quality because she relied on a direct performance assessment of writing proficiency. But from here on, the teaching, assessment, and communication processes clearly broke down.

In this book, Ken O' Connor gives voice to many of the things that went wrong in this case. Although he centers on the process of communicating about student achievement through the use of report card grades, Ken puts the grading process into a larger context. He gives attention to each of the other keys to success. He argues convincingly for an open and honest educational system—a system in which there are no surprises and no excuses. He advocates the careful articulation of appropriate achievement expectations and the unconditional sharing of those targets with students and their families. He demands rigorous achievement standards and accurate ongoing classroom assessments of student success. Finally, Ken spells out concrete procedures for transforming assessment results into grades that communicate in a timely and understandable way.

The practical guidelines offered in this book help teachers design and conduct grading practices that help students feel in control of their own academic success. These guidelines can keep students from feeling that sense of hopelessness that Krissy felt. Every teacher's goal must be to implement grading practices that lead students to feel that they can succeed if they try.

RICK STIGGINS
ASSESSMENT TRAINING INSTITUTE, PORTLAND, OREGON

Preface

In May 1990, I had the good fortune to attend a train-the-trainer workshop given by Rick Stiggins in Toronto. This sparked in me a general interest in classroom assessment, but the aspect of the workshop that really "turned me on" was the part on grading. Since then, I have read everything that I could find about grading. I also watched the passage of my own children through the school system. Each of these influences convinced me that what is needed is a practical set of grading guidelines that support learning and that teachers could apply at the classroom level, that is, in their grade books and computer grading programs.

I began to think seriously about guidelines for grading when I became one of three authors of *Assess for Success* for the Ontario Secondary School Teachers' Federation in July 1993 (Midwood, O'Connor, and Simpson 1993). What led to the real development of the guidelines was a journal article, which I read in April 1994 and which I thought was both wrong and internally inconsistent. I wrote to the editor making these criticisms, and she wrote back suggesting I write an article. At first, I ignored this suggestion, but several months later, she sent me the author's response to my criticism and again suggested that I write an article. Twice challenged, I had to respond, so I spent most of my 1994 Christmas vacation writing an article, which appeared in the May 1995 edition of the *NASSP* (National Association of Secondary Schools Principals) *Bulletin.*

Since that time, I have created staff development workshops based on the article. I have presented these workshops many times in schools and at conferences in the United States and Canada. Most of these workshops were well received and, at all of them, I received interesting comments in the session evaluations. These comments convinced me to try to reach a wider audience by turning my article and workshops into a book on grading. This I did with the first edition, which I completed in September 1998. Three years later, it was time to update and revise the book, especially to reflect the move to the results or standards-based approach to teaching and learning.

What's the Purpose of This Book?

Much of what teachers do is because that is the way it was done to them; this is no longer good enough. It is my hope that this book will lead teachers to critically examine their grading practices. Some of the ideas in this book challenge long-held beliefs and practices and create considerable cognitive dissonance.

Glickman (as cited in Bailey and McTighe 1996) said, "There are profound questions about current educational practices that need to debated" (119). The educational journal article titles and quotations on the first page of the introduction in this book demonstrate clearly that grades and grading are practices that need to be debated. Even though there are many journal articles and book chapters on the topic, grading is an aspect of education that is discussed very little by practitioners. At the four annual meetings of the Association of Supervision and Curriculum Development (ASCD) from 1996 to 1999, only 16 of more than 2,400 sessions mentioned grading in the title or description! It appears that teachers consider grading to be a private activity, thus "guarding [their] practices with the same passion with which one might guard an unedited diary" (Kain 1996, 569).

This book examines the many issues around grading and provides a set of practical guidelines that teachers may use to arrive at grades for their students. Teachers from kindergarten to college can use the ideas in this book to examine and perhaps change their own grading practices, and, even more important, to focus their discussion of this complex, confusing, and difficult issue with colleagues.

How Is This Book Organized?

An introduction sets the big picture for this book and gives readers an opportunity to identify and examine grading practices and the issues that arise from these practices. These practical grading issues lead to the need for guidelines,

and subsequent chapters provide eight guidelines. These are practical guidelines, not just broad general principles. They are important to consider as a set, but each also needs to be considered individually, which is done in chapters 1 through 8. Each of these chapters addresses three questions: What is the purpose of the guideline? What are the key elements of the guideline? What is the bottom line?

At the end of each of these guideline chapters, a reflection activity, What's My Thinking Now?, asks readers to think about the guideline and its importance and meaning to them. An example of one person's reflections on that particular guideline conclude the chapters on guidelines.

Chapter 9 provides suggestions for determining grades by bringing the application of the guidelines together. Chapter 10 examines a number of additional grading issues, including the advantages and disadvantages of different grading approaches, grade point average calculation, the use of computer grading programs, how to grade exceptional students, and legal concerns. Chapter 11 examines the broader aspects of communicating student achievement, considering topics such as expanded format reporting, informal communications, and student-involved conferencing. Conclusions and recommended actions are provided in chapter 12. In the appendices, a glossary, guidelines for grading in standards-based systems, a proposed grading policy, and an extensive bibliography provide additional information for the reader.

Changes in the Second Edition

To reflect the increasing importance of standards, the guidelines have been reorganized in this second edition. Two guidelines focus directly on the standards and their use in grading: what grades are based on (formerly guideline 4) and the reference points for determining grades (formerly guideline 6). These have been moved to be guidelines 1 and 2 respectively. The other guidelines, except for 7 and 8, have been renumbered, so 1 becomes 3, 2 becomes 4, 3 becomes 5, and 5 becomes 6. In a standards-based system, the quality of assessment becomes increasingly important. I seriously considered moving guideline 7 to number 1 or 3, but knowing the huge amount of work that has been done to improve teachers' assessment literacy, I decided to leave it where it is in the sequence.

The guidelines have been reorganized as follows:

- Guideline 1 (formerly guideline 4)
- Guideline 2 (formerly guideline 6)
- Guideline 3 (formerly guideline 1)
- Guideline 4 (formerly guideline 2)
- Guideline 5 (formerly guideline 3)
- Guideline 6 (formerly guideline 5)
- Guideline 7 (no change)
- Guideline 8 (no change)

Other important changes in this edition include:

- the addition of a section on standards in the introduction
- a new chapter 9 which describes how I believe grades should be "put together" in standards-based systems
- the inclusion of a number of expanded format report cards that have been designed to be used with standards-based curricula

How Can This Book Be Used?

The most important way to use this book is with an open mind; regardless of how many or few years of experience teachers have, they may use this book to critically examine their own practices. Throughout the book, readers will find reflection opportunities, which, it is hoped, they will use to engage themselves more thoroughly with the text. Consider creating a journal to record your thoughts in response to the questions posed in these reflection activities.

Engaging with the text can be done individually, but it is more beneficial if done in groups (e.g., the whole staff in a small school, learning teams, department or division groups, etc.). This is particularly important for the detailed analysis of each guideline at the end of chapters 1 through 8. Remember, when changing practices, start small; adapt, do not adopt; and work together. When you have finished the book, you are encouraged to complete the overview reflection at the end of chapter 12. For this book to be of real value,

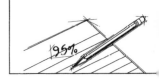

teachers must use it to critically examine and discuss the almost taboo subject of grading. It is hoped that this will lead teachers to use grading practices presented in the eight guidelines. To further encourage your interest, here are my top ten readings, which I think will be particularly helpful to you (see the bibliography for complete citation):

- "It's a Good Score: Just a Bad Grade" by R. L. Canady and P. R. Hotchkiss (1989)
- *Developing Grading and Reporting Systems for Student Learning* by T. R. Guskey and J. Bailey (2001)
- "Group Grades Miss the Mark" by S. Kagan (1995)
- "Grading: The Issue Is Not How But Why" by A. Kohn (1994)
- *Transforming Classroom Grading* by R. Marzano (2000a)
- "Guidelines for Grading that Support Learning and Student Success" by K. O'Connor (1995)
- *Student Involved Classroom Assessment* (3rd ed.) by R. J. Stiggins (2001b)
- *Honesty and Fairness: Toward Better Grading and Reporting* by G. Wiggins (1996)
- "Are Letter Grades Obsolete?" by S. Willis (1993)
- "Success for All: The Median Is the Key" by R. G. Wright (1994)

Acknowledgments

During the past eleven years, I have been on a journey—a journey of learning about assessment. This journey has been assisted by many people; it was initiated and supported over the years by Lorna Earl, formerly the research director of the Scarborough Board of Education; it was jump-started by attending train-the-trainer workshops given by Rick Stiggins, who has continued to nurture my journey by his interest in and encouragement for my work; and it was moved forward by attending workshops given by Kay Burke and Jay McTighe and by the opportunity to learn from professional friendships with Kay and Jay, as well as with Judy Arter, Kathy Busick, Anne Davies, Nancy McMunn, and Patricia Schenck. On an almost daily basis, I was assisted by Marg Daniel and Dennis Gerrard, my colleagues in the Program Department of the Scarborough Board of Education in Ontario, Canada. Other colleagues who helped me greatly include Angela Boyd, Carol Rocks, George Huff, and Peter Lipman. My journey would not have happened without my "bosses," Rollit Goldring, John Reynolds, and John Donofrio, who provided me with advice and opportunities inside and outside Scarborough.

I also benefited greatly from my ongoing collaboration with Damian Cooper then with the Halton Board of Education and Dale Midwood of the then Frontenac County Board of Education. My understanding of the practical realities of classroom assessment was enhanced by the members of the Evaluation Policy Committee of the Scarborough Board of Education and by many Scarborough administrators and teachers, especially Stella Dasko, Anita Desrosiers, Lesley Dyce, Lynn Lemieux, and Cathy Pickard. Anita, Lesley, and Lynn particularly helped me to understand assessment issues from the K–6 perspective, which is lacking from my professional background. I also gratefully acknowledge the Ontario Secondary School Teachers' Federation, which gave me my first assessment "immersion" opportunity when I was chosen to be one of the authors of *Assess for Success*. People whose work I admire and have learned from include Robert Lynn Canady, Art Costa, Robin Fogarty, Forest Gathercoal, Tom Guskey, Alfie Kohn, Bob Marzano, Jim Popham, Douglas Reeves, Spence Rogers, and Grant Wiggins. I must also express my appreciation to Rowan Amott and the staff of the Scarborough Board of Education's Professional Library who assisted me greatly finding references to enhance my workshops and my writing. I must also acknowledge my colleagues from the fourteen-month period I worked half-time in the assessment unit of the Curriculum and Assessment Policy Branch of the Ontario Ministry of Education; working at the interesting intersection between politics and education with Bruce Brydges, Micki Clemens, Marg Daniel, and Clay Lafleur was a very valuable experience which helped me to understand better what is possible and practical.

Last but not least, I must also acknowledge two school districts I have had the privilege to work with on an ongoing basis: Bay District Schools in Panama City, Florida, and the Algoma District School Board in northern Ontario. Both districts have put an amazing commitment into the professional growth of their teachers in the area of grading. I have benefited greatly from my opportunities to work with teachers in these districts, and I would like to acknowledge the leadership of Patricia Schenck, Beth Deluzain, and Lendy Willis from Bay and Gillan Richards and Mario Turco from Algoma.

There are many others I probably should acknowledge, including all those who have attended my workshops.

Although I gratefully acknowledge the contributions of all people mentioned, the responsibility for the views expressed in this book is mine and mine alone. The clarity of these views, however, is only partly due to my writing; I must acknowledge the huge contribution of my editors, Dara Lee Howard, Anne Kaske, and Kathy Siebel. It has been a delight to work with them and to see what professional editors can do to improve the original manuscript. I would also like to acknowledge Sue Schumer and Jean Ward, the acquisitions editors who made this book possible; Donna Ramirez and Carrie Straka, who helped coordinate the manuscript; and the rest of SkyLight Professional Development.

KEN O'CONNOR
SCARBOROUGH, ONTARIO

"Our knowledge base on grading is quite extensive and offers us clear guidelines for better practice." —Guskey and Bailey (2001, 145)

"Grading is not an exact science."—Judge Davis (in Bissinger 1990, 309)

"School has come to be about the grades rather than the learning." —Conklin (2001, 3)

Meets Standards

Proficient

...ellent!

"Grades are not inherently bad. It is their misuse and misinterpretation that is bad."—Guskey (1993, 7)

"Grading seems to be such an intractable problem—Trumbull and Farr (2000, xiii)

"What grades offer is spurious precision, a subjective rating masquerading as an objective assessment." —Kohn (1993b, 201)

"To ban grades entirely would be an overreaction to a flawed practice. —Busick (in Trumbull and Farr 2000, 72)

A+ 100%

"Grades are so imprecise that they are almost meaningless."—Marzano (2000a, 1)

"Letter grades have acquired an almost cult-like importance in American schools." —Olson (1995, 23)

Introduction

"I absolutely loathed giving grades to my students."—Farr (in Trumbull and Farr 2000, xiv)

"Many common grading practices . . . make it difficult for many youngsters to feel successful in school."—Canady and Hotchkiss (1989, 68)

"A lot of current practice in grading and reporting is shamefully inadequate" —Guskey and Bailey (2001, 1)

What Grading Terminology Is Needed?

REFLECTING ON . . . TITLES AND QUOTES

Ask yourself the following questions:
- ▶ What is your reaction to the titles and quotes about grades on page 1?
- ▶ What do they say about grading?
- ▶ How do you think your colleagues, students, parents, and community would react to them?

As the titles and quotes about grading on the previous page show, grading raises many concerns. One communication concern is grading terminology. The term *grading* carries different meanings for different people, while other words, such as *marking*, may sometimes mean grading, too. As McTighe and Ferrara (1995) stated, "Terms [are] frequently used interchangeably, although they should have distinct meanings" (11). Discussion of any issue or principle must proceed from a clear understanding of the meaning of the terms being used. In support of this goal, a glossary is provided at the end of the book. At this point, readers need a shared understanding of two critical terms: *grades* (or grading) and *marks* (or marking). These terms are often used interchangeably, although *grading* is used more frequently in the United States and *marking* more commonly in Canada.

REFLECTING ON . . . TERMINOLOGY

Ask yourself the following questions:
- ▶ What do you understand by the terms *grades* and *grading*?
- ▶ What do you understand by the terms *marks* and *marking*?
- ▶ Are they the same? Are they different? How?

The problem is that the terms *grades* and *grading* are often used with two meanings. For a careful analysis, it is critical to have a clear meaning for each term. In this book, grading and marking are used as follows:

> Grade(s) or grading—the number or letter reported at the end of a period of time as a summary statement of student performance.
> Mark(s) or marking—the number, letter, or words placed on any single student assessment (test, performance task, etc.).

Airasian (1994) used grading to mean "making a judgment about the quality of a pupil's performance, whether it is performance on a single assessment or performance across many assessments" (281). In most writings, the context makes clear which meaning is intended. However, this is not always the case, and, when the meaning is not clear, confusion and lack of clarity in analysis and discussion requires that the two activities be distinguished by using separate terms.

Anderson and Wendel (1988) defined marks and grades exactly opposite to the definitions used here. They agree, though, that defining terms is essential, so that "everyone operates under the same assumptions and knows exactly what meanings underlie those assumptions" (36–37).

Another definition was provided by Paul Dressel (as cited in Kohn 1993b):

> A grade can be regarded only as an inadequate report of an inaccurate judgment by a biased and variable judge of the extent to which a student has attained an undefined level of mastery of an unknown proportion of an indefinite amount of material. (201)

What Is the Context of Grading?

According to *Breaking Ranks,* the penetrating analysis of secondary schools published by the National Association of Secondary School Principals in 1996, "Teachers will integrate assessment into instruction so that assessment does not merely measure students, but becomes part of the learning process itself" (25). This quote eloquently summarizes the shift in thinking about assessment that has occurred since the 1980s and shows that a different understanding has developed about the learning process and the changes that have taken place in our economic world.

Constructivist Theories of Learning

One important understanding has been the development of constructivist theories of learning. Constructivism recognizes that learning is a process in which the learner builds personal meaning by adding new understanding to old on the basis of each new experience. This means that "learning is not linear . . . Instead, learning occurs at a very uneven pace and proceeds in many different directions at once" (Burke 1993, xiv).

Individuals experience meaningful learning when they have the opportunity to process information and relate it to their own experiences. This has significant implications for how the teaching/learning process takes place in schools.

> Learners should be able to construct meaning for themselves, reflect on the significance of the meaning, and self-assess to determine their own strengths and weaknesses. Integrated curricula, cooperative learning, problem-based learning, and whole language are just a few examples of curricula that help students construct knowledge for themselves. (Burke 1993, xiv)

Each of these approaches requires more complex assessment than traditional approaches, which emphasize simple scoring of answers or behaviors as right or wrong. More varied approaches to assessment imply that teachers will not always have neat numbers that can be "crunched" and converted into grades. Grading, therefore, also becomes a more complex activity. Teachers need to consider carefully how they will incorporate data from a broader array of assessments into their students' grades. Guidelines presented in this book help teachers do this because they are designed to support varied approaches to learning and to encourage student success, however it is demonstrated.

Brain-Based Research

The constructivist view of learning has been supported and expanded by what is often called brain-based research. This research has demonstrated that the way the brain works is much more complex than was previously acknowledged in theories of learning. Brain research shows that the ability to learn is significantly influenced by coping with emotions and the environment, by teaching the skills of thinking, and by encouraging metacognition—thinking about thinking.

The classroom environment that best facilitates the full development of the intelligences is sometimes called "brain compatible." For the brain to function fully, it is beneficial for the classroom to provide five elements: trust and belonging, meaningful content, enriched environment, intelligent choices, and adequate time. (Chapman 1993, 9)

Assessment and grading practices need to be "brain compatible." Brain-compatible assessment results from paying attention to the same elements:

Trust and belonging occurs when students are comfortable undertaking assessment activities. Students need to be in a familiar environment with opportunities to practice each assessment type before the real assessment. It has been demonstrated that unless they have had an opportunity to practice a high-stress activity in an unfamiliar environment, students perform better on the SAT when they do the test in their own classroom rather than in the school gym or cafeteria. Grading can be made brain compatible by using second chance assessment and by using the most recent information. (See chapter 5.)

Meaningful content and *enriched environment*, from an assessment point of view, mean that teachers provide assessment that promotes learning, not just assessment that is easy to score.

Intelligent choices in assessment means that teachers do not require students to demonstrate their achievement in the same way as other students; students have some choice in how they are assessed.

Adequate time refers to students' need for time to become comfortable with approaches to instruction and assessment that are new to them. It also means that students need sufficient time to be able to demonstrate their knowledge and skills in assessment situations. Students should only be required to perform in strict time-limited assessment situations if time is a critical element of the achievement being assessed. Reflective learners and slow writers often receive lower grades than they deserve as a result of being required to perform in inappropriately time-limited assessments. (This issue is addressed in greater detail in chapter 5.)

Each element of brain-compatible assessment requires that teachers be very flexible in their approach to assessment and grading. If teachers are more flexible, then there will be a greater variety of information to incorporate into their summary judgments. The guidelines in this book are designed to provide teachers with an approach to grading that allows for more than number crunching.

> **T**wo rules of thumb come from the field of brain research and enrichment. One is to eliminate the threat, and the other is to enrich like crazy.
>
> (Jensen 1998)

Multiple Intelligences

In the past, intelligence was seen as a singular entity, relatively fixed and easily measured. Gardner (1983) demonstrated that, rather than one fixed entity, there are at least eight intelligences:

- Verbal/linguistic—words, listening, speaking, dialogues, poems
- Visual/spatial—images, drawings, doodles, puzzles, visualization
- Logical/mathematical—reasoning, facts, sequencing, judging, ranking
- Musical/rhythmic—melody, beat, rap, pacing, blues, classical, jingles
- Bodily/kinesthetic—activity, try, do, perform, touch, feel, participate
- Interpersonal—interact, communicate, charisma, socialize, empathize
- Intrapersonal—self, solitude, create, brood, write, dream, set goals
- Naturalist—nature, observe, classify, hike, climb, trees, ecosystem

Knowledge of multiple intelligences requires that teachers focus on how smart students are in different ways; the focus is no longer on "how smart," but "how one is smart." Gardner believes that each person's mix of intelligences produces a unique cognitive profile. Educators should ensure that children learn by building on their strengths. Teaching to or through each of the intelligences gives students whose strengths have been undervalued in schools far greater opportunity to succeed.

Understanding multiple intelligences also means that teachers use a wide variety of instructional and assessment activities. One of the best ways to acknowledge individual differences is to encourage students to develop portfolios—purposeful collections of their work—that can show strengths, weaknesses, growth, and progress over time. See Figure Intro.1 for ways to use multiple intelligences in both instructional and assessment activities. This figure dramatically illustrates the links that can be made and the incredible variety of activities that are available to teachers to promote student success.

Each of these areas of understanding—constructivism, brain-based research, and multiple intelligences—has contributed to the realization that, in the past, educators have held a very narrow view of learning and knowledge and that this view now needs to be broadened dramatically. Teachers, for example, have focused most commonly on only two intelligences, verbal/linguistic and logical/mathematical, to the exclusion of the other six; students whose strengths are in the other intelligences have frequently not done well in school.

Portfolio Activities and Assessments for the Multiple Intelligences

Verbal/ Linguistic	Logical/ Mathematical	Visual/ Spatial	Bodily/ Kinesthetic
· tape recordings of readings · reactions to guest speakers · autobiographies · reactions to films or videos · scripts for radio shows · list of books read · annotated bibliographies	· puzzles · patterns and their relationships · mathematical operations · formulas/abstract symbols · analogies · time lines · Venn diagrams · original word problems	· artwork · photographs · math manipulatives · graphic organizers · posters, charts, graphics, pictures · illustrations · sketches · props for plays · storyboards	· field trips · role playing · learning centers · labs · sports/games · simulations · presentations · dances
Musical/ Rhythmic	Interpersonal	Intrapersonal	Naturalist
· background music in class · songs for books, countries, people · raps, jingles, cheers, poems · musical mnemonics · choral readings · tone patterns · music and dance of different cultures · musical symbols	· group videos, films, filmstrips · team computer programs · cooperative task trios · round robins · jigsaws · wraparounds · electronic mail · class and group discussions · group projects · group presentations	· problem-solving strategies · goal setting · reflective logs · divided journals · metacognitive reflections · independent reading time · silent reflections time · self-evaluations	· outdoor education · environmental studies · field trips · photographs of nature · research on ecosystems · debates on environmental issues · poems about nature

Figure Intro.1   From p. 73 of *The Portfolio Connection: Student Work Linked to Standards,* 2nd Edition, by Kay Burke, Robin Fogarty, and Susan Belgrad. © 2002, 1994 SkyLight Training and Publishing, Inc. Reprinted by permission of SkyLight Professional Development, www.skylightedu.com or (800) 348-4474.

World Economy

The world economy has changed dramatically in the 1990s and the pace of the change has continued into the new century. Globalization has given unprecedented freedom based on comparative advantage to the flow of capital and jobs between countries. For the developed world, the manufacturing sector has declined, and the service or tertiary sector, which requires higher levels of skill and knowledge, has enjoyed a huge increase. Thus, far fewer jobs are available for those who do not complete high school. The sorting function of schools—creating categories of those who leave early and find low-skill jobs, those who complete high school, and those who go on to postsecondary education—does not have the value that it did in the past. What schools now have is the orientation and expectation that students will succeed. Educators consider themselves to be in "the success business," ensuring that students have real opportunity available to them and that the economy has sufficient skilled and knowledgeable people to continue to function efficiently and effectively.

Standards

The decade of the 1990s saw a huge change in how curriculum is determined. By the end of the decade, forty-nine of fifty American states, most educational jurisdictions in Canada, and many jurisdictions in other parts of the world had developed mandatory standards for curriculum content. These "standards" have a variety of titles including standards, expectations, outcomes, learning results, or learning goals. They describe, with varying degrees of clarity and specificity, what students are expected to know and be able to do at different stages in K–12 schooling. The distinguishing characteristic of these statements compared with previous organizers for curriculum content is that the focus is on outputs—what students will know and do—rather than on inputs—the opportunities that will be provided to students and/or what teachers are expected to do. Generally speaking, standards consist of *content standards* at various grade levels—the what—and *performance standards*—descriptions of how good is good enough. These two types of standards should form the basis of assessment, both classroom and large-scale. The connections are shown in Figure Intro.2.

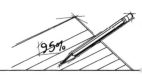

Assessment, Evaluation, and Reporting Connections Chart

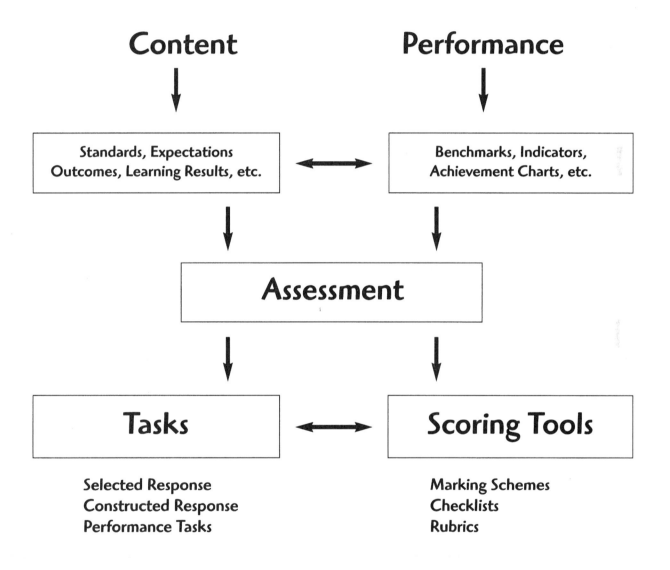

STANDARDS

Content

Performance

| Standards, Expectations Outcomes, Learning Results, etc. | Benchmarks, Indicators, Achievement Charts, etc. |

Assessment

Tasks

Scoring Tools

Selected Response
Constructed Response
Performance Tasks

Marking Schemes
Checklists
Rubrics

Figure Intro.2

Schmoker (2000) believes that the "standards movement (is) among the most radical and promising movements in the history of education" (49). Not everyone would give standards such a ringing endorsement but there is widespread agreement that standards have a number of benefits. Standards provide:

- clear focus on what students should know and be able to do;
- common direction for all schools in an educational jurisdiction;
- greater equity in learning goals for all students;
- a consistent basis for communication about student achievement to and among stakeholders; and
- an explicit and external basis for judging the success of teaching and learning.

Marzano (2000a) notes that the standards movement is not "problem free." Standards are criticized as:

- "glorified wish-lists" (Popham, 2000); there are too many standards and many are not well written or sufficiently succinct;
- straitjackets for teachers who take the life out of the classroom;
- hoops for students to jump over because "the bar has been raised;" and
- responsible for the explosion of testing at district, state, and national levels.

Reeves (2001) suggests that such criticisms of standards and their use are "a good rationale for the improvement of standards . . . they are not arguments for the rejection of standards" (6). He suggests that "the adoption of standards retains large amounts of . . . discretion, and individual judgment" (1996/98, 2) but that it is appropriate to have some limits on teachers' individual freedom in curricula decision making. Another way of putting this is that the standards determine the *what,* but teachers still have great freedom in determining the *how.* Undoubtedly improvements need to be made in standards, such as a review and revision of the content and number of standards in each jurisdiction. But even while there are too many standards, school districts and teachers can prioritize the standards so that there is appropriate emphasis on the more important standards. Suggestions for possible classifications and rationale are shown in Figure Intro.3. Standards will be appropriately emphasized when they are seen as the primary focus for classroom assessment rather than for large-scale assessment (Reeves 2001).

Prioritizing Standards

Where there are too many standards, prioritize using one of these approaches:

Understanding by Design[1]
Enduring understandings
Important to know and do
Worth being familiar with

Popham[2]
Essential
Very desirable
Desirable

Reeves[3] Three Tests
Endurance
Leverage
Required for next level

[1] From Wiggins, G. and J. McTighe. 1998. *Understanding by Design,* Association for Supervision of Curriculum Development, Alexandria, VA. Pg. 15. Used with permission.
[2] From Popham, W. J. 2000. "Assessing Mastery of Wish-List Content Standards." *NASSP Bulletin,* December, 30–36. Used with permission.
[3] From Reeves, D. B. 2001. "Standards Make a Difference: The Influence of Standards on Classroom Assessment." *NASSP Bulletin,* January, 5–12. Used with permission.

Figure Intro.3

To be effective, standards-based reform will require the previously mentioned improvements in detail or usage as well as an approach to lesson and unit design that replaces teachers' absolute individual freedom and the tyranny of the textbook with a "design down" or backwards design approach. This involves the following sequence:

- selection of the standard(s) as a base for planning;
- identification of how and how well students will be expected to demonstrate their knowledge and skills; and
- instructional planning that is focused on "how to get them there," that is, the instructional strategies, topics, theme, and resources that will be used to illuminate the standards.

The logic of "design down" suggests a planning sequence for curriculum. This sequence has three stages:

1. Identify desired results.
2. Determine acceptable evidence of achievement.
3. Plan learning experiences and instruction.

It is important to remember that "[achievement] standards can be raised only by changes that are put into effect by teachers and students in classrooms" (Black and Wiliam 1998, 148). The move to standards-based systems seems to hold promise if teachers are assisted appropriately in aligning curriculum instruction, assessment, grading, and reporting. If this alignment occurs, teachers will truly be able to "work smarter, not harder." It will also be easier for teachers to separate their dual classroom roles of coach/advocate and judge because of the clear focus on publicly articulated learning goals known to all. In this context, it should also be easier for students to see assessment as something that is done *with* them (to improve their learning) rather than something that is done *to* them (to find out what they don't know.) For maximum benefit to be obtained, it will be necessary that the purpose for grades and reporting clearly be the communication of achievement of the standards. "If grading and reporting do not relate grades back to standards, they are giving a mixed message. Our grading practices must reflect and illuminate those standards" (Busick 2000, 73).

How Do These Concepts Affect Assessment?

The economic changes, together with the development of standards and the new understandings about learning, are leading to significant changes in the ways children are taught and the ways in which they are assessed. There has been a move to authentic learning—learning that is relevant to students and to the real world—and to authentic assessment—assessment that provides students with opportunities to demonstrate what they know, can do, and are like. (See Figure Intro.4 for a graphic illustration of the characteristics of authentic assessment.) These approaches have moved assessment away from emphasis on paper-and-pencil methods (especially an almost exclusive reliance on multiple choice questions) toward the use of a broader array of assessment methods with an emphasis on performance assessment.

Current Methods

All of these changes and their impact on schools lead to the conclusion that "the primary purpose of classroom assessment [must now be] to inform learning, not to sort and select or justify a grade" (McTighe and Ferrara 1995, 11).

Criteria for Authentic Assessment

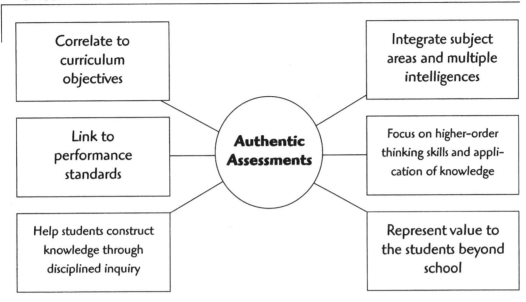

Correlate to curriculum objectives	Integrate subject areas and multiple intelligences
Link to performance standards	Focus on higher-order thinking skills and application of knowledge
Help students construct knowledge through disciplined inquiry	Represent value to the students beyond school

Authentic Assessments

Figure Intro.4   Adapted from p. 11 of *The Portfolio Connection: Student Work Linked to Standards,*
2nd Edition, by Kay Burke, Robin Fogarty, and Susan Belgrad. © 2002, 1994 SkyLight
Training and Publishing, Inc. Reprinted by permission of SkyLight Professional
Development, www.skylightedu.com or (800) 348–4474.

The focus of traditional grading practices is to sort, select, and justify. Traditional grading practices emphasize the use of scores from assessments that are easy to quantify, such as selected response items, especially multiple-choice questions. Teachers "become 'bean counters' . . . adding up all the marks, bonus points, and minus points before using the calculator to divide by the total number of entries—to the second decimal point, of course" (Burke 1993, 140). This approach was consistent with the competitive mentality prevalent in schools and society. However, as McTighe and Ferrara suggested, this approach is not compatible with the role grading could play, given what is now understood about the nature of learning and the type(s) of assessment that encourages and supports real learning. It is, therefore, necessary to move away from traditional grading and, as much as is possible, use grading in the service of learning. This book provides many suggestions about ways in which grading can be used to inform learning.

REFLECTING ON . . . ASSESSMENT METHODS

Use the checklist shown in Figure Intro.5 to identify the assessment methods you use in your classroom.

Assessment/Evaluation Checklist

TYPES OF STUDENT ASSESSMENT

Personal Communication
- ❏ Instructional questions
- ❏ Conferences
- ❏ Questionnaires
- ❏ Response journals
- ❏ Learning logs
- ❏ Oral tests/exams

Performance Assessment (using rubrics, checklists, rating scales, and anecdotal records)
- ❏ *Written Assignments*
  - ❏ Story
  - ❏ Play
  - ❏ Poem
  - ❏ Paragraph(s)
  - ❏ Essay
  - ❏ Research paper
- ❏ *Demonstrations* (live or taped)
  - ❏ Role play
  - ❏ Debate
  - ❏ Reading
  - ❏ Recital
  - ❏ Retelling
  - ❏ Cooperative group work
- ❏ *Presentations* (live or taped)
  - ❏ Oral
  - ❏ Dance
  - ❏ Visual (photos or video)
- ❏ *Seminars*
- ❏ *Projects*
- ❏ *Portfolios*

Paper-and-Pencil Tests/Quizzes
- ❏ True/false
- ❏ Matching items
- ❏ Completion items
- ❏ Short answer
- ❏ Visual representation
- ❏ Multiple choice
- ❏ Essay style

Figure Intro.5

SkyLight Professional Development

Why Grade?

Through such reflection and discussion with colleagues, you will find that there are many purposes for grading. To understand this fully, it is helpful to consider classifications from two sources. According to Gronlund and Linn in their classic text, *Measurement and Evaluation in Teaching* (1990), there are four general uses for grading:

- *instructional uses,* to clarify learning goals, indicate students' strengths and weaknesses, inform about students' personal-social development, and contribute to student motivation;
- *communicative uses,* to inform parents/guardians about the learning program of the school and how well their children are achieving the intended learning goals;
- *administrative uses,* to include "determining promotion and graduation, awarding honors, determining athletic eligibility, and reporting to other schools and prospective employers" (429); and
- *guidance uses,* to help students make their educational and vocational plans realistically.

A second source, Guskey (1996), summarized the purposes of grading as follows:

- *communicate* the achievement status of students to parents and others;
- *provide information* that students can use for self-evaluation;
- *select, identify, or group* students for certain educational paths or programs;
- *provide incentives* to learn; and
- *evaluate* the effectiveness of instructional programs (17).

Both of these classifications were developed relative to the broader, double meaning of grading; when the narrower, single meaning of grading employed in this book is used, all of the purposes still apply, although some uses apply more to marks than to grades, for example, self-assessment. Also note that the use of grades, especially traditional grades, for accountability purposes is of very limited value.

It is clear from these two classifications that grades serve many different purposes. Therein lies the basic problem with grades—to serve so many purposes, one letter or number symbol must carry many types of information (achievement, effort, behavior, etc.) in the grade. Putting together such a variety of information makes it very difficult to clearly understand what grades mean. In order to achieve this clarity, a definitive prioritization of the purpose of grades is needed. "The primary purpose of . . . grades is to *communicate* [emphasis added] student *achievement* to students, parents, school administrators, post-secondary institutions, and employers" (Bailey and McTighe 1996, 120).

> *Communication is also the purpose that best fits with what grades are—symbols that summarize achievement over a period of time.*

Communicating student achievement is the primary purpose of grades. Simply stated, if clear communication does not occur, then none of the other purposes of grades can be effectively carried out. Communication is also the purpose that best fits with what grades are—symbols that summarize achievement over a period of time. Communication is most effective when it is clear and concise; grades are certainly concise, and they can be clear communication vehicles if there is shared understanding of how they are determined and, thus, what they mean. Instructional and guidance uses not only need to be based on grades with clear meaning, but also are best served by much more information than symbols provide. The administrative uses of grades are really a form of communication and are best served when communication is clear. The other purposes of grades are also best served when communication is the focus—clarity about student achievement enables all the participants in the educational endeavor to do what is needed to support learning and encourage success.

Acknowledging that the primary purpose of grades is communication helps to point teachers in some very clear directions concerning the ingredients of grades and the use of grades at different levels within the school system. Emphasizing communication about achievement means that clarity is needed about what achievement is (see chapter 3). This emphasis is reflected in the analysis of grading and the grading guidelines presented in this book.

What Are the Underlying Perspectives on Grading?

The following sections explore seven perspectives, which were developed from a variety of assessment specialists including Stiggins, McTighe, and Guskey. They provide both a clear indication of the philosophy that underlies the approach to grading advocated in this book and a vehicle for addressing some of the myths about grades and some of the criticisms of grading.

REFLECTING ON . . . THE SEVEN PERSPECTIVES

THE SEVEN PERSPECTIVES ON GRADING:

1. Grading is not essential for learning.
2. Grading is complicated.
3. Grading is subjective and emotional.
4. Grading is inescapable.
5. Grading has a limited research base.
6. Grading has no single best practice.
7. Grading that is faulty damages students—and teachers.

Without reading any further, what is your reaction to these seven perspectives? With what perspectives do you agree? Disagree? Which ones are you not sure about? Keep a record of your initial reaction as you read the rest of this section.

Perspective One: Grading Is Not Essential for Learning

Although many teachers appear from their actions to believe otherwise, "teachers do not need grades or reporting forms to teach well, and students can and do learn well without them" (Guskey 1996, 16). Proof of this can be found in co-curricular activities, such as teams and clubs, and in interest courses, such as night school craft courses. In each of these situations, excellent teaching and superb learning take place—without grades. The problem in the school system is that, as soon as grades are introduced, teachers, parents, and students emphasize grades rather than learning. Teachers usually say this happens because grades motivate. Kohn (1993b) believes very strongly that grades should be abolished because grades serve as extrinsic motivators and destroy positive, intrinsic motivation. Kagan (1994), however, suggested that "if a student is performing a behavior and enjoys it and happens to receive praise or recognition, the recognition will not necessarily erode intrinsic motivation" (16.8). Brookhart (1994) offers another view, saying

> . . . Cognitive evaluation theory suggests that if students get feedback that helps them make progress, then motivation and control should increase. . . . Students will behave because their efforts will cause learning, and because enhancing perceived competence is motivating in and of itself. Students will perceive grades and other assessments which teachers use to provide informational feedback as more soundly based and reliable than grades and other assessments used to provide controlling feedback. (296)

The issue of motivation and learning is of vital importance in this analysis of grading. It is important to acknowledge several facts:

- Teachers need to learn more about motivation so that they can use knowledge rather than perception to guide their practices.
- Students—and parents—have been taught to overvalue grades. Although it will not be easy, if teachers grade better, both may learn to value grades more appropriately.
- Good grades may motivate, but poor grades have no motivational value. In fact, the only grades that do motivate are those that are higher than a student usually receives, or As.
- Educators must emphasize that learners are responsible for learning. It is then clear that the learner must be motivated by the intrinsic interest and the worth of what is being learned, not by the carrot-and-stick approach that emphasizes gold stars and As. Kohn (1993b) suggested that what matters is the three Cs of motivation: content (things worth knowing), choice (autonomy in the classroom), and collaboration (learning together).

Further, Stiggins (1999, 192) points out that "students succeed academically only if they want to succeed and feel capable of doing so. If they lack either desire or confidence, they will not be successful. Therefore, the essential question is a dual one: How do we help our students want to learn and feel capable of learning?"

Students' responsibility for their own learning can be achieved most effectively by consciously involving students in the assessment process. Students should be involved in designing or selecting assessment strategies, developing criteria, keeping records of their achievement, and communicating about their learning (Stiggins 2001b).

Perspective Two: Grading Is Complicated

Much grading is done in a mechanistic way, using formulas to produce the final grade as merely the result of arithmetic calculations. Teachers and students, therefore, come to believe that grading is simple; in fact, it is extremely complicated. Grades are shorthand; they are symbols that represent student performance. In order to arrive at grades, hundreds of decisions have been made along the way; the final grade could be very different if any of those choices had been made differently. In particular, the decisions that are made about how the numbers are "crunched," or manipulated, are critical. This issue is addressed in chapters 6 and 9, with suggestions about how to manipulate numbers in ways that support student learning better than traditional grading practices.

Perspective Three: Grading Is Subjective and Emotional

Rather than looking at the volume and complexity of the decisions about calculations, this perspective focuses on decisions about what is included in grades and the why of calculations. Because grades are usually the result of at least some numerical calculation, teachers often claim that grades are objective measures of student performance. Kohn (1993b) counters this claim: "What grades offer is spurious precision, a subjective rating masquerading as an objective assessment" (201). Grades are as much a matter of values as they are of science— all along the assessment trail, the teacher has made value judgments about what type of assessment to use, what to include in each assessment, how the assessment is scored, the actual scoring of the assessment, and why the scores are to be combined in a particular way to arrive at a final grade. Most of these value judgments are professional ones; these are the professional decisions that teachers are trained (and paid) to make. It should be acknowledged that grades are, for the most part, subjective, not objective, judgments.

> **T**he question is not whether it is subjective, but whether the scoring system is defensible and credible.
>
> (Wiggins 2000)

Many other educators support this view. Marzano (2000a) notes that "the current system based on points and percentages is inherently subjective" (61). Davies (2000) says, "Teachers' professional lives might be more pleasant if evaluating and reporting could be tidy and objective; but they aren't. Evaluation is inherently subjective" (68). Thus, we must acknowledge and not apologize for the subjective nature of grading. What we must strive for are defensible and credible decisions throughout the assessment process. As the National Council of Teachers of Mathematics (NCTM 1995) stated: "Teachers can be fair and consistent judges of student performance."

It should also be acknowledged that, although most teachers' decisions are based on professional judgment, some are based on emotion. Teaching is and, it is hoped, always will be an interpersonal activity. How we feel about the individuals and the groups being assessed sometimes affects our judgment. Again, the point here is not that this is wrong, but that all involved need to acknowledge that giving and receiving grades is not a purely objective act—it has a significant emotional component. The subjective and emotional aspects of grades have implications for how grading is done; grading will contribute to more effective learning when this perspective is acknowledged rather than denied.

It is also important to note that "subjectivity becomes detrimental (only) when it translates to bias" (Guskey and Bailey 2001, 330). This does not mean that fairness means treating all students the same. As Gathercoal (1997) points out in his wonderful book *Judicious Discipline*, "consistency in education is providing the professional specialization and skills needed to help each student believe success is possible" (48). Gathercoal also notes that "the group must learn to trust that decisions regarding exceptions [to the rules] will be fair for all as professional judgments are made for individuals caught up in any number of diverse and often complex circumstances" (67–68).

Perspective Four: Grading Is Inescapable

Willis (1993) listed the following criticisms of grades:

- Grades are symbols, but what they represent is unclear.
- Grades sort students rather than help them to succeed.
- Grades give little information about student strengths and weaknesses.

- Grades are arbitrary and subjective.
- Grades undermine new teaching practices.
- Grades demoralize students who learn slower.

Many educators believe that grades should be abolished. Although this might be desirable, especially for younger students, it simply is not going to happen in the foreseeable future in most educational jurisdictions. In fact, almost everywhere that schools or school systems have tried to remove grades from report cards, they have been faced with community reaction so strongly negative that educators have been forced to return to traditional grades. Olson (1995) gave a clear example of this in a blow-by-blow description of what happened in Cranston, Rhode Island, when a parent-teacher committee proposed a report card without traditional grades for elementary schools. The committee prepared for the change very thoroughly, including piloting the new report cards. However, when the new format was adopted, the uproar in the community forced the school system to return to the former reporting methods.

Grading practices are inherently subjective— this is not a denunciation but a truth that needs to be told.

(Farr 2000)

Wiggins (1996) stated that "trying to get rid of familiar letter grades . . . gets the matter backwards while leading to needless political battles. . . . Parents have reasons to be suspicious of educators who want to tinker with a 120-year-old system they think they understand—even if we know traditional grades are often of questionable worth" (142). Getting it backwards means that it is inappropriate to focus on trying to eliminate grades; it is more productive to make grades better. Wiggins went on to say that "what critics of grading must understand [is] that the symbol is not the problem; the lack of stable and clear points of reference in using symbols is the problem" (1996, 142). These concerns are addressed in chapters 1, 2, and 8.

Wiggins (1996) made another basic point: "grades or numbers, like all symbols, offer efficient ways of summarizing" (142). Although traditional grades may be of questionable worth, they have a long history. It is not worth fighting against this history; rather, it is worth fighting to make grades meaningful and more supportive of learning. That is what this book is about. What is needed are "thoughtfully designed grading and reporting systems that emphasize the formative and communicative aspects of grades (which) can maintain students' focus on important learning goals." (Guskey and Bailey 2001, 20). Furthermore, "the harmful effects of grades can be eliminated by changes in grading systems that provide more chances for success, more guidance, feedback, re-instruction, and encouragement" (Haladyna, 1999, 12).

Perspective Five: Grading Has a Limited Research Base

"What a mass and mess it all was." This is how Middleton (quoted in Guskey 1996, 13) described the literature on grading practices—in 1933! Writing in 1995, Reedy said, "since the introduction of percentage grades in public high schools in the early 1900's, grading and grade reporting have recycled rather than evolved" (47). That there has been no real change over a period of almost one hundred years probably stems from the fact that there is relatively little pure research on grading practices. As can be seen from examining the resources in the bibliography, many journal articles and reports have been written on grading, but most of them, including this book, are summaries of previous work and the opinion(s) of the author(s) on how grading should be done. Logical and well explained as the articles and reports may be, they do not have the weight or authority provided by research. Teachers freely ignore the advice of authors, even those they acknowledge as experts. Stiggins, Frisbie, and Griswold (1989) identified nineteen grading practices that measurement experts agreed were desirable. When they examined the actual practices of a group of teachers, they found that teachers ignored the expert advice for eleven of these grading practices. Stiggins et al. suggested three reasons for this situation: recommendations may be opinion or philosophical position rather than established fact; recommendations may be unrealistic in actual classroom practice; and recommendations may be outside the knowledge or expertise base of teachers.

Frary, Gross, and Weber came to similar conclusions in their 1992 study and stated that "large proportions of teachers hold opinions and pursue practices contrary to what many measurement specialists would recommend" (2).

Perspective Six: Grading Has No Single Best Practice

The lack of a research base and the fact that every method of grading has advantages and disadvantages means that there is no one way to grade. The private nature of grading and the dramatic inconsistency in approaches within departments in high schools and colleges and between classrooms in elementary schools means that there are major problems educators need to address.

This is especially so where grades are "high stakes," that is, when grades serve as more than communication with students and parents. Thus, when grades are the prime or major component of the decision-making process (e.g., for college admission), there needs to be greater consistency, at least within a school and, one hopes, across a school district. Ideally, there will be principles that could be agreed on and that would lead to consistency across many, or even all, educational jurisdictions. That is the basic purpose behind this book—to provide guidelines that all teachers can follow. Because they are guidelines, not rules, teachers may adapt them to different grade levels and subjects.

Perspective Seven: Grading that Is Faulty Damages Students and Teachers

The flush rose on Alan's face. His hands quivered. "It's not fair," he shouted. "I worked hard. I didn't deserve a B+. This will wreck my chances for Harvard."

Mr. Beaster stood silent. As Alan took a breath, Beaster interjected, "Alan," he began, "your grade. . . ."

Alan glared. "It's not my grade. I worked for an A. I deserve an A. I need it. This is the last semester. The good colleges will look at my grades. If you don't give me an A, my class rank drops." Again Mr. Beaster tried to interrupt, but Alan kept on, nostrils flaring, his face now beet red, "You're cheating me," he screeched. "You're ruining my life. My father will kill me. There's no way this grade is O.K. If you liked me you would give me an A. You're not fair."

"Alan," countered Beaster, "I'm not going to debate this grade with you. If you want to discuss it when you're calm, I'll be glad to."

"Bull____ . You'll never change it," Alan pouted as he turned to leave. "You teachers are all alike."

_____

Carmela stared at the floor. Mrs. Martinez sat beside her. Carmela did not move. "Carmela, what am I going to do with you?" Mrs. Martinez asked. "Your grades are getting worse. You are a bright girl. You should be doing better. You are not a D student."

Carmela still did not move. "I do care," she thought, "but it's not so easy. It never has been easy. I've got more to think about than school. School doesn't help me make the dinner or watch my brothers and sisters at night—especially when there is no dinner. And even if I do study, I'm always getting a C or D. So why bother? I can do C or D without studying." (Bellanca 1992, 297)

These two stories illustrate some of the problems with traditional grading practices. Alan had no concept of what good work was or how his grades were calculated. He had developed the idea that school was only about grades, not learning, and that teachers "gave" good grades to students they liked rather than those who produced quality work. Carmela had different problems; there were too many other things in her life for her to be able to show her ability by producing quality work on demand. Rather than becoming angry, as Alan did, she developed a sense of the inevitable—whatever she did she would get Cs or Ds, so there was no point in trying to improve.

Overemphasis on grades and faulty grading practices have detrimental effects on student achievement, motivation, and self-concept, as can be seen in these examples. Faulty grading also damages the interpersonal relationship on which good teaching and effective learning depend. This problem occurs at least partly because of teachers' dual roles as coach and judge. Unfortunately, these roles frequently conflict and, as a result, teacher–student relationships are damaged. Many of the problems illustrated by Alan's and Carmela's stories may be at least alleviated and possibly even eliminated if grading practices that support learning and student success are used.

These perspectives on grading contrast with traditional perspectives on grading. Traditional grading is normally seen as being essential for learning ("If I don't give them grades, they won't do the work") and as straightforward and scientific ("The formula says; the calculator shows . . ."). If one followed the first three perspectives to their logical conclusion, a strong case could be made against grading; but the fourth perspective means that, as it is virtually impossible to do away with grades, it is necessary to find ways to make grades more meaningful. Here, making grades more meaningful means to develop grading practices that support learning and encourage student success. Teachers must not see grades as weapons of control, but rather use grading as an exercise in professional judgment to enhance learning. If teachers acknowledge the seven perspectives in their dealings with parents, students, and other teachers, grades can become a positive rather than a punitive aspect of educational practice.

REFLECTING ON . . . THE PERSPECTIVES

Now that you have read about each of the perspectives, what do you think?

▶ With which perspectives do you now agree? Disagree?

▶ Which perspectives in the list are you now not sure about?

▶ How did your thinking change from when you first read the list?

Grading Practices and Guidelines

This section actively engages readers in analyzing grading practices. It begins with some factual data about grading practices. Readers then examine their own beliefs about grading and their own grading practices. Seven case studies provide opportunities to analyze grading practices and identify grading issues—the what, how, and why of grading. Readers might keep a list of the issues that they identify to compare with a list provided in the text on page 37. Having identified grading issues, one looks for solutions. One solution is practical guidelines that teachers may use in their classrooms and in their grade books. A set of eight such guidelines is introduced in this section and examined in detail in chapters 1 through 8.

How Is Grading Done?

Robinson and Craver (1989, 26) reported the use of letter and percentage grades at various grade levels in the United States in 1988. Figure Intro.6 shows the usage levels for the two most prevalent grading symbol systems: letters and percentages. Unfortunately, there was no comparable report in the 1990s. The information in Figure Intro.6 demonstrates that letter or percentage grades were given to 15% to 20% of kindergarten students; 55% to 70% of students in grades 1– 3; and 80% to 100% of students in grades 4–12.

There is no reason to believe that the proportions have changed dramatically since Robinson and Craver's 1989 report. We are, therefore, examining an educational practice that is a significant fact of life for most students, parents, and teachers in North America.

Reported Use of Grading Symbols at Different Grade Levels

Grade	Letter	Percentage
Kindergarten	14.8%	4.8%
Grades 1–3	55.4%	15.6%
Grades 4–6	79.2%	20.7%
Grades 7–9	81.9%	26.8%
Grades 10–12	80.2%	28.5%

*Percentages may total more than 100% because some districts may use more than one grading symbol system at a grade level.

Figure Intro.6   Glen E. Robinson and James Craver. 1989. *Assessing and Grading Student Achievement.* Arlington, VA: Educational Research Service. Reproduced with permission.

How Do YOU Grade?

"[Grading] practices are not the result of careful thought or sound evidence, . . . Rather, they are used because teachers experienced these practices as students and, having little training or experience with other options, continue their use" (Guskey 1996, 20). This statement is unfair to many teachers, but it is certainly true for some teachers.

REFLECTING ON . . . YOUR GRADING PRACTICES

▶ What are the principles on which your grading practices are based?

▶ What are your actual grading practices? Do you just crunch numbers?

▶ What were or are the main influences on your grading principles and practices?

▶ How do your grading principles and practices compare with those of other teachers in your school?

One of the best ways to analyze grading practices (and the principles behind them) is to analyze a set of marks and grades and identify the issues that arise from such an analysis. Following are eight case studies that give us the opportunity to analyze grading practices and discover grading issues.

Case Study 1: Interim Report Card Grade

Case study 1 considers the impact of a zero mark on a grade and the possible impact on a student of grade reporting very early in a course/year.

The marks in Figure Intro.7 were given to a student in a senior science class on an interim report card (after four weeks of 76-minute classes) in a school with a semester block schedule.

This case study dramatically illustrates the effect of assigning a zero for a missed test. The student has six marks of 90% or higher, two marks in the 80s,

Scores

Task	Mark/Total Possible	Percentage
Tests (50%)		
Symbols	16/20	80
Matter	0/68 (absent)	0
Reactions	35/50	70
Daily Work (25%)		
Assignment	10/10	100
Homework	9/10	90
Homework	9/10	90
Atom Quiz	9/10	90
Moles Quiz	5/8	62.5
Homework	9/10	90
Lab Work (25%)		
MP/BP	18/20	90
Superation	20/24	83.3
Reactions	7/10	70
Periodicity Check	10/10	100

Figure Intro.7

and no mark lower than 62.5%; but, the interim grade is lower than all except the lowest mark! A grade like this could have a devastating effect on students, causing them to give up. This student is achieving well, but the grade suggests otherwise—because of a missed test.

REFLECTING ON . . . CASE STUDY 1

▶ What grade would you give the student? Why?

▶ The actual grade the student received was 68.1%. What is your reaction to this grade? Was this grade a fair reflection of the student's overall achievement?

▶ If the zero was not included the grade would be 81.6%. Would this be a fairer reflection of the student's overall achievement?

▶ What grading issues arise from this case study?

Case Study 2: Chris Brown's Science Class

Case study 2 considers the marks and grades of a teacher using a very traditional approach to grading. The student marks have been arranged so that, for most students, there are some obvious problems with their performance and/or the way it is graded.

The marks and grades in Figure Intro.8 are for Chris Brown's science class in Ontario. If you are not a science teacher, put the appropriate items for your subject in place of the lab reports, care of equipment, and so forth. Note carefully the information that is shown below the grade book extract regarding the miscellaneous items, the way absence is dealt with, and the grading scale. Enter to the right of the chart the letter grade each student would get using the grading scale in use in your district/school.

One A, one B, four Cs, and a D in Ontario—but, did they go to the right students? Marg got a D, but on her achievement alone she probably deserved an A. Lorna got an A, but had only a 60% average on tests and exams; is she a weak student who is a teacher's pet—one who receives good marks on the things she can get help on—or is she a very capable student who suffers from severe test anxiety? Kay and Peter have the same grade but Kay is getting high 80s at the end, whereas Peter is receiving failing marks; is this fair? These are just some of the considerations that arise from an analysis of this case study.

Scores

Name	Lab Reports										Total	Tests/Exams			Total	Miscellaneous*						Final Total	Final Grade		Your District
out of	10	10	10	10	10	10	10	10	10	10	100	50	50	100	200	20	20	20	20	20	100	400	%	Letter	
Robin	6	6	6	7	6	6	5	6	6	6	60	33	39	81	153	15	15	12	0	10	52	265	66	C	
Kay	2	3	5	8	9	7	6	5	6	10	61	11	29	86	126	15	13	18	10	10	66	253	63	C	
Marg	10	10	A	10	10	A	10	A	A	A	60	50	A	100	150	0	0	0	0	15	15	225	56	D	
Dennis	9	8	9	10	9	10	9	8	9	8	89	24	24	49	97	20	17	17	20	20	94	280	70	B	
Peter	10	10	9	9	8	8	7	7	6	5	79	45	36	32	113	20	10	15	10	5	60	252	63	C	
Lorna	10	10	10	10	10	10	10	10	10	10	100	32	29	59	120	20	20	20	20	20	100	320	80	A	
John	8	8	7	9	9	10	8	8	9	8	84	32	30	57	119	20	8	7	0	5	40	243	61	C	

A = Absent = 0 (for Lab Reports and Tests/Exams)

*Miscellaneous

1–Attendance; 2–Care of Equipment; 3–Attitude/Participation; 4–Notebook; 5–Reading Reports (4x5 marks)

Letter Grade Legend (in Ontario)

A = 80%–100%; B = 70%–79%; C = 60%–69%; D = 50%–59%; F = 0%–49%

Figure Intro.8   Adapted from Todd Rogers, University of Alberta. Used with permission.

REFLECTING ON . . . CASE STUDY 2

▶ Do the grades awarded fairly reflect the results from which they were derived for each student?

▶ If you answered "yes," for which students? Why?

▶ If you answered "no," for which students? Why?

▶ What grading issues arise from this case study?

Case Study 3: Hiring a Student

Very often, secondary report cards give little more information than the student's grade and a three- or four-word comment. Case study 3 provides an opportunity to analyze how grades are calculated and whether grades provide meaningful information to potential employers, the students themselves, and their parents.

Scenarios

AUTO MECHANICS

	Student #1 71%		Student #2 52%

WEIGHTS

Scenario	Practical	Theory	Grade
A	25%	75%	
Student 1	0/25	71/75	71%
Student 2	25/25	27/75	52%
B	50%	50%	
Student 1	0/50	47/50	47%
Student 2	50/50	18/50	68%
C	75%	25%	
Student 1	0/75	24/25	24%
Student 2	75/75	9/25	84%

Figure Intro.9

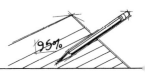

Figure Intro.9 may appear to present an extreme example, but there have been—and probably still are—many classrooms where this situation exists. This case study illustrates the critical connection between teacher's intent and how grades are actually calculated.

REFLECTING ON . . . CASE STUDY 3

► To which student would you give a job at the local auto repair shop based on the information from Scenario A?

► Study the additional information in Scenarios B and C. Which student would get the job now?

► What grading issues arise from this case study?

Case Study 4: Anita's Grade?

Case Study 4 provides many numbers and therefore many possibilities for how grades are calculated—number crunching again!

The teacher of this class bases grades only on unit tests, but believes in multiple assessment opportunities, when it is feasible. Thus on test 2, there are questions on unit 1 and unit 2, on test 3 there are questions on units 1, 2, and 3, and on test 4, there are questions on all four units. This gives students four opportunities to demonstrate their knowledge and skill on unit 1, three opportunities on unit 2, two opportunities on unit 3, but only one opportunity on unit 4. This approach yields many numbers for Anita, as shown in Figure Intro.10.

Tests

Unit	Test Score (percentage)			(B)
1	50/100 (50)	30/50 (60)	30/40 (75)	23/25 (92)
2		30/50 (60)	23/33 (70)	21/25 (84)
3			20/30 (67)	19/25 (76)
4				17/25 (72)
Test Average (A)	50%	60%	71%	81% (C)

Figure Intro.10

Using traditional approaches, there are at least three alternatives for calculating the final grade for Anita:

Alternative A: use the average mark on each test, that is,

(50 + 60 + 71 + 81)/4 = 66%

Alternative B: use the final mark on each unit, that is, the marks for each unit on test 4, that is, (92 + 84 + 76 + 72)/4 = 81%

Alternative C: use the mark for the first test on each unit, that is,

(50 + 60 + 67 + 72)/4 = 62%

As you can see, these three approaches result in a final grade for Anita that ranges from 62% to 81%, a variation of almost 20%.

One would hope that the teacher would use alternative B because it is the option that provides multiple opportunities and supports the teacher's intent. However, there are many teachers who would use alternative A, and some who would use alternative C, even though it completely negates the multiple assessment opportunities.

REFLECTING ON . . . CASE STUDY 4

▶ Which grade would you give to Anita? Would you use alternative A, B, C, or something else? Why?

▶ What grading issues arise from this case study?

Case Study 5: All or Some

Another aspect of number crunching is presented in this case study.

Imagine you are going to go skydiving. Presumably, you will want to have a parachute that has a very good chance of opening properly. The skydiving company has provided you with the assessment scores of three students from a recent parachute-packing course. These three are the only people they employ to pack parachutes, so you have to have a parachute packed by one of them—unless you want to jump without a parachute! Please note the competency/mastery level for each assessment, as shown in Figure Intro.11, and carefully consider which student you want to pack your parachute.

Parachute-Packing Test Scores

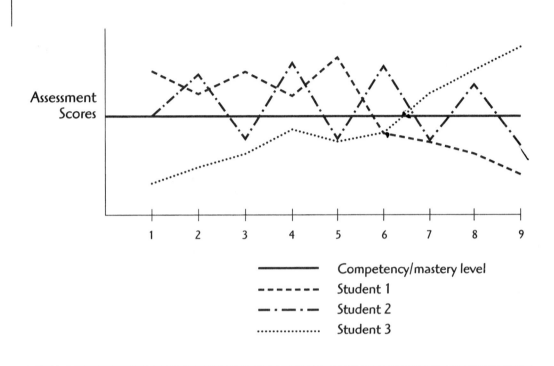

Assessment
Scores

——————— Competency/mastery level

– – – – – – Student 1

— · — · — Student 2

················ Student 3

Figure Intro.11   Adapted from A. Davies. 2000. *Making Classroom Assessment Work.*
Merville, BC, Canada: Connections Publishing.

REFLECTING ON . . . CASE STUDY 5

▶ Which student will you choose to pack your parachute? Why?

▶ If these were scores in a typical teacher's grade book, which students would pass? Which students would fail?

▶ Is there any discrepancy between your answers to question 1 and 2? If so, why does this discrepancy occur?

Case Study 6: Grading Scales

What does A mean? What does F mean? For fifty and more years, as a student and as a teacher in Australia and in Canada, I have known that an A has been 80% and an F has been less than 50%. Anything different is very hard for me to comprehend. The familiar becomes the norm—but is it right? Case study 6

demonstrates that letter grades, honors, and pass/fail mean very different things in different educational jurisdictions.

Figure Intro.12 shows grading scales used in North America at five different places. You may use the last row to enter the grading scale used in your district/school.

Grading Scales

	Symbol Conversion				
Source	A	B	C	D	F
Ontario	80–100%	70–79%	60–69%	50–59%	<50%
Ruth Evans*	90–100%	80–89%	70–79%	60–69%	<60%
Rick Werkheiser*	93–100%	85–92%	78–84%	70–77%	<70%
Pam Painter*	95–100%	85–94%	75–84%	65–74%	<65%
R. L. Canady**	95–100%	88–94%	81–87%	75–80%	<75%
Your District	_____	_____	_____	_____	_____

*From the Internet, *The School House Teachers' Lounge* (Nebraska)
**Canady, R. L., and P. R. Hotchkiss. 1989. *Phi Delta Kappan* September, 68–71.

Figure Intro.12   Robert Lynn Canady and Phyllis R. Hotchkiss, "It's a Good Score: Just a Bad Grade," September, 1989, pg. 68–71. *Phi Delta Kappan.* Reproduced with permission.

An A can mean anything from 80% to 95%, and a failing grade can be anywhere between 49% and 74%. What do these variations mean? For example, is a 49% in Ontario the same as 74% in the district identified by Canady and Hotchkiss (1989) as having the highest grade equivalents? There is no way of knowing this without comparing marked student work from both jurisdictions, but the wide variation makes one wonder about the meaning of grades.

REFLECTING ON . . . CASE STUDY 6

> ▶ What is your reaction to the wide variation in grading scales?
> ▶ What letter grade would Anita (case study 4) get if she were in each of these school jurisdictions?
> ▶ What grading issues arise from this case study?

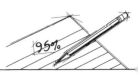

Case Study 7: Grading Plans

Case study 7 looks at the recipes teachers use to "cook up" their grades. This case study lets teachers examine how their recipe—or plan—compares with those of their colleagues.

In most traditional grading situations (see Figure 1.1), teachers have a recipe or plan for the ingredients in their grades. These usually include some assessment methods and some student behaviors. In addition to the components of grades, such plans usually include some indication of the relative importance of each component by giving it a (percentage) weight.

There is clearly no right answer or perfect grading plan, but for those who teach the same grade or course(s) in the same school and, ideally, in the same school district, it would not be unreasonable to expect that there would be some basic similarities or discernible patterns in their grading plans. If no similarities exist, serious professional discussion about how grading is carried out is needed.

REFLECTING ON . . . CASE STUDY 7

See Figure Intro.13, Grading Inventory, to identify the grading "recipe" you use. Ask colleagues to share their inventories with you. (If your categories do not appear on Figure Intro.13, enter your categories at the bottom.)

▶ What similarities or differences exist between your inventory and your colleagues' inventories?

▶ Why do the differences exist? Should the differences exist?

▶ What grading issues arise from this case study?

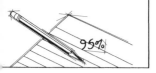

Grading Inventory

Items Included in Grades	Percentages Allocated			
	Self	Teacher #1	Teacher #2	Teacher #3
Exams				
Tests				
Projects · individual · group				
Demonstrations/Oral Presentations				
Written Assignments · small writing tasks · writing folders or portfolios · essays				
Class Participation and Effort · whole class discussions · group discussions · homework · notebook · attendance, punctuality				
Peer Assessment				
Self-Assessment				
Additional Categories				

Figure Intro.13

Case Study 8: Grading Practices That Inhibit Learning

Canady and Hotchkiss (1989) identified twelve grading practices that inhibit learning (see Figure Intro.14 on page 38). Many of these are, or were, quite common practices that many—maybe even most—teachers would consider acceptable and normal. The fact that Canady and Hotchkiss labeled them as practices that inhibit learning requires teachers to carefully analyze their own grading practices.

The grading practices in numbers 2, 3, 4, and 9 in Figure Intro.14 were all part of my practices when I was a classroom teacher just a few years ago. Most teachers will probably admit that they use at least one-third of the practices listed at least some of the time. The grading guidelines presented in this book, when fully implemented, eliminate most of these learning inhibiting practices.

REFLECTING ON . . . CASE STUDY 8

▶ Does Figure Intro.14 reflect any practices you used in the past?

▶ What grading issues arise from this case study?

Grading Issues

The case studies have identified the issues listed below.

- Basis for grades—Standards (learning goals) or assessment methods?
- Reference points—what performance standards?
- Ingredients—achievements, ability, effort, attitude, behavior?
- Sources of information—methods, purposes?
- Changing grades—all or more recent evidence?
- Number crunching—calculation? method?
- Assessment quality
- Student understanding and involvement

Although this list is general, I believe it includes all the major grading issues. (An expanded version of this list with the specific concerns that arise out of each issue can be found at the end of this introduction on page 46, Figure Intro.18.)

Grading Practices That Inhibit Learning

1.	Inconsistent grading scales	The same performance results in different grades, in different schools or classes.
2.	Worshipping averages	All of the math to calculate an average is used, even when "the average" is not consistent with what the teacher knows about the student's learning.
3.	Using zeros indiscriminately	Giving zeros for incomplete work has a devasting effect on averages and often zeros are not even related to learning or achievement but to nonacademic factors like behavior, respect, punctuality, etc.
4.	Following the pattern of assign, test, grade, and teach	Students are often told to read material and prepare for a test. The real discussion and teaching then takes place—after the test. It is far more logical to teach before testing, but we continue to an alarming extent to follow the pattern of assign, test, grade, and teach.
5.	Failing to match testing to teaching	Too many teachers rely on trick questions, new formats, and unfamiliar material. If students are expected to perform skills and produce information for a grade, these should be part of the instruction.
6.	Ambushing students	Pop quizzes are more likely to teach students how to cheat on a test than to result in learning. Such tests are often control vehicles designed to get even, not to aid understanding.
7.	Suggesting that success is unlikely	Students are not likely to strive for targets that they already know are unattainable to them.
8.	Practicing "gotcha" teaching	A nearly foolproof way to inhibit student learning is to keep the outcomes and expectations of their classes secret. Tests become ways of finding out how well students have read their teacher's mind.
9.	Grading first efforts	Learning is not a "one-shot" deal. When the products of learning are complex and sophisticated, students need a lot of teaching, practice, and feedback before the product is evaluated.
10.	Penalizing students for taking risks	Taking risks is not often rewarded in school. Students need encouragement and support, not low marks, while they try new or more demanding work.
11.	Failing to recognize measurement error	Very often grades are reported as objective statistics without attention to weighting factors or the reliability of the scores. In most cases, a composite score may be only a rough estimate of student learning, and sometimes it can be very inaccurate.
12.	Establishing inconsistent grading criteria	Criteria for grading in schools and classes often change from day to day, grading period to grading period, and class to class. This lack of consensus makes it difficult for students to understand the rules.

Figure Intro.14

Robert Lynn Canady and Phyllis R. Hotchkiss, "It's a Good Score: Just a Bad Grade," September, 1989, pg. 68–71. *Phi Delta Kappan.* Reproduced with permission.

REFLECTING ON . . . GRADING ISSUES

▶ How does the list of grading issues on page 37 compare with your list? Which issues that you identified are included?

▶ Which issues that you identified are not included?

Basis for Grades

Traditionally, grades have been based on assessment methods, but in standards-based systems it is questionable whether this is the appropriate link. In order for grades to reflect standards directly and not just by chance, grades must be based directly on the standards. If there are a limited number of standards (no more than seven or eight), grades should be based on the standards themselves, but in most standards documents there are so many standards that they need to be organized by strand. Another important consideration is that the basis for grades is usually also used as the base for reporting. Therefore, basing grades on standards also gives us the most appropriate base for reporting in standards-based systems.

Reference Points

In order for grades to have any real meaning, they must have some point of reference or comparison: norm, criterion, or self-referenced. Traditionally, grades have been norm-referenced, that is, they were based on comparing the individual with a group. This frequently involved the use of the bell curve or some modification of the curve.

With the introduction of state and local standards, grades are increasingly based on these standards and so are criterion-referenced. Even where there are no published standards, teachers use a criterion-referenced approach when they provide their students with rubrics—scoring scales that clearly indicate the criteria for quality work. Classroom teachers determine most criterion-referenced standards, so variability from teacher to teacher is still a major issue. The concerns arising from this problem are discussed in chapter 2.

Self-referencing, which compares students with their own previous performance, can also provide valuable information.

The issue that needs to be considered is which type of reference point to use to determine grades and which type to use only in report card comments.

Ingredients

Teachers include and mix many ingredients to arrive at grades. Student characteristics often used in the mix are achievement, ability, effort, attitude, behavior, participation, and attendance. These ingredients are included because grades serve so many purposes. The result is that grades frequently become almost meaningless for their main purpose—communication. This is clearly illustrated in Rick's Mysterious Falling Grade, a case that begins chapter 3.

In order to provide effective communication, grades must be clearly understood by the message senders (teachers and schools) and by the message receivers (students, parents, college admissions officers, employers, etc.). "To develop this shared understanding, there must be a consistent and limited basis for what is included in grades; instead of including everything, we must limit the variables or valued attributes that are included in grades" (O'Connor 1995, 94).

Frisbie and Waltman (1992) identified a large set of evaluation variables, which includes everything (or almost everything) students do in the classroom and the school. This large set of evaluation variables is reduced to a smaller subset of reporting variables. The size of this subset depends on the type of reporting to parents done by each school/district. Care should be taken to ensure that the most highly valued variables are included. The last step is to select a subset of the reporting variables as the grading variables. The grading variables should be the "status indicators at the end of the learning experience" (Frisbie and Waltman 1992, 38).

Guskey (1994) provided another approach to identifying the ingredients in grades. He identified progress criteria (for improvement scoring or learning gain); process criteria (for work habits, attendance, participation, effort, and so forth); and product criteria (for final exams, overall assessments, or other culminating demonstrations of learning).

Frisbie and Waltman's and Guskey's concepts are combined as shown in Figure Intro.15. Figure Intro.15 shows that in Frisbie and Waltman's terms, Guskey's process and progress criteria are the reporting variables, and the product criteria are the grading variables. This combination identifies

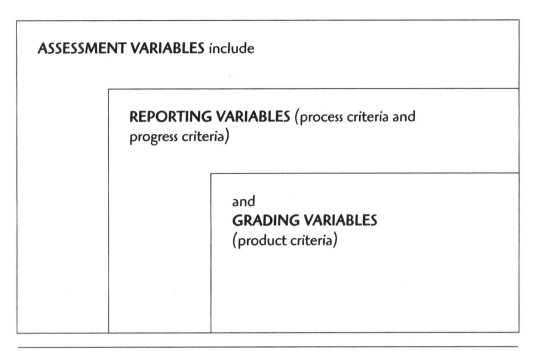

ASSESSMENT VARIABLES include

REPORTING VARIABLES (process criteria and progress criteria)

and
GRADING VARIABLES
(product criteria)

Figure Intro.15   Adapted with permission from K. O'Connor "Guidelines for Grading that Support
Learning and Student Success." *NASSP Bulletin,* (May 1995): 91–101,
National Association of Secondary School Principals.

variables that are separated for grading and reporting purposes. The interaction shown in Figure Intro.15, however, is rather simplistic, as some process variables may be assessed over time as part of stated learning goals, and, therefore, legitimately may be considered as grading variables. This more complex and more realistic identification of grading and reporting variables is illustrated in Figure Intro.16. By definition, in standards-based systems, the content standards now define achievement and should be the only grading variables.

Sources of Information

Teachers have many possible sources of information about student achievement. Teachers use a wide variety of assessment methods, but not all sources of information need be included in grades. They decide which sources of information to include based on the reliability and validity of the data and the purpose of the assessment. Teachers make these decisions consciously and carefully.

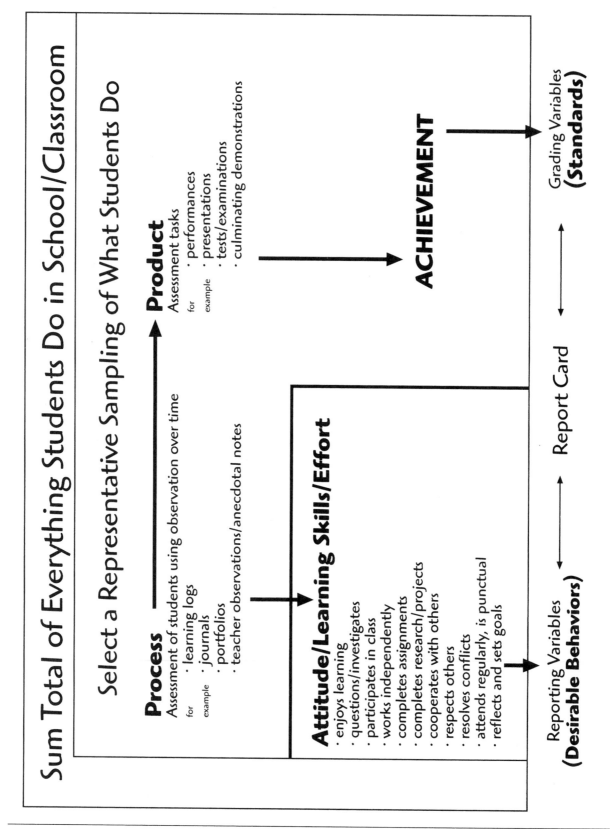

Sum Total of Everything Students Do in School/Classroom

Select a Representative Sampling of What Students Do

Process

Assessment of students using observation over time

for example
- learning logs
- journals
- portfolios
- teacher observations/anecdotal notes

Product

Assessment tasks

for example
- performances
- presentations
- tests/examinations
- culminating demonstrations

→ **ACHIEVEMENT** → Grading Variables **(Standards)**

Attitude/Learning Skills/Effort

- enjoys learning
- questions/investigates
- participates in class
- works independently
- completes assignments
- completes research/projects
- cooperates with others
- respects others
- resolves conflicts
- attends regularly, is punctual
- reflects and sets goals

→ Reporting Variables **(Desirable Behaviors)**

Report Card

Figure Intro.16   Adapted with permission from the work of K. O'Connor and Damian Cooper, Assessment Consultant.

Changing Grades

Teachers tend to include everything that they score in student grades. The issue to consider is whether all these data are necessary or appropriate. The amount of data needed is only that which enables confidence that any further information will confirm the previous judgment. Focus should be on the most consistent level of performance, especially toward the end of any learning (grading) period, because this is the information that tells whether the learning goals have been met.

Number Crunching

The case studies demonstrated that there are a variety of ways numbers can be "crunched." They also demonstrated that, depending on the distribution of student scores and the method chosen, students can receive very different grades from the same set of scores. Thus the methods chosen and a number of other aspects of number crunching, including the weighting of the various components, are very important considerations in the determination of grades.

Assessment Quality and Record Keeping

Because there are many ingredients in grades, even if only achievement information is used, teachers must ensure that the evidence comes from assessments that meet standards of quality. If, for example, assessment is not matched appropriately to teaching, student achievements will be measured incorrectly and the evidence used to determine grades will be inaccurate.

Record keeping is also important. The complexity of learning goals requires that teachers base grades on complete and accurately tabulated records—on paper, on a computer, or both. It is not justifiable for data that go into a grade to come off the top of a teacher's head at the end of the grading period.

Student Understanding and Involvement

Frequently students do not understand how the grades they receive are determined. This occurs because either the grading procedures are not discussed with them or the procedures are too complicated to be understood. The issue is how teachers may best ensure that students understand their grades. If grades are to serve learning, students must understand and be involved in the whole assessment process.

Guidelines for Grading

Grading issues can be addressed in a variety of ways. To avoid the misuse and misinterpretation of grades, a set of grading guidelines that address the practical concerns of teachers is needed.

In 2000, Trumbull noted that there had been a virtual revolution in assessment practices in the decade of the 1990s, but that grading practices evolved only slowly (Trumbull and Farr 2000).

Traditional grading practices need to change so that grading aligns with standards and supports current assessment and evaluation philosophy and practices. The grading guidelines in Figure Intro.17 were developed with these principles in mind. Some of them require radical changes in teacher practices, especially at the high school and college levels, and in school and

Guidelines for Grading in Standards-Based Systems

**To Support Learning
To Encourage Student Success**

1. Relate grading procedures to learning goals (i.e., standards).

2. Use criterion-referenced performance standards as reference points to determine grades.

3. Limit the valued attributes included in grades to individual achievement.

4. Sample student performance—do not include all scores in grades.

5. Grade in pencil—keep records so they can be updated easily.

6. Crunch numbers carefully—if at all.

7. Use quality assessment(s) and properly recorded evidence of achievement.

8. Discuss and involve students in assessment, including grading, throughout the teaching/learning process.

A more detailed version of these guidelines can be found in Appendix 2: Guidelines for Grading in Standards-Based Systems.

Figure Intro.17

district policies. The guidelines are organized in approximate order of importance to the implementation of standards, and to the support of student learning and success. The order also relates to where most change from traditional grading practices is needed—relatively few teachers using traditional approaches to grading use guidelines 1 through 6, whereas many (maybe most) teachers already follow guidelines 7 and 8. Each guideline stands on its own, but there is significant interconnection between the guidelines, and together they make a coherent group.

The specific relationships between the grading issues identified and the guidelines are shown in Figure Intro.18 on page 46. Each issue relates primarily to one guideline. Some of the specific concerns that arise out of each issue also are listed.

This set of grading guidelines has been modified considerably from those proposed by Gronlund and Linn (1990), but it is important to acknowledge that their list was the starting point. Guidelines such as these are more practical than most guidelines found in the literature on grading. The guidelines are intended to provide practical guidance to teachers as they decide how to grade students' achievement—and can actually be used by teachers in their grade books or in setting up their computer grading programs. Guidelines also should have school and/or district policy status, so that students and parents can understand the grading practices used in their classrooms, and so that they can expect grading practices that are consistent among all teachers in each school. Currently, teachers are "all over the book"; these guidelines should at least get teachers in the same chapter and, eventually, on the same page!

In chapters 1 through 8, each guideline is examined individually in detail.

REFLECTING ON . . . THE GUIDELINES

▶ What *is* your initial reaction to each of the guidelines for grading in Figure Intro.17? Why?

▶ Think in terms of what *is* Positive, what *is* a Concern, and what *is* just Interesting (PCI). List your reflections for later reference.

Relationships Between Grading Guidelines and Issues/Concerns

Guideline	Issue(s)	Concern(s)
1	**Basis for grades** Assessment Methods or Learning Goals	which groupings—standards, strands?
2	**Reference points** Standards—norm or criterion referenced	performance standards—what? how good is good enough? to curve or not to curve (bell, that is)?
3	**Ingredients** Achievement, Behavior(s)	learning skills/work habits/effort late assignments/extra credit group grades/marks
4	**Sources of information** Formative, Summative Variety	tests? quizzes? homework? how much data? variety: paper-and-pencil, performance assessment, personal communication
5	**Changing grades**	second- or multiple-opportunity evaluation, recent or all information method of calculation
6	**Number crunching** Mean, Median, Mode	role of professional judgment effect of zeros/missed work # points on scale
7	**Quality** **Record keeping**	e.g., fairness—time on tests management/tracking system(s)
8	**Student understanding**	clear criteria how much student involvement?

Figure Intro.18

Chapter 1

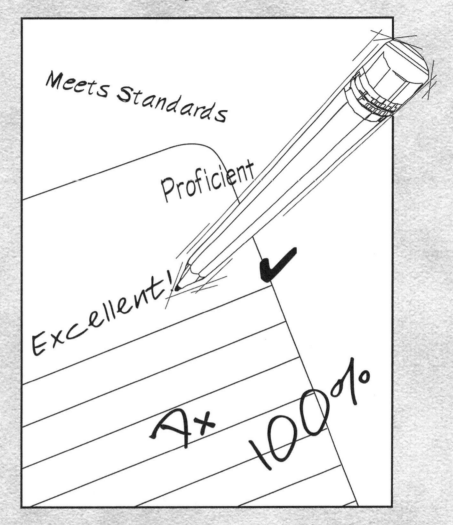

Linking Grades

The best referencing system for grading is . . . learning goals.
—MARZANO (2000a, 33)

Guideline:

1

Relate grading procedures to learning goals (i.e., standards).

THE CASE OF . . .

Michael's Amazing Passing Grade

In grade 9, in a program that introduced students to the wide range of possibilities open to them, Michael was required to take a course in a vocational area. Michael chose auto mechanics, even though he had very little interest or skill in this area. During the six weeks of the class, he completed two poor quality repairs of simple problems, both of which deservedly received very low marks. School procedures established a highly structured assessment schedule, which provided four days of written exams at the middle and at the end of each semester. School policy also required that exams be held in each subject and that their scores count for 50% of the final grade. The auto mechanics exam included questions about safety procedures and how to make simple repairs. This assessment was easy for Michael because he had a good memory and wrote well. Michael

received 50/50 on the exam, which was added to his performance marks. This combination resulted in an overall passing grade, which Michael clearly did not deserve, as the main goal of the course was for students to perform quality repairs.

What's the Purpose of the Guideline?

This guideline requires that grading procedures be aligned with stated learning goals. This alignment is direct, and the contribution of each learning goal to the final grade is direct. For example, if the primary learning goal in a course is practical demonstration of skills, then the final grade in that course should be based on direct observation of those skills and evaluation of the products that result from those skills.

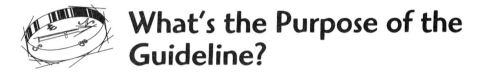

What Are the Key Elements of the Guideline?

As noted earlier, most school districts and states/provinces now have clearly stated learning goals. Different words are used to describe these goals. In most places, standards are still the descriptor of choice, but in many places, other words, such as learning results and expectations, are used. It does not matter much which word is used; the concept is that at either the local or state level, specific learning targets have been established, often on a grade-by-grade basis. In this chapter, to simplify a confusing situation, I use *learning goals* as a generic term; however, when other sources are quoted, alternative terms to learning goals will be retained.

> **T**his guideline requires that grading procedures be aligned with stated learning goals. The contribution of each learning goal to the final grade is direct.

Learning Goals

Grades should be effective communication vehicles, and the methods used to determine them need to provide optimum opportunities for student success and to encourage learning. For this to happen, the meaning of grades must be clear, which requires that, in addition to all the issues dealt with in guidelines 3, 4, and 5, grades must be directly related to the learning goals for each grading period in each classroom. Teachers must understand clearly what learning results are expected and then base their grading plans on these learning goals.

Grading Plan

Off Target: Methods of Assessment

Before discussing an appropriate basis for determining grades, let's briefly discuss what not to use. Simply said, do not base a grading plan on methods of assessment, as illustrated in Figure 1.1.

Traditional Plan for Middle School Grading

Evaluation Category	Expected Range
1. **Quizzes/tests/exams**	20–30%
2. **Written assignments** creative or explanatory paragraphs, essays, notes, organizers, writing folios, portfolios	15–25%
3. **Oral presentations or demonstrations** brief or more formal presentations or demonstrations, role-playing, debates, skits, etc.	15–25%
4. **Projects/assignments** research tasks, hands-on projects, video- or audiotaped productions, analysis of issues, etc.	10–20%
5. **Cooperative group learning** evaluation of the process and skills learned as an individual and as a group member	5–15%
6. **Independent learning** individual organizational skills, contributions to class activities and discussions, homework, notebooks	5–15%
	70–130%

Note: Aspects of this plan conflict with other grading guidelines in addition to guideline 1.

Figure 1.1

With this type of plan, it is extremely difficult to appropriately emphasize each learning goal because the primary focus is on the methods of assessment. Each learning goal may be assessed in a number of ways; for example, there may be questions on tests/exams, written assignments, and demonstrations for each goal. However, to align assessment with the desired emphasis on each goal over several methods of assessment is extremely difficult.

On Target: Learning Goals

A much better approach is to use the learning goals as the basis for grades. In this approach, some aspect of the organizational structure of the learning goals is the basis for grades for the year or for each grading period. This can be determined by teachers working collaboratively; for example, all the grade 3 teachers in a school or district or all the grade 9 science teachers meet to discuss what is the most appropriate base for grades. This discussion may be the best professional dialogue teachers engage in, because they have to be very clear about what goals are important at what point in the school year, and they have to be prepared to support their own views while respecting the opinions of others. Another very important benefit of this approach is that there will be much greater consistency across a school or district than occurs with traditional, largely private, approaches to grading.

> **G**rades must be directly related to the learning goals for each grading period.

Ideally, the organizational structure chosen should be at the most specific and detailed level of the learning goals because, as Marzano (2000a) points out, "a problem that makes the traditional system highly ineffective . . . is the mixing of different types of knowledge and skills" (13). He further points out that "the construct of academic achievement is not a simple one" and "to provide effective feedback to students, teachers must keep track of those factors they wish to include in grades" (40). Thus the most appropriate way to organize a grading plan would be to base it on individual standards or benchmarks. This is being done with increasing frequency by elementary schools and is reflected in a report card such as the one in Figure 11.2-1 on page 214. In order to effectively complete such a report card, each teacher would need to use a tracking sheet for each student with horizontal rows for each of the standards included on the report card (see Figures 1.2–1.4). Unfortunately, in many jurisdictions there are just too many standards and/or teachers have too many students to be able to manage tracking of every standard for every student, so they must find a compromise. This generally means using the strands in the content standards or the basic organizing structure from the performance standards. Three examples of such approaches are provided in Figures 1.2, 1.3, and 1.4. Also, for high school teachers who teach so many students that having a separate page for each student is impractical, an example of a single tracking sheet for each class can be found on page 193, Figure 9.4b.

Illinois has five strands (and many standards) in its state goals for language arts:

1. Read with understanding and fluency.
2. Read and understand literature.
3. Write to communicate.
4. Listen and speak effectively.
5. Acquire, assess, and communicate information.

Figure 1.2 shows the approach and a tracking sheet that a teacher could use to record the achievement evidence for each strand. Each component of every assessment would have to link to one of the five strands. A grade could then be determined for each strand and/or an overall grade could be determined for language arts. The former is more desirable as it provides more useful information, but the approach taken would depend largely on the nature of the report card being used by the school or district.

The Wisconsin Mathematics Academic Standards have six strands as follows:

A. Mathematical Processes
B. Number Operations and Relationships
C. Geometry
D. Measurement
E. Statistics and Probability
F. Algebraic Relationships

Figure 1.3 shows an approach and a tracking sheet that would be appropriate for this subject. The same considerations and possibilities exist as for Illinois language arts, but, in addition, the way assessment results would be recorded is shown. On September 1st a test was administered which included standards from the geometry and measurement strands, so scores are recorded for those two strands. Then on September 8th a performance assessment was

Summary of Evidence for Illinois Language Arts

	Student: _____										
ACHIEVEMENT EVIDENCE											
Assessments / Strands											Summary
Read with understanding and fluency.											
Read and understand literature.											
Write to communicate.											
Listen and speak effectively.											
Acquire, assess, and communicate information.											
Comments											
										Overall Grade	

Figure 1.2

Summary of Evidence for Wisconsin Mathematics

	Student:	

ACHIEVEMENT EVIDENCE

Assessments / Strands	9/1 Test	9/8 PA												Summary
Mathematical Processes		3												
Number Operations and Relationships														
Geometry	$\frac{15}{20}$													
Measurement	$\frac{19}{20}$	4												
Statistics and Probability		3												
Algebraic Relationships														
Comments														

REPORT CARD GRADE
Most consistent level of achievement with consideration for more recent

Figure 1.3

completed that included standards from the mathematical processes, measurement, and statistics and probability strands with rubric scores (on a four-point scale) recorded for each strand. Over the grading period, this approach would be continued so at the end grades for each strand assessed during the grading period could be determined and, if necessary, an overall report card grade could also be determined.

A somewhat different approach can be found in Ontario, Canada (Figure 1.4). For all elementary and secondary subjects, achievement charts (see an example in chapter 2, Figure 2.6, on pages 76–77) have been developed which provide the performance standards. Each chart has descriptors of four levels of achievement for each of four categories of knowledge and skill. At the elementary level, the categories are different for each subject, but at the secondary level the categories are consistent across all fifteen disciplines included in the secondary curriculum. Expectations (as learning goals are called in Ontario) have to be classified into the most appropriate category, and then an approach identical to those for Illinois language arts and Wisconsin mathematics can be followed. Further examples of similar approaches can be found in Reeves (2000, 13) and Marzano (2000a, 106–118).

One possible drawback of this approach is that there is some additional bookkeeping, but, especially if rubrics are used, it takes less time to score assessments, which can be balanced against the additional time taken to record scores. In addition, while every strand or category should be assessed enough times over a year or course to make valid and reliable judgments of achievement, it is not essential that there be scores or grades for each strand/category in each grading period.

If overall grades are required, another aspect of this approach which teachers need to consider is whether each strand or category is of equal significance or whether some strands or categories are more important for the whole year or for any particular grading period. It is usually best to start from the position that each strand or category is of equal significance, making appropriate adjustments if it is obvious from the emphasis in the curriculum policy or in the way the subject is taught that one or more strands or categories are of greater significance than others. An example of this uneven distribution is the recommendation from the provincial association for physical and health education (PHE) teachers in Ontario that the application category be assigned a weight of 60-65% for grade 9 and 10 PHE.

> **T**he use of columns in a grade book to represent standards instead of assignments, tests, and activities, is a major shift in thinking for teachers.
> (Marzano and Kendall 1996, 150)

Summary of Evidence for Ontario Secondary

													Summary
Student: _____													
ACHIEVEMENT EVIDENCE													

Assessments / Knowledge/ Skill Categories													Summary
Knowledge/ Understanding													
Thinking/Inquiry													
Communication													
Application													
Comments													
							Most consistent level of achievement with consideration for more recent						

Figure 1.4

If grading plans are approached in this fashion, the learning goals become the set and the assessment methods become the subset. As has been shown, teachers identify for each assessment what components (or questions) fit with what learning goals and then record separate scores for each.

A detailed examination of this approach to grading is provided by Marzano and Kendall (1996), who said that "first and foremost, the teacher must stop thinking in terms of assignments, tests and activities to which points are assigned, and start thinking in terms of levels of performance in the declarative and procedural knowledge specific to her subject area" (147). They also acknowledged that "the use of columns in a grade book to represent standards, instead of assignments, tests, and activities, is a major shift in thinking for teachers" (150).

Related issues raised by Marzano and Kendall are how final grades are determined, and how student performances are reported. The first issue is dealt with in chapter 9, and the latter issue in chapter 11. It is sufficient to note here with regard to reporting that if grades are related to learning goals it is, at the very least, highly desirable, if not essential, that report cards provide opportunities for teachers to provide specific information on each learning goal in addition to an overall grade.

> **G**rading is an exercise in professional judgment, not just a mechanical, numerical exercise.

Learning Goals and Passing Grades

A final issue that needs to be considered in connection with this guideline is whether students should receive credit for a course if they have not demonstrated mastery of the critical learning goals. In the example in Figure 1.2, there are five strands in Illinois language arts. Although unlikely, it would be possible for a student to obtain very low scores on two strands, while obtaining sufficiently high scores on the other strands to obtain a passing grade. Teachers and schools need to decide if this is acceptable. If they really believe all or some strands are critical, then students will not obtain credit unless they have achieved a reasonable level of competence—ideally mastery—on each of those strands. If teachers use this approach, it obviously complicates the grading process, but it does support the concept that grading is an exercise in professional judgment, not just a mechanical, numerical exercise.

It also illustrates the interconnectedness of the grading guidelines because guidelines 4 and 5 become absolutely critical. Formative assessment has to be used to provide information to students and to teachers about progress (guideline 4), and students need to have growth acknowledged appropriately and have varied opportunities to demonstrate competence (guideline 5).

 ## What's the Bottom Line?

- Teachers should link grades to learning goals (standards, expectations, outcomes, etc.), not assessment methods.
- Teachers should have a clear understanding of what learning results are expected.
- Reporting should allow for detailed information on learning goals.
- Credit should be granted only when students have mastered the critical learning goals. (Mastery is the ideal.)

This guideline has these practical implications:

- Teachers use grade books where the columns primarily represent the learning goals and secondarily represent assessment methods.
- Teachers use an expanded format for reporting.

What's My Thinking Now?

**GUIDELINE 1: Relate grading procedures to learning
goals (i.e., standards).**

Analyze guideline 1 for grading by focusing on three questions:

Why use it?

Why not use it?

Are there points of uncertainty?

After careful thought about these points, answer these two questions:

Would I use guideline 1 now?

Do I agree or disagree with the guideline, or am I unsure at this time?

See the following for one person's reflections on guideline 1.

 # A Reflection on Guideline 1

WHY USE IT?

- links to basis for curriculum, instruction, and assessment
- realistically reflects intentions of course/grade
- provides clear goal/focus
- students know why they received grade
- consistency and fairness
- makes teachers accountable

WHY NOT USE IT?

- loss of creativity
- too great a shift in thinking/practice
- learning goals often vague
- community reaction
- huge amount of work to select learning goals, develop grading plan, etc.

POINTS OF UNCERTAINTY

- clarity of learning goals?
- fair to all learning styles?
- weighting learning goals?
- mastery or pass/fail?
- how many learning goals?

Chapter 2

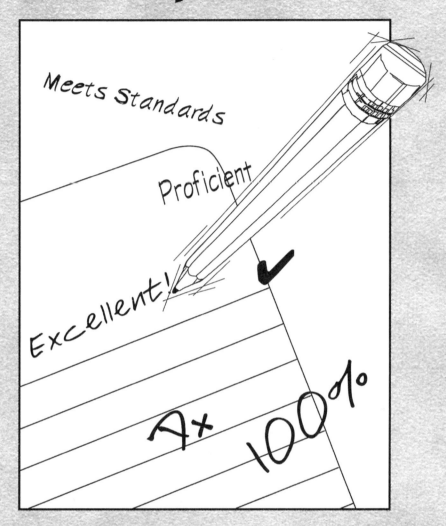

Using Performance Standards

Show us what good work looks like and what we have to do to get there.

—8-YEAR-OLD STUDENT

Guideline:

2

Use criterion-referenced performance standards as reference points to determine grades.

THE CASE OF . . .

Sally's Shocking Grade

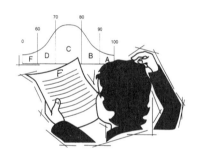

Sally was a very capable mathematics student in a small school in a high-income suburb. The school believed that the way to ensure maximum student effort was to use a bell curve to distribute grades. Sally's junior math class was taught by Mrs. Jones, who was generally acknowledged to be an excellent teacher, and had only ten students in the class. Sally really enjoyed the class, believed she was learning effectively, and appeared to be achieving well as all her quiz, test, and performance scores were more than 90%. She was absolutely shocked when she received her first quarter report card, and her math grade was an F. Her parents immediately called the school to inquire why their daughter received a failing grade. They were informed that Sally's marks were the lowest in the class, thus she fell into the lowest category on the bell curve. Sally doubled her efforts in the second quarter, but she was in a class with nine absolutely

brilliant math students, so at the end of the quarter, she was still in last place and received another F. Her parents could not accept this and arranged for Sally to transfer to a school with a semester program. Sally enrolled in the same math course and continued to perform at the same level as she had in her previous school. In this school, Sally's 90% marks were the highest in the class, and she received a grade of A+! The difference in the two situations was not Sally's achievement, but rather the ability of her classmates. In both schools, Sally's grades were not fair or accurate representations of her mathematics achievement.

What's the Purpose of the Guideline?

This guideline supports learning and encourages student success by ensuring that grades depend on clear, public performance standards and the student's own achievement, not on how that achievement compares with other students' achievement. Under this guideline, there is no artificial rationing of high (or low) grades as there is when relative standards (norm-referencing or the bell curve) are used to distribute grades.

What Are the Key Elements of the Guideline?

Everybody believes in standards, preferably high standards. But often it is not clear what is meant by standards. The use of standards always involves comparison and judgment because we are trying to answer the questions, How good is it? or How good is good enough? So the key question is: What reference points should we use? Guideline 1 dealt with content standards; this guideline deals with performance standards.

Developing Standards: Five Methods

One might suggest that these questions are impossible to answer, but here are five ways of approaching performance standards and standard setting:

1. Develop a norm.
2. Develop a criterion.
3. Use tacit knowledge.
4. Describe verbally.
5. Use key examples.

This five-fold classification is helpful because it shows a variety of performance standards or standard-setting approaches. Let us review each method in more detail.

Standard Based on a Norm

A *norm* is usually a number (often a mean) that is used as a standard against which performance is measured or compared (e.g., IQ test scores). Norms always compare performance with performances of others and are used appropriately in competitions when ranking is necessary. The concept of norms is expressed most clearly in the bell curve or so-called "normal distribution." This concept holds that there will be an equal number of high and low performers and that, on any performance, a population will be spread as shown in Figure 2.1.

Normal Distribution or Bell Curve

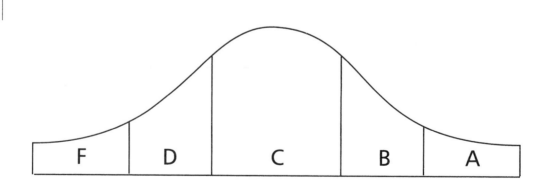

Figure 2.1

Standard Based on a Criterion

A *criterion* is a reference point, often a number, against which performance is measured, for example, words per minute in keyboarding. Criterion-referenced standards also compare, but the comparison is with a performance level, not the performance of others. For example, the world-class standard for the 100 meters is 10 seconds. Any runner near this time is a world-class sprinter, but we would not expect a twelve-year-old runner to perform at this level. We can, however, use the world-class time as a basis for criterion-referenced standards at various age groups.

Standard Based on Tacit Knowledge

Tacit knowledge belongs to the expert or connoisseur. These standards may begin as criterion-referenced standards but, in their highest form, reside only in the head of the expert. This level of knowledge comes only as a result of many years of study and/or practice. An example of this standard is judging Olympic figure skating.

> **In** *the real world, standards often involve combining several of these approaches.*

Standard Based on Verbal Description

Verbal description involves statements that make a standard explicit, public, and accessible, so that the standard is known and can be met and challenged, for example, by prior learning assessment.

Standard Based on Key Examples

Key examples of performance or behavior can be shown in various formats, including visual or text form, to help people recognize the standard when they see it. Examplars are not standards but rather represent standards, for example, videotaped performances of oral presentations.

Standard Based on Combinations of Methods

In the real world, standards often involve combining several of these approaches. In figure skating, experts apply criteria, using their tacit knowledge to arrive at a score on technical merit and artistic impression for each performance; however, to arrive at the final result for the competition, each skater's scores are compared with all the other skaters' scores to rank them (ordinals) and to determine the final placing for each skater for that performance. It is also worth noting that the expert's tacit knowledge has been developed from verbal descriptions of the criteria and also from many hours of study of key examples, either in live performances or on video.

Setting Performance Standards for the Classroom

The question that has to be addressed is: How should performance standards be established in and for the classroom?

Using Self-Referencing

One standard that has a place is self-referencing—for example, How is Sally doing today compared with how she did yesterday? How is she doing this month compared to last month? Last year? But even in this use of standards, decisions are made about what type of performance standard to use—for example, Is Sally compared with others? with performance criteria? based on expert knowledge, descriptions and/or exemplars?

Using Norm Referencing

Traditionally, the bell curve has been used to assign marks and grades, especially at the college level. This approach has many problems, which are eloquently summarized by both Guskey and Bellanca:

> Grading on a curve makes learning a highly competitive activity in which students compete against one another for the few scarce rewards (high grades) distributed by the teacher. Under these conditions, students readily see that helping others become successful threatens their own chances for success. As a result, learning becomes a game of winners and losers; and because the number of rewards is kept arbitrarily small, most students are forced to be losers. (Guskey 1996, 18–19)

> Grades, especially those based on the competitive curve, create fearsome anxieties for students . . . as well as for teachers. In our highly individualistic society, the grading curve exacerbates the most negative aspects of competition. Because the grading curve brands winners and losers, it works against the goal of successful learning for all students. . . . For every student who wins with an A, there is one who loses with a B, C or F. As the top scorers become more enamored of their successes in school, one by one, the bottom dwellers give up and go elsewhere. (Bellanca 1992, 299)

Glasser (1990) expressed this idea more simply when he said, "no student grade should ever depend on what other students do" (108).

In addition to this philosophical argument, there are also technical reasons why the use of the bell curve is inappropriate. In order to establish a normal distribution, the sample size must be large (at least several hundred, preferably thousands). It is simply wrong to grade on the curve if the population size is small. To be technically correct, one could use the curve at the classroom level, but only for very large classes, for example, all freshman English students in a very large high school or college. Even in this situation, philosophical (and practical) considerations should lead teachers away from the bell curve. Consider this: The class whose marks/grades are curved may be the best—or worst—the school has ever had. If it is the best, many students receive much lower grades than they really deserve; if it is the worst, many students receive much higher grades than they really deserve.

Pratt (1980) illustrates this unappealing situation. He describes the distributions of grades for two consecutive presentations of the same course by the same instructor. The first semester class was very weak, achieving final scores of 0% to 55%; the second semester class was much stronger, achieving final scores of 40% to 100%. The instructor followed his usual practice of bell curving the results and giving students final letter grades of A to F. In this somewhat extreme example, students who received an F in the second semester would have received an A with the same score in the first semester!

It is clear from this example that grading on a curve tells very little about what students know or are able to do. Grades are meant to be vehicles of clear communication— grading on the curve does not meet this standard because it often provides grades that are almost meaningless as measures of achievement.

An argument often made for the use of norm referencing in classroom grades is that it maintains standards. As noted earlier, this is not always the case—if you have a very weak class, students who do not deserve A's will get them if the bell curve is used. An extreme example of this occurred in California immediately after World War II. Many returning servicemen (and they were almost all men!) enrolled in college as a result of the GI bill; at this time, virtually all colleges used the bell curve. Aware of this, some men had

> **G**rading on a curve tells very little about what students are able to do.

their wives to enroll in the same courses as they did. Because the wives did no work and therefore got the F's on the curve, the husbands were guaranteed higher grades!

As Rick Stiggins said in a workshop presentation in Toronto in May, 1992, "There is no pedagogical, psychological, or scientific reason to assume in advance that achievement will be distributed in any way—whether normally or skewed in some direction—before instruction begins." Therefore, norm referencing, or the bell curve, is not appropriate at the classroom level. He went on to say, "Standards ought to be reflected, not in some . . . assumption of what the distribution of grades should be, but in clear, rigorous targets for students. Grading should be based on clear, high quality assessment of students' achievement with respect to that target."

Using Criterion Referencing

If norm referencing does not work, then we must use criterion-referenced standards. At times, these standards involve numbers, but more often they are verbal descriptions of various levels of performance developed from the tacit knowledge of experts (teachers, in collaboration with their students) supported by key examples of quality products, performances, or behaviors (see Figure 2.7 on page 80).

It is difficult—if not impossible—to achieve complete agreement on what quality is. Decisions do have to be made, and the performance standards chosen will have much greater credibility if they are public.

The more people involved in the discussions and decisions on these criterion-referenced standards, the better. Determining the performance standards, whether for grade 1 visual arts, senior mathematics, or college biology, is not an easy task. Equally vital is that the criterion-referenced standards have credibility with the students, teachers, parents, and the community where they are used. Spady (1991) suggested the "criteria need to be focused on the true culminating outcomes of significance for our students—not on all the daily details and work tasks" (44). A generic rather than a task-specific approach may help, but it is extremely difficult—if not impossible—to achieve complete agreement on what quality is. Decisions do have to be made, and the performance standards chosen will have much greater credibility if they are public and if the process by which they were determined is open and accessible. This does not mean that there needs to be a public standard-setting process for each assessment used, but teachers need to be able to align the standards they are using with publicly available performance standards.

REFLECTING ON . . . SAMPLE SCENARIOS

Take a minute to consider these situations:

1. What do you think would happen in your school if you did an outstanding job, all the students in your class were highly motivated and did an outstanding job, and all the students received grades of 90% or higher?

2. What do you think would happen in your school if you did a good job, most of the students in your class were unmotivated and did a poor job, and almost all the students received failing grades?

If the school's objective for grades is to support learning and encourage success, situation 1 needs to be celebrated. But situation 2 needs to be carefully examined, and program decisions need to be made to try to ensure that it does not happen again.

Far too often, however, neither situation would be allowed. In situation 1, administrators frequently lower student grades or at least severely question the teacher. As Juarez (1990) pointed out "normative grading forces the teacher into the absurd 'Catch 22' position of not being viewed as successful unless a percentage of his or her students are unsuccessful" (37). In situation 2, student grades would probably be raised and the teacher's competence doubted.

> **There should be no artificial rationing of high or low marks or grades.**

Neither of these administrative decisions is acceptable. If all students perform at a high—or at a low—level, then they should receive the appropriate marks and grades. There should be no artificial rationing of high or low marks or grades. This is particularly important in the so-called subjective subjects, such as English and history; students must be able to receive 100% in these subjects in the same way as students get 100% in the so-called objective subjects, such as mathematics and physics. Marks or grades of 100% do "not indicate perfection, but rather that the student has achieved all 'objectives' at the highest standard identified" (Pratt 1980, 257).

It is also critical that there be no grade rationing in different years in school or college. It appears that many high school teachers, and particularly first-year college teachers, claim they have high standards because their class averages are low, many students fail, and few students receive A's. Bonstingl

(1992) examines this view thoughtfully and somewhat humorously in a chapter titled The Bell Curve Meets Kaizen (*kaizen* means continuous improvement). He posed this question: "Why does it seem the farther we get from first grade, the less likely we are to view education's central purpose as nurturing people's innate potential through the development of patterns of success, and the more likely we are to view education as a judgmental, gatekeeping function?" (2–3)

> **M**arks and grades must reflect actual student performance based on publicly available criterion-referenced standards, not artificially determined distributions.

Marks and grades must reflect actual student performance based on publicly available criterion-referenced standards, not artificially determined distributions. Cereal and car makers strive to produce 100% of their products with a grade of A; educators must strive for this as well, and not be satisfied with class averages of about 70%, which is often the case. Teachers must be careful that they do not have a bell curve lurking in the back of their minds; they must be prepared to give students the grade they deserve based on comparison with absolute (criterion-referenced), not relative (norm-referenced), standards.

Performance Standards

Figure Intro.2 (see the Introduction, page 9) illustrates that standards have two critical components—content and performance standards. All standards-based jurisdictions have content standards but, even when they say they have them, relatively few have real performance standards. One state, for example, has an excellent definition of performance standards on the cover of its standards document, but when you look inside, the so-called performance standards are just content standards in greater detail. The net result of this gap is that performance standards are often still left to the individual teacher to establish and apply. This is unsatisfactory and should be seen as unacceptable, because if standards-based reform is to achieve its promise, there must be clear, agreed upon performance standards so that judgments of quality are as consistent as possible by each teacher for every student. As Stiggins (2001a) asks, "How are teachers to provide dependable information about student achievement if targets are not defined?" (16).

Figure 2.2 provides some possibilities for establishing performance standards. The cruise line's idea of performance standards is based on passengers' expectations, while the hotel's is based on satisfaction linked to a percentage

Establishing Performance Standards

When establishing performance standards, it is necessary to ask the following questions:

How good is good enough?
What reference points do we use?

Cruise Line

Above Expectations
Met Expectations
Below Expectations

Hotel

100% — Very Satisfied
60% — Somewhat Satisfied
40% — Neither Satisfied nor Dissatisfied
20% — Somewhat Dissatisfied

Traditional School Approaches

90–100%	— Outstanding	Excellent
80–89%	— Above Average	Good
70–79%	— Average	Satisfactory
60–69%	— Below Average	Poor
>60%	— Failing	Unacceptable

Standards-Based Approaches

(may be described by levels or linked to %)

Advanced	Above standard*
Proficient	Meets standard
Developing	Below but approaching standard
Beginning	Well below standard

*Standard has to be defined. For example, Ontario defines standards as "well prepared for next grade or course."

Figure 2.2

scale. In education, we have used brief descriptors often linked to letter or percentage grades. In the past, these scales often used "average" for the middle category, but with criterion-referenced standards this is inappropriate, so we need to use descriptors such as advanced, proficient, developing, and beginning. There are a wide variety of scales like this currently in use (see Figure 2.3) and while they provide a starting point, to be truly useful the scales need to include additional descriptive words to make the performance standards clearer (see Figure 2.4). Carr and Farr also provide an example of performance standards (2000, 198). The more detailed this description is, the better. Also, it is better if the descriptors or abbreviations are used on report cards rather than traditional letter grades because the words are more affirming, especially for young children (Guskey and Bailey 2001). There are some words, however, that it is probably best to avoid, such as "exceeding" or "extending," because it is often unclear what is necessary to meet these descriptors. It is particularly important that the highest level be attainable by students achieving at a grade level. For example, the highest level at, say, grade 4, does not mean that students have to be achieving at a grade 5 level.

Possible Titles for Performance Standard Levels

Advanced	Advanced	Above standard	Exceptional	Consistently
Proficient	Proficient	At standard	Proficient	Usually
Partial	Approaching	Approaching	Progressing	Sometimes
Minimal	Below	Well below	Beginning	Seldom

Note: The performance standard levels are what Guskey and Bailey (2001, 75) call "categorical grading labels"; some of these examples are quoted from that source.

Figure 2.3

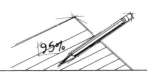

Sample Set of Performance Levels

Beginning
Limited mastery of essential knowledge and skills; may require assistance or extended time in applying knowledge and skills

Progressing
Partial mastery of essential knowledge and skills; partial success in tasks using this knowledge or skill

Proficient
Solid academic performance, demonstrates competency of subject matter knowledge, applies such knowledge to real-world situations

Advanced
Superior performance, in-depth understanding, application of knowledge and skills to develop new understanding and solutions

Figure 2.4   Adapted from the Nebraska Department of Education, 2000.

One concept that is often included in performance standards is the idea that there is a level that is the objective for all or most students. This is usually the second highest level so that the highest level is above this standard, while the lower levels are approaching and well below this objective standard. As indicated in Figure 2.2, in Ontario this is called "the provincial standard" and is defined as being "well prepared for the next grade or course." This may seem a little vague, but I believe that it is a concept that we have always used, and thus has real meaning for students, parents, and teachers. It has rarely been suggested that grades just at the passing level mean a student is achieving well or even satisfactorily—these descriptors have been reserved for higher achievement levels and that is what is happening frequently now with performance standards.

To be really useful for students, parents, and teachers, performance standards should be described in even greater detail. One way to do this is with descriptive grading criteria (see Figure 2.5). Descriptors like these could be adapted for any grade or subject. Another approach is the one being used in the Province of Ontario. Brief descriptors of five levels—one to four, plus failing—are provided, along with detailed achievement charts with descriptors for each of the four levels of achievement for a number of criteria within four categories of knowledge and skill. See Figure 2.6 for an example. These achievement charts provide fairly broad general descriptors, but when read horizontally, a relatively clear quality progression can be seen for each criterion. Their greatest value, however, is when they are read vertically so that one gets a real sense of performance at each level. Read this way, the charts can give students, parents, and teachers a real sense of "fourness" or "A" level achievement. These achievement charts also form the base from which to develop classroom scoring tools, be they traditional marking schemes, checklists, or fully developed rubrics.

Ideally, exemplars or anchor papers that enable students and teachers to see actual examples of performance at various levels should support rubrics and other scoring guides. Exemplars provide aiming points and then take-off points for students as they deepen their understanding of what quality is and what level of achievement is possible. For teachers, exemplars provide a base for consistency in scoring; in fact, the more teachers can do collaborative scoring and discuss actual work samples in relation to exemplars the more consistent scoring will become.

Performance Standards—When?

One difficult aspect of performance standards that must be addressed is deciding whether performance standards refer to the time of each report or whether they should be considered in relationship to year-end standards. There is no easy answer to this dilemma, but whichever approach is taken it must be made very clear to all involved, especially parents of young children.

Sample Descriptive Grading Criteria

Students receiving a grade demonstrate most of the characteristics most of the time.

A
- Exhibits novel and creative ways to show learning.
- Enjoys the challenge and successfully completes open-ended tasks with high quality work.
- Test scores indicate a high level of understanding of concepts and skills.
- Assignments are complete, high quality, well organized, and show a high level of commitment.
- Almost all the learning goals are fully or consistently met and extended.

B
- Exhibits standard ways to show learning.
- Enjoys open-ended tasks, but needs support in dealing with ambiguity.
- Test scores indicate a good grasp of concepts and skills.
- Assignments are generally complete, thorough, and organized.
- Most of the learning goals are fully or consistently met.

C
- Needs some encouragement to show learning.
- Needs support to complete open-ended tasks.
- Test scores indicate satisfactory acquisition of skills and concepts.
- Assignments are generally complete, but quality, thoroughness, and organization vary.
- More than half of the learning goals are fully or consistently met.

D
- Occasionally shows learning after considerable encouragement.
- Needs support to begin, let alone complete, open-ended tasks.
- Test scores indicate weak acquisition of skills and concepts.
- Assignments are widely varied in quality, thoroughness, and organization.
- Only a few of the learning goals are fully or consistently met.

F
- Rarely shows learning.
- Unable to begin, let alone complete, open-ended tasks.
- Test scores indicate very weak grasp of concepts and skills.
- Assignments show poor quality and are frequently incomplete.
- None or almost none of the learning goals are fully or consistently met.

Figure 2.5   Adapted from original work by Sharon Anderson, Dave Layzell, and Bob Belcher.

Achievement Chart — Grades 9–10, Science

Categories	50–59% (Level 1)	60–69% (Level 2)	70–79% (Level 3)	80–100% (Level 4)
Knowledge/ Understanding	**The student:**			
– understanding of concepts, principles, laws, and theories (e.g., identifying assumptions; eliminating misconceptions; providing explanations)	– demonstrates limited understanding of concepts, principles, laws, and theories	– demonstrates some understanding of concepts, principles, laws, and theories	– demonstrates considerable understanding of concepts, principles, laws, and theories	– demonstrates thorough understanding of concepts, principles, laws, and theories
– knowledge of facts and terms	– demonstrates limited knowledge of facts and terms	– demonstrates some knowledge of facts and terms	– demonstrates considerable knowledge of facts and terms	– demonstrates thorough knowledge of facts and terms
– transfer of concepts to new contexts	– infrequently transfers simple concepts to new contexts	– sometimes transfers simple concepts to new contexts	– usually transfers simple and some complex concepts to new contexts	– routinely transfers complex concepts to new contexts
– understanding of relationships between concepts	– demonstrates limited understanding of relationships between concepts	– demonstrates some understanding of relationships between concepts	– demonstrates considerable understanding of relationships between concepts	– demonstrates thorough and insightful understanding of relationships between concepts
Thinking/Inquiry	**The student:**			
– application of the skills and strategies of scientific inquiry (e.g., initiating and planning, performing and recording, analyzing and interpreting, problem solving)	– applies few of the skills and strategies of scientific inquiry	– applies some of the skills and strategies of scientific inquiry	– applies most of the skills and strategies of scientific inquiry	– applies all or almost all of the skills and strategies of scientific inquiry
– application of technical skills and procedures (e.g., microscopes)	– applies technical skills and procedures with limited competence	– apples technical skills and procedures with moderate competence	– applies technical skills and procedures with considerable competence	– applies technical skills and procedures with a high degree of competence
– use of tools, equipment, and materials	– uses tools, equipment, and materials safely and correctly only with supervision	– uses tools, equipment, and materials safely and correctly with some supervision	– uses tools, equipment, and materials safely and correctly	– demonstrates and promotes the safe and correct use of tools, equipment, and materials

Figure 2.6

76

SkyLight Professional Development

Categories	50–59% (Level 1)	60–69% (Level 2)	70–79% (Level 3)	80–100% (Level 4)
Communication	**The student:**			
– communication of information and ideas	– communicates information and ideas with limited clarity and precision	– communicates information and ideas with moderate clarity and precision	– communicates information and ideas with considerable clarity and precision	– communicates information and ideas with a high degree of clarity and precision
– use of scientific terminology, symbols, conventions, and standard (SI) units	– uses scientific terminology, symbols, conventions, and SI units with limited accuracy and effectiveness	– uses scientific terminology, symbols, conventions, and SI units with some accuracy and effectiveness	– uses scientific terminology, symbols, conventions, and SI units with considerable accuracy and effectiveness	– uses scientific terminology, symbols, conventions, and SI units with a high degree of accuracy and effectiveness
– communication for different audiences and purposes	– communicates with a limited sense of audience and purpose	– communicates with some sense of audience and purpose	– communicates with a clear sense of audience and purpose	– communicates with a strong sense of audience and purpose
– use of various forms of communication (e.g., reports, essays)	– demonstrates limited command of the various forms	– demonstrates moderate command of the various forms	– demonstrates considerable command of the various forms	– demonstrates extensive command of the various forms
– use of information technology for scientific purposes (e.g., specialized databases)	– uses technology with limited appropriateness and effectiveness	– uses technology with moderate appropriateness and effectiveness	– uses appropriate technology with considerable effectiveness	– uses appropriate technology with a high degree of effectiveness
Making Connections	**The student:**			
– understanding connections among science, technology, society, and the environment	– shows limited understanding of connections in familiar contexts	– shows some understanding of connections in familiar contexts	– shows considerable understanding of connections in familiar and some unfamiliar contexts	– shows thorough understanding of connections in familiar and unfamiliar contexts
– analysis of social and economic issues involving science and technology	– analyzes social and economic issues with limited effectiveness	– analyzes social and economic issues with moderate effectiveness	– analyzes social and economic issues with considerable effectiveness	– analyzes complex social and economic issues with a high degree of effectiveness
– assessment of impacts of science and technology on the environment	– assesses environmental impacts with limited effectiveness	– assesses environmental impacts with moderate effectiveness	– assesses environmental impacts with considerable effectiveness	– assesses environmental impacts with a high degree of effectiveness
– proposing courses of practical action in relation to science- and technology-based problems	– extends analyses of familiar problems into courses of practical action with limited effectiveness	– extends analyses of familiar problems into courses of practical action with moderate effectiveness	– extends analyses of familiar problems into courses of practical action with considerable effectiveness	– extends analyses of familiar and unfamiliar problems into courses of practical action with a high degree of effectiveness

Figure 2.6 continued)

Carr and Farr (as cited in Trumbull and Farr 2000, 200) suggest that there are three alternatives:

1. achievement at the time of the report—what they call period-referenced scores;
2. progress toward grade level proficiency—what they call progress-referenced scores; and
3. year-end grade level proficiency—what they call standards-referenced scores.

Each alternative has advantages and disadvantages; the main problems (Carr and Farr as cited in Trumbull and Farr, 2000, 201) are as follows:

1. the need for specific performance standards for each reporting period,
2. the difficulty of getting teacher consistency from descriptors that are usually rather vague, and
3. parental understanding—or lack of understanding—of why even good students may get no better than twos on the first report card

I believe the most practical approach is to consider that progress reports are for the content standards introduced or developed in that reporting period and that grades reflect achievement relative to the standard at that point in the school year. I know that this introduces an element of uncertainty or inconsistency, but it seems to me that it is the fairest to students and clearer for parents. Probably the best approach is to provide two scores or grades: one period-referenced score and one standards-referenced score. An example would involve using a one-to-four scale for period-referenced scores and a plus and minus scale (++, +, −) for standards-referenced scores. Guskey and Bailey (2001, 99) provide an excellent example of a report card that used this approach in their thought-provoking book, *Developing Grading and Reporting Systems for Student Learning.*

Establishing Scoring Criteria

Another dimension of this guideline should also be considered. If grades are related to learning goals, it is critical that teachers mark each assessment on clear, pre-established criteria (targets, standards). The use of detailed rubrics

or scoring guides is essential, and it is ideal to have students involved in the development of the rubrics or scoring guides (see chapter 8). These scoring guides must be based on the more general performance standards that have been established at the state/province, district, or school level. For an example, see Figure 2.8 on page 81.

This is the complete opposite of the approach recommended by Mahon (1996) who said "teachers, like magicians, are ill-advised to reveal too many tricks of the trade" (280). If we want grades with meaning and if we want assessment to contribute to learning, Mahon is wrong. As Stiggins says in almost every workshop he presents, "students can hit any target they can see and which stands still for them." But teachers have to provide this clarity and consistency in the form of rubrics and detailed scoring guides. Then students know what is expected and have some chance of producing it. Students also are able to use summative assessments to contribute to their growth by answering what Fogarty and Bellanca (1987, 227) called Mrs. Potter's Questions:

1. What were you expected to do?
2. In this assignment, what did you do well?
3. If you had to do this task over, what would you do differently?
4. What help do you need from me?

Clear criteria or targets also help us to deal with the issue of what grades mean because they provide "stable and clear points of reference," which Wiggins (1996, 142) said are often lacking but are necessary for symbols like grades to have meaning. A rubric for expository writing, Figure 2.7, is provided as an example for teachers to use in developing their own rubrics and scoring guides. Further useful information can be found in Danielson (1997), and discussion of the use of scoring guides and many sample rubrics can be found in Arter and McTighe (2001).

What's the Bottom Line?

What standards should be used? Teachers should use criterion-referenced (or absolute) performance standards that are public, based on expert knowledge, clearly stated in words or numbers, and supported by exemplars or models.

Expository Writing Assessment

Name _____ Date _____

Assignment _____

Assessor: Teacher ☐ Peer ☐ Self ☐   Put a ✓ mark in the appropriate box for the level of performance for each criterion.

Criteria for Expository Writing	Levels of Performance for Each Criterion			
Structure—introduction means that the first sentence(s) clearly state(s) the main idea(s)	The introduction is missing.	The introduction is included but is unclear or off topic.	The introduction is included but is somewhat unclear.	The introduction clearly states the main idea(s).
Structure—conclusion the last sentence(s) clearly summarize(s) the main idea(s)	The conclusion is missing.	The conclusion is included but is unclear or off topic.	The conclusion is included but is somewhat unclear.	The conclusion clearly summarizes the main idea(s).
Supporting sentences, reasons or arguments means that the sentences developing the main idea are clear and related to the main idea in a logical fashion	Supporting sentences, reasons, or arguments are mainly unclear and unconnected to the main idea.	Supporting sentences, reasons, or arguments are occasionally unclear and may be unconnected to the main idea or disorganized.	Supporting sentences, reasons, or arguments are usually clear and connected to the main idea in an organized way.	Supporting sentences, reasons, or arguments are always clear and connected to the main idea in an organized way.
Evidence and examples means the use of specific related facts, examples, or evidence to develop or support sentences, reasons, or arguments	No relevant, clear facts, examples, or evidence are given to support the arguments.	Some evidence is given as support. Many pieces of evidence are missing or irrelevant.	Most sentences, reasons, or arguments are developed or supported by relevant evidence and examples.	All sentences, reasons, or arguments are developed or supported by relevant evidence and examples.
Mechanics of writing means the use of correct spelling and grammar, such as sentence structure and proper wording	Major repeated errors in spelling and/or grammar.	Some significant errors in spelling and/or grammar.	Few significant errors in spelling and/or grammar.	No significant errors in spelling and grammar.
Additional criteria (developed by the teacher and students)				

Comments and Suggestions for Improvement:

Figure 2.7   Adapted with permission, © 1995 from Toronto District School Board, Ontario, Canada.

SkyLight Professional Development

Pennsylvania Performance Standards

ADVANCED
Students achieving at the advanced level demonstrate superior academic performance. Advanced work indicates an in-depth understanding or exemplary display of the skills included in the Pennsylvania Academic Content Standards.

These students:
- demonstrate broad in-depth understanding of complex concepts and skills
- make abstract, insightful, complex connections among ideas beyond the obvious
- provides extensive evidence for inferences and justification of solutions
- demonstrate the ability to apply knowledge and skills effectively and independently by applying efficient, sophisticated strategies to solve complex problems
- communicate effectively and thoroughly, with sophistication

PROFICIENT
Students achieving at the proficient level demonstrate satisfactory academic performance. Proficient work indicates a solid understanding or display of the skills included in the Pennsylvania Academic Content Standards. This is the accepted grade-level performance.

These students:
- can extend their understanding by making meanngful, multiple connections among important ideas or concepts and provide supporting evidence for inferences and justification of solutions
- apply concepts and skills to solve problems using appropriate strategies
- communicate effectively

BASIC
Students achieving at the basic level demonstrate marginal academic performance. Basic work indicates a partial understanding or display of the skills included in the Pennsylvania Academic Content Standards. Students achieving at this level are approaching acceptable performance but have not achieved it.

These students:
- demonstrate partial understanding of basic concepts and skills
- make simple or basic connections among ideas, providing limited supporting evidence for inferences and solutions
- apply concepts and skills to routine problem-solving situations
- communicate in limited fashion

BELOW BASIC
Students achieving at the below basic level demonstrate unacceptable academic performance. Below basic work indicates a need for additional instructional opportunities to achieve even a basic understanding or display of the skills included in the Pennsylvania Academic Content Standards.

These students:
- demonstrate minimal understanding of rudimentary concepts and skills
- occasionally make obvious connections among ideas, providing minimal evidence or support for inferences and solutions
- have difficulty applying basic knowledge and skills
- communicate in an ineffective manner

Figure 2.8

Used with permission by Jacques Gibble, Supervisor of Curriculum and Instruction, Donegal School District, Mount Joy, PA.

What's My Thinking Now?

GUIDELINE 2: Use criterion-referenced performance standards as reference points to determine grades.

Analyze guideline 2 for grading by focusing on three questions:

Why use it?

Why not use it?

Are there points of uncertainty?

After careful thought about these points, answer these two questions:

Would I use guideline 2 now?

Do I agree or disagree with the guideline, or am I unsure at this time?

See the following for one person's reflections on guideline 2.

 # A Reflection on Guideline 2

WHY USE IT?

- clear to all what the standards are
- all learners may be successful
- emphasizes self-assessment and growth, not competition
- makes marking/grading more consistent
- contributes to improved quality of work

WHY NOT USE IT?

- time consuming to develop criteria, rubrics, etc.
- who says what quality is?
- doesn't teach competitiveness students need in "real" world
- standards may be set too high or too low
- need for flexibility, creativity

POINTS OF UNCERTAINTY

- differences between teachers and school on what is quality
- what do parents and the next level of educators expect?
- subject requirements vary, some more subjective than others
- variation in ability between and within classes
- can all students get As?

Chapter 3

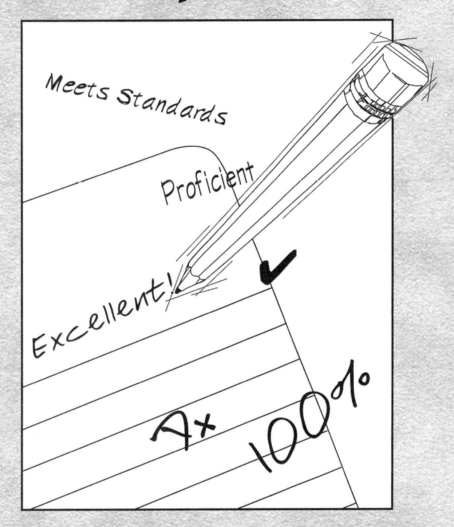

Grading Individual Achievement

In a standards-based accountability system, achievement alone should be the basis for grades. If behavior or effort is to be rated, it should be reported separately.

—TRUMBULL (IN TRUMBULL AND FARR 2000, 36)

Guideline:

3

Limit the valued attributes included in grades to individual achievement.

THE CASE OF . . .

Rick's Mysterious Falling Grade

The report card mathematics grade that Rick received in December in grade 8 was about 25% lower than the grade he received in June at the end of grade 7. His parents were very concerned because Rick had always enjoyed mathematics and achieved at a high level. They went to the parent-teacher conference wondering whether he needed a tutor. When they put this question to his teacher, she said that this was not necessary. She went on to say that his mathematics results were excellent; all his test scores were more than 90%, but that he had received low marks for participation, effort, group work, notebook, homework, and so forth. Rick's parents felt the grade was very misleading because it did not indicate clearly Rick's level of mathematics achievement.

 # What's the Purpose of the Guideline?

This guideline is critical because, among the many purposes for grades, the first is communication—with students, parents, and many others—of the achievement status of each student.

 # What Are the Key Elements of the Guideline?

Grading Achievement Only

For grades to have real meaning, they must be relatively pure measures of each student's achievement of the learning goals for each course. From a philosophical perspective, achievement may be defined narrowly as knowledge, somewhat more broadly as knowledge and skills, or most broadly as knowledge, skills, and behavior. The breadth of definition of achievement depends on the stated, clearly understood learning goals. For example, in a senior mathematics or science course, achievement may be defined quite narrowly, whereas in a freshman drama, environmental studies, or physical education course, achievement could, and probably should, be defined more broadly. The breadth of definition of achievement varies with the grade level and the nature of the course.

> **For** grades to have real meaning, they must be relatively pure measures of each student's achievement of the learning goals.

Practically speaking, this philosophical perspective is now virtually irrelevant in most jurisdictions because achievement is now defined by the standards so that achievement equals standards. (See Figure Intro.16 on page 42.)

Grading Viewpoints

A number of viewpoints relevant to this guideline can be found in the literature on grading. Stiggins and Knight (1997) described the situation portrayed in Rick's Mysterious Falling Grade as grade pollution. They said "when the object is effective communication [of achievement] . . . schools [should] adopt grading policies that permit teachers to indicate each student's current level of academic achievement with nothing else factored in to interfere with that message" (61).

Brookhart (1994) stated that teachers' grading practices often combine a variety of factors "into composite scores of questionable validity and uncertain meaning" (299). Bailey and McTighe (1996) noted that "grades often reflect a combination of achievement, progress, and other factors. . . . this tendency to collapse several independent elements into a single grade may blur their meaning" (121). Cizek (1996a) found that teachers created what he calls "an uncertain mix." By an uncertain mix, he means that they "combined the marks they had assigned to individual assignments and tests . . . with three other kinds of information:

- formal achievement-related measures (attendance, class participation);
- informal achievement-related measures (answers in class, one-on-one discussions); and
- other informal information (impressions of effort, conduct, teamwork, leadership and so on)" (104–105).

He concludes that "this mix of factors is difficult to disentangle."

Hensley et al. (1989) reported that "class attendance and 'dressing out' were the most frequently used variables in the assessment of students in physical education classes" (38). Matanin and Tannehill (1994) supported this finding, stating that "factors that stood out as consistent contributors to students' grades in physical education were attendance, appropriate attire, behavior, and effort" (401). Canady, in a workshop in Toronto in June 1996, described this as determining grades on whether their shorts were clean and whether their socks matched!

Gronlund and Linn (1990) stated that

... letter grades are likely to be most meaningful and useful when they represent achievement only. If they are contaminated by such extraneous factors as effort, the amount of work completed (rather than the quality of the work), personal conduct and so on, their interpretation will be hopelessly confused. When letter grades combine various aspects of pupil development, not only do they lose their meaning as a measure of achievement, but they also suppress information concerning other important aspects of development. (437)

> **G**rades often reflect a combination of achievement, progress, and other factors. . . . this tendency to collapse several independent elements into a single grade may blur their meaning. (Bailey and McTighe 1996, 121)

A Critical Grading Concept: Achievement

The basic concepts embodied in this guideline are illustrated in Figure Intro.16 on page 42. This diagram shows that teachers make some sort of assessment of everything that students do in the school or classroom (the outer rectangle), but from that entirety, they select a representative sampling of what students do to grade and/or to report. The grading variables concentrate on achievement of the process and product learning goals, whereas attitude, learning skills, and effort are seen primarily as reporting variables. *Achievement* demonstrates knowledge, skills, and behaviors that are stated as learning goals for a course or unit of instruction, which in most jurisdictions means the standards.

> **Grades are limited to individual achievement and are not used as punishment.**

This guideline does not imply that grading is simply a clinical, objective procedure. There is a great deal of professional judgment involved in grading, as teachers develop an assessment plan (guideline 8), choose or develop the assessment instruments (guideline 7), evaluate the process and product components of grades (guidelines 4 and 5), and record the results after deciding how to combine the scores and determine grades (guidelines 1, 2, and 6). These aspects are considered in discussions of these guidelines.

A critical aspect of guideline 3 is this: Grades are limited to individual achievement and are not used as punishment for poor attendance, inappropriate behavior, or lack of punctuality. These are discipline problems and, although they usually impact achievement, they should be dealt with as such. Most schools have rules or student codes of behavior that set standards and penalties; penalties for rule or code infractions should not be academic penalties. Lowering grades simply because of poor attendance, misbehavior, or lateness distorts achievement; grades then do not have clear meaning. Bobby's C may reflect his consistent achievement at that level, whereas Ann's C, although she consistently achieves at an A level, results from her many absences, frequent lateness, and misbehavior. This mixed result is inconsistent with this guideline; schools or districts that have such penalties in their grading policies need to move them to their discipline policies and also ensure that their formal and informal communication vehicles allow them to report poor behavior, attendance, and lateness in an accurate and timely manner.

Hills (1991) provides an excellent analysis of how to deal with attendance.

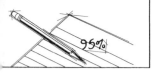
If the desired behavior or competency is to attend class regularly, then have that as a written objective and base grades on it. (For most courses above the primary grades, this approach would be absurd.) If the desired behavior or competency is a skill in the topic under study, such as effective behavior in an operating room, then base the grade solely on the level of skill achieved in that behavior. If a student is able to develop that skill without attending, then his or her attendance is irrelevant as far as an evaluation of competence is concerned. If some students are truant, and if this situation influences the behavior of other students, then you have a disciplinary problem, and you should deal with it as a disciplinary matter, not as an academic matter. If the student cannot be evaluated on something like skill and effectiveness in the operating room because no one has seen him or her function in one, then no grade should be given at all. You have no basis for determining a level of competency, so you should not pretend otherwise. (541)

Students' grades appear on their personal report cards and therefore should not be contaminated by the achievement (or lack of achievement) of other students.

A particularly difficult aspect of misbehavior is the issue of cheating, because it crosses the line between behavior and achievement. Schools and districts need procedures to deal fairly and appropriately with cheating, including plagiarism. This can be achieved best by having a clear district or school policy on academic honesty. As with other misbehavior, cheating is primarily a discipline problem, but it clearly is reasonable to have more direct academic consequences for this than for other behavioral problems. An excellent case study that illustrates this issue can be found in Busick and Stiggins (1997, 109–110).

Grading Individuals

Another extremely important aspect of this guideline is the emphasis on grading individuals on their personal achievement rather than grading individuals on their group's achievement. With the increasing importance of the ability to work effectively with others in school and at work, this emphasis on individual achievement may seem strange. But remember that students' grades appear on their personal report cards and therefore should not be contaminated by the achievement (or lack of achievement) of other students.

Concerns About Group Grades

It is unfortunate that group marks are one of the reasons why students and parents give group work a bad name. Cooperative learning—despite its importance for the development of capable citizens and productive employees and its value to learning as shown by a significant body of research—has struggled against this legacy.

In his excellent article, Kagan (1995) provided strong criticism of eight arguments for group grades (Figure 3.1). He also gave seven reasons why he is "unequivocally opposed to group grades" (69; see Figure 3.2). Then he suggested "alternative ways to accomplish the same goals" (71). (Please note that in most cases, Kagan uses *grade* to mean what this book calls *mark*.) Kagan also suggested that cooperative learning skills could be rewarded through a variety of other recognition approaches that are more effective than group grades. He said that it is preferable to give students a mark in "group skills" or marks in specific cooperative skills.

Rather than use group marks, Kagan proposed several alternatives:

1. Follow an approach similar to Kohn's 3 Cs: collaboration—learning together; content—things worth knowing; and choice—autonomy in the classroom (1993a, 212–221). This approach ensures that "we will not need grades to motivate students" (71).
2. Provide formal feedback in written form on students' cooperative learning skills. Kagan believes students will work very hard if they know in advance that such feedback will occur.
3. "Meet with students individually after asking them to set their own goals" (71). This type of self-assessment promotes real learning.

Marking Cooperative Learning

How then should cooperative learning be marked? Obviously, the key is to focus on assessing the skills of each student as an individual. One way to do this is to use an observation sheet such as the one shown in Figure 3.3.

While students are working on a cooperative learning task, the teacher walks around the classroom and records information on each group.

Kagan's Critique of Group Grades

ARGUMENT		COUNTER ARGUMENT
The real-world argument—Preparing students for the real world requires that they develop cooperative learning skills; in the real world, teams are rewarded for their group effort.	BUT	"In the real world there are many unfair practices, . . . that doesn't justify unfair practices in the classroom."
The employment skills argument—Grading the social skill of cooperation, which is highly desired by employers, shows students that it is important.	BUT	"Group grades don't necessarily foster social skills," and "group grades on academic projects do not fairly assess the cooperative skills of individuals because, for example, if most members of the group cooperate very well, everyone in the group—even the least cooperative student—receives a high grade. The reverse is also true and is probably a more serious problem."
The motivation argument—Students won't work together unless it counts in the grade.	BUT	"There are many better ways to motivate students."
The teachers' workload argument—Some teachers prefer marking groups because it is faster than marking many individual papers.	BUT	"This is not a legitimate short cut. Group grades tell us nothing reliable about individual performance."
The grades-are-subjective-anyway argument	BUT	"The sometimes subjective nature of grading does not justify using a method that is even less precise."
The grades-aren't-that-important argument	BUT	"Try explaining it to the parents of a student who, based on his or her grades [which included group marks for cooperation], has just narrowly missed being accepted to a desired college."
The credit-for-teamwork argument	BUT	"Individuals should be given credit for their individual work, not a free ride on the work of others."
The group-grades-are-a-small-factor argument—Some argue that it is all right to use group marks because they rarely have a significant impact on the final grade.	BUT	"Very occasionally is far too often if it means giving individual grades that do not reflect individual performances."

Figure 3.1   From Kagan, Spencer. "Group Grades Miss the Mark." *Educational Leadership* 52(8): 68-71. Reprinted with permission of the Association for Supervision and Curriculum Development. © 1995 by ASCD. All rights reserved.

Kagan's Seven Reasons for Opposing Group Grades

1 **No fair.** Group grades are so blatantly unfair that on this basis alone they should never be used.

2 **Group grades debase report cards.** If the grade a student gets "is a function of who the student happens to have as a teammate," then no one can use the grades in a meaningful way.

3 **Group grades undermine motivation.** There are two problems here: (1) group grades penalize students who work hard but have cooperative learning partners who don't, and (2) they reward students who don't work hard but have hard-working partners. Both scenarios have undesirable effects on student motivation.

4 **Group grades convey the wrong message.** Grading practices send students messages about what is valued. The basic point of the guidelines presented in this book is that grading should emphasize and support learning and success, but if grades "are partially a function of forces entirely out of their control," it sends entirely the wrong message to students.

5 **Group grades violate individual accountability.** This is a key principle of cooperative learning. If it is applied effectively and appropriately, students are likely to achieve more; if not, students will find ways to manipulate the situation to their personal advantage.

6 **Group grades** are responsible for parents', teachers', and students' resistance to cooperative learning.

7 Group grades may be challenged in court.

Figure 3.2   From Kagan, Spencer. "Group Grades Miss the Mark." *Educational Leadership* 52(8): 68–71. Reprinted with permission of the Association for Supervision and Curriculum Development. © 1995 by ASCD. All rights reserved.

Group Cooperative Learning Assessment

Assessor: Teacher ☐   Peer ☐   Self ☐

Put the appropriate symbol in the boxes for each student.

Evidence of skill observed ✓   Not observed yet ✗

Cooperative learning skill / Names of students in the group	Student 1	Student 2						
Stays focused on task								
Fulfills assigned role								
Contributes ideas and solutions								
Works well with others (listens, shares, and supports others)								
Shows interest and involvement								
Additional skills (developed by teachers and students)								

Figure 3.3   Reprinted with permission, ©1995 Toronto District School Board, Ontario, Canada.

Observations may be made by the teacher, by students of other students, or by students of themselves, but are restricted to two or three skills at one time. Feedback is given to individuals, to groups, and to the class as a whole. After students practice their cooperative skills and observation skills, then a sheet, patterned on Figure 3.3, can be used to summarize each student's achievement in this area. If teamwork or cooperative skills are part of standards, this summary can be converted to marks (see chapter 6) for inclusion in student grades. If, however, these characteristics are not specifically mentioned in your standards, then evidence of these skills should only be used in the comments or learning/social skills part of the report card.

> **B**onus marks distort achievement grades because they mix other factors with achievement. It is better not to use them.

Sheeran (1994) suggested a variety of approaches to assessing cooperative learning. He emphasized individual accountability and positive interdependence. However, a number of the methods he suggested are of dubious merit because they are based on the concept of individuals receiving bonus marks when group goals are achieved, such as an average score on a test. This is inappropriate for two reasons: (1) an individual's mark depends on the efforts of others, and (2) bonus marks are not acceptable in any circumstances. Although positive, bonus marks distort achievement grades because they mix other factors with achievement. It is better not to use them—if students do something worthy of extra credit, consider it to be a reporting variable and recognize the exceptional achievement with either a formal (report card) or informal (note or phone call) communication.

Another approach to marking group projects was suggested by Culp and Malone (1992). For them, student contributions to such projects "fall into four main categories, most of which are usually included in standards: creativity/ideas contributed, research/data collection, writing/typing/artwork, and organizing/collating" (35). Students rate each other's contributions in each category with the total for each category for all students adding up to one hundred percent. Comparisons are made between student and teacher ratings to ensure that they are fair. The average for each student is then converted to a percentage mark. Culp and Malone also suggested that keeping scores over several projects provides useful information—students learn more about themselves. They see that individuals contribute differently to the team, and they may identify specific skills they might want to strengthen (1992, 36, 59).

One very significant positive aspect of Culp and Malone's approach is that it overcomes a problem that is seen frequently in the marking of cooperative learning—the rationing of success. They overcome the problem by giving a mark of 95% to each student in a group of four whose average contribution is 21% or greater. However, if a percentage contribution of 21% or higher is considered to be exemplary performance, the mark should be 100% for two reasons: (1) students are not arbitrarily penalized, and (2) the maximum score should always be attainable. To paraphrase Stiggins (1993), any student who hits the goal should get the highest possible mark.

> **A**ny student who hits the goal should get the highest possible mark.

Another very appropriate approach suggested by Burke (1999) is shown in Figure 3.4. The template provides a way for ensuring that, as the name of the strategy—cooperative *learning*—implies, the focus of the cooperative phase is on learning which is followed by individual assessment. Benevino and Snodgrass (1998) support this approach with a number of suggestions about how individual accountability can be ensured: "teacher monitoring of (cooperative) activity work; and essay response based on questions formulated during the activity; a class discussion of the questions and responses generated; and a (test) on the content" (146).

In conclusion, note that "a carefully constructed cooperative environment that offers challenging learning tasks, that allows students to make key decisions about how they perform, and that emphasizes the value (and skills) of helping each other to learn" (Kohn 1991, 86) is far more important than coming up with the perfect way to mark. The various aspects of cooperative learning (see Figure 3.3) can then be included in grades or learning skills depending on whether they are part of the standards or not. This is a difficult aspect of marking and grading. The principle to keep in mind is to emphasize individual achievement within the cooperative learning setting.

What Should Not Be in Grades?

Effort, participation, attitude, and other personal and social characteristics need to be reported separately from achievement. Figure 3.5 shows a very inappropriate grading plan for a performance subject.

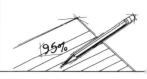

Creating Performance Tasks

Create a meaningful performance task for your subject area.

Subject Area: _____Health_____   Grade Level: _____8th Grade_____

Task Description: As part of the school's Health Fair Week, students will develop a plan for eliminating all smoking areas from local businesses. The project will include: 1) a presentation; 2) a brochure; 3) a letter to the community newspaper; 4) a 5-minute video "selling" the students' ideas to the business owners.

Direct Instruction for Whole Class: The whole class will be involved in the following learning experiences:
· Guest lecture from the school nurse on the effects of secondhand smoke
· Training in computer graphic design
· Lectures and discussions on the health risks related to smoking

---

Group Work: Students may select their group.

Group One	**Group Two**	**Group Three**	**Group Four**
Research facts and statistics about effects of smoking.	Prepare charts and graphs on health risks of smoking in a brochure.	Summarize the key research points in a letter to the editor of the local newspaper.	Prepare a five-minute video to present to business owners.

Individual Work: In addition to the group project, each student will complete the following individual assignments:
1) A poster that integrates the most essential facts, statistics, quotes, and visuals to argue for a smoking ban in all public businesses in the area; 2) a portfolio that contains selected assignments from the unit as well as student reflections on each artifiact.

Methods of Assessment
· Teacher-made test on the health risks of smoking
· Rubrics to assess each of the four group projects
· Checklist to assess criteria for poster and portfolios

Figure 3.4   From p. 80 of *The Mindful School: How to Assess Authentic Learning,* 3rd Edition, by Kay Burke.
© 1999, 1994, 1993 SkyLight Training and Publishing Inc. Reprinted by permission of SkyLight Professional Development, www.skylightedu.com or (800) 348-4474.

Sample Grading Inventory

In this extract from an actual high school grading inventory for a performance subject, the asterisked items should NOT be included in grades.

	% of grade
*Daily activities	40%
Major projects and performances	30%
Journals (reflections on projects and performances)	10%
*Attendance and punctuality	20%

Attendance Scale	Late (Tardiness) Scale
20 marks—perfect attendance	Subtract 1/2 mark—first tardy
16 marks—3 absences	Subtract 1/2 mark—second tardy
12 marks—4 absences	Subtract 1 mark—tardies
8 marks—5 absences	thereafter
4 marks—6 absences	
0 marks—7 absences	

Figure 3.5

REFLECTING ON . . . GRADING PLANS

Consider the effects of the grading plan shown in Figure 3.5 on the following scenarios, in which a block schedule with 70 classes can be assumed:

Scenario 1— a student who missed 10% of the classes would be able to receive a grade of no more than 80%, even if he or she got perfect marks in all other aspects of the course.

Scenario 2—a student who missed 7% of the classes and who was late for 10% of the classes would be able to receive a maximum grade of 82%.

Are these fair results?

▶ Does this inventory produce grades with clear meaning?

▶ Does a procedure like this promote attendance and punctuality?

▶ Does a procedure like this honor learning?

Effort

Hard work (effort), frequent responses to teacher questions, intense involvement in class activities (participation), and a positive, encouraging, friendly, and happy demeanor (attitude) are all highly valued attributes. However, they should not be included directly in grades, because they are very difficult to define and even more difficult to measure.

Stiggins (1997) provided a detailed analysis of the arguments for and against including these factors in grades. With regard to effort, he said that definitions of trying hard vary greatly from teacher to teacher, and so, if effort is included in the grade, "we add noise into the grade interpretation process" (418). *Noise* means "static, not clear meaningful signals" (413). He also noted that "students can manipulate their apparent level of effort to mislead us" (418).

Participation

Stiggins (1997) suggested that participation is often a personality issue—some students are naturally more assertive while others are naturally quieter. This is often related to gender and/or ethnicity, and so we run the risk of these biases if we include effort and participation in grades. Another problem is that "factoring effort into the grade may send the wrong message to students. In real life just trying hard to do a good job is virtually never enough. If we don't deliver relevant, practical results, we will not be deemed successful, regardless of how hard we try" (418).

> **F**actoring effort into the grade may send the wrong message to students. In real life just trying hard to do a good job is virtually never enough. (Stiggins 1997, 418)

The inclusion of attitude presents similar problems; positive attitude has many dimensions, is very difficult to define, and is extremely difficult to measure. It is also very easy to manipulate—students can fake a positive attitude if they think or know it will help their grade.

To a considerable extent, personal and social characteristics do contribute to achievement, but including a mark for attitude as part of a mark for a product blurs the assessment of the product and affects the validity and thus the meaning of the grade. Also, including a mark for effort or any of these characteristics means a double benefit for successful students and double (or triple or quadruple) jeopardy for less successful students. This is clearly unfair.

Several authors, including Marzano (2000a) and Halydana (1999), have suggested compromises in this area such that teachers may include behavioral components in grades, but I believe such compromises are inappropriate.

Halydana (1999) classifies criteria for grading as supportable, arguable, and unsupportable. His arguable list includes violation of deadlines, class participation, extra credit, improvement, and attendance. I believe that all of these should be placed clearly in the unsupportable category. Strong effort, active participation, and positive attitude are highly valued attributes, but if grades are to have clear meaning they should not be included in grades; they are *reporting* variables, not grading variables. These attributes need to be assessed as accurately and rigorously as possible and reported separately and regularly. Examples of reporting procedures that include these student characteristics can be found in Figure 11.2–1 on page 214–215.

Late Work

A major problem that overlaps both parts of this guideline is the issue of submitting required work on time. The following late homework policy for one college course was found on the Internet:

> Homework turned in for grading in class on the date due will incur no penalty. Otherwise the following grade reductions are in effect:
> - up to one day—a 5 percent reduction;
> - two days late—a 10 percent reduction;
> - three days late—a 20 percent reduction;
> - four days late—a 40 percent reduction; and
> - five days late—an 80 percent reduction.

> Homework extensions are only granted *before* homework is due. Do not attempt to obtain an extension on or after the due date.

Strong effort, active participation, and positive attitude are highly valued attributes, but they are reporting variables, not grading variables.

At the high school level in my former school district, penalties for handing work in late have been as high as 10% per day to a maximum of 50% (including weekend days!).

There are two problems with these approaches. First, the penalty that students receive distorts their achievement and thus contributes to a mark and, ultimately, to a grade that does not have clear meaning. Second, the punitive nature of the penalty provides a powerful disincentive for students to complete any work after it is more than one or two days late. In both examples, no intelligent student would bother completing the work after three days. Such policies are obviously opposed to a learning/success orientation—that the work is done and that learning occurs holds more importance than when the work is done and when learning occurs. This does not mean

that handing work in on time is not important, but as I once heard Joel Barker say, "It is best to do it right and on time, but it is better to do it right and late than the reverse."

In the school or college situation, there are several important considerations about due dates for student work. One is that required work is sometimes part of an instructional sequence and so needs to be submitted before marked work is returned. A second consideration is that teachers need to have a reasonable workload—they cannot be expected to mark huge amounts of work on the last day or two of a grading period.

In both situations, the concept of an absolute deadline after which no work will be accepted for inclusion in grades—in that grading period—may be appropriate and/or necessary. This does not mean that students automatically receive zeroes or severe penalties. In the case of work in an instructional sequence, this type of work usually has a formative purpose and so should not be included in grades anyway (see chapter 4); all the teacher needs to do is record that the work was not done or was handed in late. In the case of a lack of time for the teacher to grade, the most appropriate approach would be to record an incomplete and include the mark in the student' s grade in the next grading period, when the teacher has had a reasonable amount of time to assess the student's work.

A third consideration for due dates is that these are frequently quite arbitrary, especially for major performance assessments such as term papers. In these—and in fact, in all—situations, teachers should encourage students to submit work on time, but if they do not, teachers should keep penalties as small as possible. For example, the teacher might deduct 1% or 2% per day to a maximum of 10%; record the fact of the tardiness; and consider the fact as a reporting, not a (major) grading, variable.

Think of your favorite author—let us call her Margaret. Imagine that when Margaret was in high school, she was a brilliant writer but always handed work in late. Using the punitive procedures described earlier, although receiving As or 90% or more on each piece of writing, Margaret would probably have received relatively low grades because her marks would have been reduced one or two letter grades, or 20% to 30%. The final grade would give no idea of her high quality of work or of her tardiness problem. Far better that Margaret get the 90% or better that she deserved as marks and that the report card state "95%, Margaret is a brilliant writer but she always hands her work in late."

> *The intent is that tardiness be dealt with appropriately, so grades have meaning and communicate clear, easily interpretable information about achievement, and second, that the procedures used are likely to assist students to eliminate the problem.*

Now we have real information. If she is going to be a novelist or a playwright, it is not much of a problem—publishers have deadlines, but for novels and plays, the deadlines are often flexible. If, however, she has applied to be a journalist on a daily newspaper or to be an advertising copywriter, she will probably not be hired because in those occupations the deadlines are as important as the quality of the writing.

It must be emphasized again that the intent here is not to encourage students to hand work in late. The first intent is that tardiness be dealt with appropriately, so grades have meaning and communicate clear, easily interpretable information about achievement. The second intent is that the procedures used are likely to assist students to eliminate the problem. Years and years of teachers using penalties shows that they do not work and that they basically give students excuses to not do the work. A far more positive approach is one that has been developed in the York Region School District in Ontario. The approach, developed by Cathy Costello with assistance from Barry McKillop, is titled "Creating a Culture of Responsibility." Just the name itself indicates the orientation of this approach. An adapted version is provided as Figure 3.6. Further details can be found in their excellent article in the classroom assessment issue of *Orbit,* published by Ontario Institute for Studies in Education of the University of Toronto (Costello and McKillop 2000).

Another author who illuminates this topic with clear logic and support for students is Forest Gathercoal in his wonderful book *Judicious Discipline* (1997), a must-read, at least for all school administrators with responsibility for discipline. He notes that

> "lowering achievement grades for misbehavior does not always teach responsibility, but it always does pass on misinformation. By accepting and not grading down late work, educators send a professional message to students that completing assignments, receiving teacher feedback, and being fairly educated are all important to their educational success." (142, 143).

An interesting source for teachers' ideas on the subject of late work is the "Teacher Talk" section of January 2000 edition of *Classroom Notes Plus* published by the National Council of Teachers of English. This section contains ideas from an online discussion, "How Do You Handle Late Work." Views range from open submission to advocating severe penalties and everything in between.

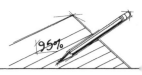

Getting Work In On Time

1. Set clear and reasonable timelines with some student input.

2. Ensure that the expectations for the task/assignment are clearly established and understood.

3. Support the students who will predictably struggle with the task without intervention.

4. Find out why other students' work is late and assist them.

5. Establish the consequences for late work, such as:
   - after school follow-up
   - make-up responsibility within a supervised setting
   - parent contact
   - notation in the mark book for each assignment which is late
   - "grades" on a learning skills/work habits section of the report card
   - comments on the report card that reflect chronic lateness

6. Provide the opportunity for students to extend timelines:
   - student must communicate with the teacher in advance of the due date
   - student must choose situations carefully as this extension may only be used once/twice per term/semester

7. If all the above "fails" (i.e., work is still late/not done), use small mark penalties/deductions which do not distort achievement or motivation.

Figure 3.6

Adapted from "Creating a Culture of Responsibility" with permission from the York Region District School Board, Ontario, Canada.

What's the Bottom Line?

What should be in grades? Grades should include achievement only, based on standards, or when lacking definitive standards, defined as broadly or narrowly as professional judgment dictates.

What should not be in grades? Effort, attitude, behavior, attendance, punctuality, tardiness, and so forth should not be in grades. These should be assessed and reported on separately. (See chapter 11.)

 What's My Thinking Now?

GUIDELINE 3: Limit the valued attributes included in grades to individual achievement.

Analyze guideline 3 for grading by focusing on three questions:

Why use it?

Why not use it?

Are there points of uncertainty?

After careful thought about these points, answer these two questions:

Would I use guideline 3 now?

Do I agree or disagree with the guideline, or am I unsure at this time?

See the following for one person's reflections on guideline 3.

 # A Reflection on Guideline 3

WHY USE IT?

- based on standards
- very clear, concrete, and specific
- clarifies priorities
- gives "pure" grades
- gives a clear picture of student achievement, whereas mixing achievement and effort gives a muddy picture of both
- more accountability for really knowing student strengths and weaknesses

WHY NOT USE IT?

- attitude and effort important in student's future
- lack of clear definition of achievement
- participation and achievement so closely linked
- report card does not allow separation of achievement and effort
- school and district policy

POINTS OF UNCERTAINTY

- where do participation and effort fit?
- how to include growth?
- how to include critical employability skills?
- how to report in a manageable way?
- students need to see consequences of their behavior in an obvious way

Chapter 4

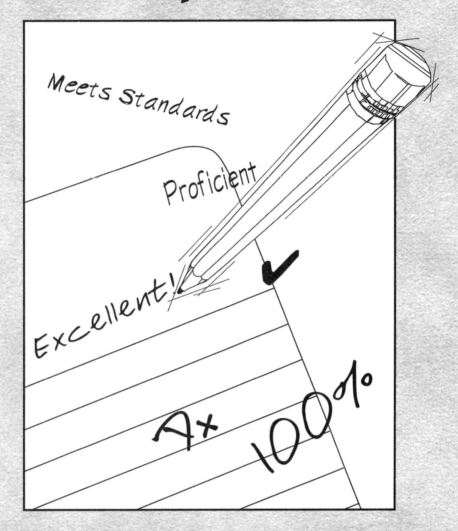

Sampling Student Performance

We know that students will rarely perform at high levels on challenging learning tasks at their first attempt. Deep understanding or high levels of proficiency are achieved only as a result of trial, practice, adjustments based on feedback, and more practice. Performance-based instruction underscores the importance of using assessments to provide information to guide improvement throughout the learning process, instead of waiting to give feedback at the end of instruction.

—MCTIGHE (1996/1997, 11)

Guideline: **4**

Sample student performance—do not include all scores in grades.

THE CASE OF . . .

Heather's Grim Grade

Heather is a very bright girl who generally achieves at a very high level. She has always liked and done well in English. On her first report card in grade 11 English, she gets a C; both her parents and Heather are shocked and upset by the low (for her) grade. They express their concern to her teacher, who provides them with a computer printout showing how Heather's C was calculated. What is revealed is that the marks for virtually every piece of work that was done were included in the letter grade. First drafts, experimental pieces, quizzes on spelling and grammar—marks for all of these were included. Heather did not do well on any of these, but her unit tests, final drafts, and a major project all received marks of 85% or better. Heather likes to experiment and to take risks on creative tasks; she also needs a lot of practice to understand concepts and detail. By including all the scores from the formative assessments in her grade, her teacher had emphasized Heather's weaknesses as a learner.

What's the Purpose of the Guideline?

This guideline requires that teachers have a clear understanding of the need for a variety of assessment strategies and the purpose of each assessment. It is essential that teachers recognize that different assessment strategies will reveal evidence of students' strengths and weaknesses and that they distinguish clearly between *formative* and *summative* assessment. The issue of variety in assessment will be dealt with in chapter 7. The major focus of this chapter is the need for appropriate use of formative and summative assessment. Formative assessment should be used primarily to give feedback to students (and teachers) on the progress of learning, whereas summative assessments are used to make judgments about the amount of learning and so are included in grades. This approach deals with two serious problems: (1) the "does-this-count?" syndrome exhibited by students and (2) the "I-have-too-much-marking" syndrome exhibited by teachers. In high schools, this may be the single most important guideline because many secondary teachers have a strong tendency toward putting a number on everything students do and putting everything into the grade.

> **It *is essential that teachers distinguish clearly between formative and summative assessment.***

What Are the Key Elements of the Guideline?

Formative Versus Summative Assessment

It is essential that educators clearly understand the concepts of formative and summative assessment (see Figure 4.1). Also see the glossary at the end of this book for more definitions of terms used.

Formative. Assessment designed to provide direction for improvement and/or adjustment to a program for individual students or for a whole class, that is, quizzes, initial drafts/attempts, homework, and questions during instruction.

Summative. Assessment/evaluation designed to provide information to be used in making judgments about a student's achievement at the end of a

Comparison of Formative and Summative Assessments

	Formative	Summative
Purpose	To monitor and guide a process/product while it is still in progress	To judge the success of a process/product at the end (however arbitrarily defined)
Time of assessment	During the process or development of the product	At the end of the process or when the product is complete
Types of assessment techniques	Informal observation, quizzes, homework, teacher questions, worksheets	Formal observation, tests, projects, term papers, exhibitions
Uses of assessment information	To improve and change a process/product while it is still going on or being developed	Judge the quality of a process/product; grade, rank, promote

Figure 4.1

Adapted from P. W. Airasian, *Classroom Assessment*, 2d ed. (New York: McGraw-Hill, 1994), 136. Used with permission.

period of instruction, that is, tests, exams, final drafts/attempts, assignments, projects, performances.

Teachers need a very clear vision of their purpose for each assessment. If assessment is principally to inform learners about their strengths and weaknesses as well as inform teachers about how successful instruction is as it proceeds, then assessment is formative. On the other hand, if assessment is primarily to inform about the achievement status of the learner, then it is summative. Obviously some overlap occurs, particularly with summative assessment.

Assessing Process and Product

It is also extremely important that teachers do not equate process with formative assessment and products with summative assessment. Process may and should be assessed both formatively and summatively; similarly, products may be assessed both formatively and summatively. Furthermore, summative assessments are not only tests and exams—there are a huge variety of assessment methods that can be used summatively (see Figure 4.2).

A Performance May Be . . .

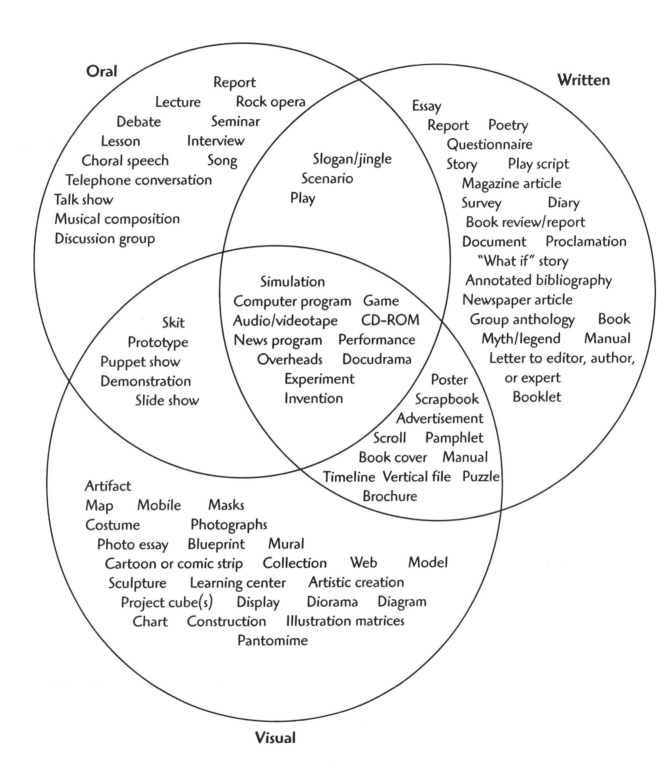

Oral / **Written** / **Visual**

Oral:
- Report
- Lecture
- Rock opera
- Debate
- Seminar
- Lesson
- Interview
- Choral speech
- Song
- Telephone conversation
- Talk show
- Musical composition
- Discussion group

Written:
- Essay
- Report
- Poetry
- Questionnaire
- Story
- Play script
- Magazine article
- Survey
- Diary
- Book review/report
- Document
- Proclamation
- "What if" story
- Annotated bibliography
- Newspaper article
- Group anthology
- Book
- Myth/legend
- Manual
- Letter to editor, author, or expert
- Booklet

Oral ∩ Written:
- Slogan/jingle
- Scenario
- Play

Oral ∩ Visual:
- Skit
- Prototype
- Puppet show
- Demonstration
- Slide show

Oral ∩ Written ∩ Visual (center):
- Simulation
- Computer program
- Game
- Audio/videotape
- CD-ROM
- News program
- Performance
- Overheads
- Docudrama
- Experiment
- Invention

Written ∩ Visual:
- Poster
- Scrapbook
- Advertisement
- Scroll
- Pamphlet
- Book cover
- Manual
- Timeline
- Vertical file
- Puzzle
- Brochure

Visual:
- Artifact
- Map
- Mobile
- Masks
- Costume
- Photographs
- Photo essay
- Blueprint
- Mural
- Cartoon or comic strip
- Collection
- Web
- Model
- Sculpture
- Learning center
- Artistic creation
- Project cube(s)
- Display
- Diorama
- Diagram
- Chart
- Construction
- Illustration matrices
- Pantomime

Figure 4.2   Reprinted with permission, © 1995 Toronto District School Board, Ontario, Canada.

A good example of a process that can be assessed formatively and summatively is student use of safety skills in a laboratory or vocational program. Starting on the first day, the teacher introduces students to critical safety skills. Students are given or develop clear criteria indicating levels of performance, possibly in the form of a rubric that describes various levels of quality. Students practice their safety skills daily as the teacher observes and feeds back to them information as to their strengths and weaknesses. The teacher keeps track of these observations—these records could be anecdotal, symbols (– or x), level scores (1–4), or numbers (e.g., 7/10). This process continues over a number of weeks. Near the end of the first grading period, the teacher announces that, for several specific days, the same criteria and the same observations will be used to assess students' safety skills and that the scores are to be included in their grades. This period of observation becomes the summative assessment of their process skills. No scores from the practice weeks are included in the grade. These scores are used instead to provide valuable reporting information about growth and progress.

> **T**oo often, educational tests, grades, and report cards are treated by teachers as autopsies when they should be viewed as physicals. (Reeves 2000, 10)

An example of a performance that can be assessed formatively and summatively is a student seminar presentation (individual or group). Usually, these major projects are scheduled far in advance, so students need some guidance to keep them on track. The teacher may provide students with a schedule for checking such things as hypothesis, first draft, audiovisual needs, and second draft. Students might also have a practice presentation. For each of these steps, and for the presentation, students have clear criteria indicating various levels of performance. As with the safety skills, the teacher provides students with feedback on each of these steps to help them develop their performance. The teacher keeps records of these process steps, using symbols, scores, marks, or anecdotal notes. None of these will be included in students' grades; instead, they will be used for reporting purposes. The only mark included in a student grade is the mark for the actual seminar presentation—the summative assessment of the product. Most students need to follow the process steps, and the quality of their final performance depends to a great extent on how diligent they have been in following them. There are, however, some students who may be able to present a high-quality seminar without following some, or even all, of the recommended process steps. Because it is the seminar presentation that counts, students do not suffer lower grades because they did not follow the suggested steps.

Johnson's Mileposts and Checkpoints

Johnson (1996) provided labels for planned use of formative and summative assessment. He says we should consider assessments as mileposts (summative) or as checkpoints (formative). He suggested that teachers plan a number of milepost assessments for each course and then "design appropriate checkpoints—those activities which prepare students for the Milepost Assessment" (23). He goes on to say that checkpoints

> . . . allow both the teachers and students to gauge a student's progress toward successfully completing the Milepost Assessment. In this way, curriculum, instruction, and assessment are all of the same cloth; students and teachers work together, searching for answers to essential questions, solutions to problems, [and] developing skills to apply—all the while using content as the vehicle which drives the work. (24)

Notice that distinguishing between formative and summative assessment requires careful planning. When a teacher knows what summative assessment will be used, he or she can ensure that students have the appropriate practice opportunities.

Many assessments are designed to provide information so that teachers can adjust instruction and students can improve performance. This should be the prime purpose of quizzes.

The Role of Formative Assessment

Feedback—The Main Product

Many assessments are designed to provide information so that teachers can adjust instruction and students can improve performance. For example, this is—or should be—the prime purpose of quizzes. Teachers give a quiz during the instructional process to see how students are doing with their learning. If the class average is 90%, the teacher knows to move on rapidly, but if the average is 30%, some reteaching using different teaching/learning strategies is called for.

Similarly, individual students are informed on how they are doing and so can act appropriately. The teacher, of course, also uses information about individual students for remediation or enrichment. The same considerations apply to teacher questions, most homework (Nottingham 1988), many worksheets, most teacher observation, and initial student attempts at any activity, such as writing, constructing a map, or completing lab reports. Stiggins, Frisbie, and Griswold (1989) suggested that we consider these as "learning activities and not as assessments per se" (8). Figure 4.3 identifies the similarities and differences between teaching/learning activities and summative assessment. The relationships involved are shown clearly in Figure 4.4: after initial instruction and formative assessment, all students receive further instruction. Those who were successful receive enrichment, while those who need improvement participate in correctives (i.e., reinstruction in a different way—not just slower or louder!) and may take more formative assessment. When they are ready, students take the summative assessment(s) and either move on to new instruction or to further correctives.

Stiggins, Frisbie, and Griswold's concept of distinguishing clearly between learning and assessment also applies to most assessments by peers and self. This information primarily improves learning and thus is considered as formative, not summative, assessment. Peer assessment and/or self-assessment should be included in grades only rarely when such assessment is a stated learning goal and when students have had many opportunities to practice it. Then, we know that the likelihood is high that the assessment will be of high quality.

A Comparison of Teaching/Learning and Summative Assessment Activities

Common Elements
· focused on expectations
· engaging for students
· enhance students' knowledge and skills

Teaching/Learning Activities	Summative Assessment Activities
· introduction, instruction or practice for students learning knowledge and/or skills	· students demonstrate knowledge/skills on which they have had opportunity to practice
· introduce criteria, allow for feedback, self-assessment, and guided practice	· are based on known criteria
· focus on individual or group learning	· focus primarily on individual student performance
· may be narrow in focus—introduce or provide practice for specific skills and knowledge	· usually broader—integrate important skills and knowledge
· information for report card comments	· information for report card grades and comments

Figure 4.3

The Role of Formative and Summative Assessment

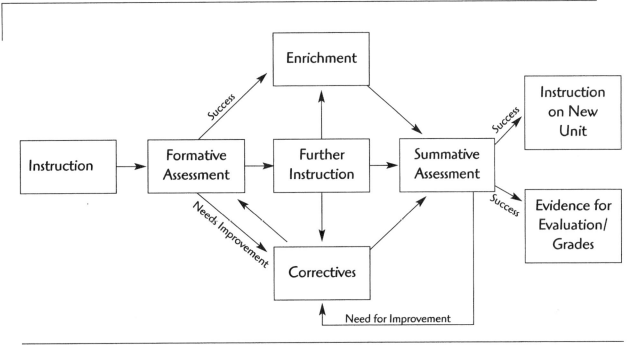

Figure 4.4 Adapted from Guskey, T. R. and J. M. Bailey. *Developing Grading and Reporting Systems for Student Learning*. p. 98, © 2001 by Sage Publications, Inc. Reprinted with permission of Corwin Press, Inc.

The importance of feedback and the role of formative assessment have been highlighted by Black and Wiliam (1998) in their very important article "Inside the Black Box." These two researchers looked at a huge number of studies done over a ten-year period and discovered strong evidence that improving formative assessment leads to huge gains in student achievement. They found that this was true for all students, but they also found "that improved formative assessment helps low achievers more than other students and so reduces the range of achievement while raising achievement overall" (141). Another important finding was that "the giving of marks and the grading function were overemphasized, while the giving of advice and the learning function are underemphasized" (142). They suggested that these deficiencies could be reduced by a "culture of success," "advice on what (each student) can do to improve," and "self-assessment by pupils" involving "thoughtful reflection in which all pupils can be encouraged to take part" (142, 143). All of this means that if teachers want students to be successful, they must do more to involve students in the assessment process so that they understand when assessment is formative and can then benefit from feedback and ultimately achieve at a much higher level. This will only happen if formative assessment is risk-free (i.e., it is not part of grades).

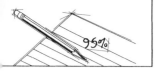

The Role of Coaching

In activities such as band and basketball, students understand that practice counts, not directly but indirectly. It is practice that makes the spring concert great or enables the team to make the playoffs. Because we put a mark that counts directly on everything students do in the classroom, we contradict the value that practice usually represents to students. Coaching of the type that we see in band and basketball is needed in the classroom. It will not be easy,

> *Coaching of the type that we see in band and basketball is needed in the classroom.*

but, through an educative process, students may again understand that doing worksheets, doing their homework, and trying their best on quizzes that do not count directly in their grade is practice and will lead to much better performance on the summative assessments that do count in grades. (Note: For those students who do well on formative assessments and not as well on summative assessments, teachers must carefully consider the concerns addressed in chapters 5 and 6.)

Feedback as Motivation

Feedback in the form of words can be very motivational. After a score of 7 out of 10 has been put on a small assignment, there is not much more that can be said. If, however, teachers indicate one or two strengths and one or two weaknesses, they have the basis for discussions with individual students to help them improve their work. The basic principle at work here is that words open up communication, whereas numbers close it down—prematurely at that.

Marking Quantity

A very common complaint of teachers at all levels is that they have too much marking. This is often true—because they mark too much! It is not necessary, from a measurement point of view, to mark everything students do. Assessment can be reliable as long as there are several samples of each type of work from each student.

Marking everything is not necessary from an educational point of view. Many teachers claim they must mark everything so that students will do the work. But, as has been indicated, this does not provide good information to students and, according to many experiments, damages motivation (Kohn 1993b). "The more feedback helps students view a grade as their own responsibility and as amenable to sustained and consistent effort, the more they will see school achievement as having an internal locus and being stable and

controllable" (Brookhart 1994, 294). A much better approach, thus, is for teachers to check students' work regularly without always providing marks. This lightens a teacher's workload in a number of ways:

- Some work can simply be recorded as done or not done.
- Some work—for example, first drafts in creative writing—can be skimmed for a general overall impression rather than examined for the detail that is necessary to arrive at a score.
- Some work may be assessed by focusing on one or two key characteristics rather than everything. Strengths and weaknesses in essential aspects can be identified clearly in this approach.
- Some work may be assessed by peers, which gives students important practice in identifying strengths and weaknesses while appropriately reducing a teacher's marking burden.

> **W**ords open up communication, whereas numbers close it down.

Compared to marking everything, each of these approaches saves time and is more beneficial to students because most teachers are very conscientious when marking work that will be included in student grades. As Chapman (1993) said, ". . . daily quizzes, interim tasks, single journal entries and other contributing pieces and checks for understanding may merit a + or a – mark, but don't merit intense bean counting. Because teachers are not accountants, it is not helpful if they have to spend long hours entering a [mark] for every classroom activity" (222).

The Role of Mistakes

A very important concept that is also honored by this guideline is the idea that mistakes are our friends. Spady (1987) noted that mistakes are "inherent elements in the journey toward learning competence" (11). The problem with including everything, Spady stated, is that grades "label those mistakes failures and make their consequences *irreversible,* [which] is counter to the notion of human growth and our inherent potential for change and improvement" (11). North Americans, in particular, need to change their beliefs about errors and develop strategies that allow errors to be used effectively. In their research into the results of TIMSS 3, Stigler and Stevenson (1991) found that "for Americans, errors tend to be interpreted as an indication of failure in learning the lesson. For Chinese and Japanese, they are an index of what still needs to be learned. These divergent interpretations result in very different reactions

to the display of errors—embarrassment on the part of American children, calm acceptance by Asian children. They also result in differences in the manner in which teachers utilize errors as effective means of instruction" (44). Clearly a large step in the right direction would be using formative and summative assessment appropriately.

Homework

Many teachers inappropriately include homework as a specific part of grades. Most of the time, homework is formative and therefore should not be part of a grade. "Homework should be a risk-free chance to experiment with new skills. Homework should require students to apply what they have learned so they find out what they really do understand and can return to class to ask questions about what was not understood" (Carr and Farr 2000, 200).

Concern About Excluding Formative Assessment Scores

It is very important to emphasize that excluding formative assessment scores from grades does not mean that they are unimportant. Formative assessments are critical to the learning process, because "they provide feedback when it is still possible to influence the process, and are at the heart of teaching" (Airasian 1994, 136). Teachers must emphasize this to students and to parents to develop a new understanding of what counts. Guskey and Bailey (2001) suggest that "most students need to be shown the explicit benefits of putting forth appropriate effort on formative assessment" (31). However, they also acknowledge that "many teachers have found when students understand the purposes of formative assessments and see the direct payoff they derive from the feedback offered by such assessments, motivation is no longer a problem" (50). Anecdotal evidence of this is provided by the experience of the modern language department at Rutherford High School in Panama City, Florida. Led by department head Sandy Wilson, all teachers in this department have made a clear distinction between formative and summative assessment. They have found (and I have heard students attest) that students here discovered that this approach is very beneficial to their understanding of language and that they approach summative assessments with great confidence. It is essential that teachers know which students are doing well and which are not. This knowledge allows all concerned to build on the strengths and correct the weaknesses of individual students.

> **E**xcluding formative assessment scores from grades does not mean that they are unimportant.

The Role of Summative Assessment

Performance—Data Source for Grades

What does count for grades are the performances that students give to demonstrate the knowledge, skills, and behaviors they have acquired as the result of instruction and practice. These demonstrations usually occur at toward the end (however arbitrarily the end is defined) of a unit, a course, or a grading period.

Variety of Summative Assessments

This guideline does not emphasize just exams and unit tests. There are many possible summative assessments, especially if teachers use performance assessment (see Figure 4.2). For most subjects, teachers should use a combination of assessment types:

- paper-and-pencil tests—primarily for knowledge;
- performance assessment—primarily for application of knowledge and to recognize skills and behaviors; and
- personal communication—to evaluate aspects of all types of learning goals.

> **W**hat does count for grades are the performances that students give to demonstrate the knowledge, skills, and behaviors they have acquired as the result of instruction and practice.

Good examples of varied summative assessments are those drivers complete before they can obtain a driver's license. First, there is usually a written test on the rules of the road and common driving situations. This is often followed by an eye test, and finally, there is a performance assessment of the critical skill—driving. Student drivers must pass all three tests to obtain a license. This model may be applied in the classroom when we want students to demonstrate their knowledge, skills, and behaviors.

Also note that most people take lessons and practice for a long time before they try the driving test. While they are doing this, the instructor provides them with feedback. Instructors do not give each lesson a mark to be factored in with the score on the driving test that determines if the license will the issued!

It must be emphasized again that guideline 4 supports learning and encourages student success by giving students opportunities to practice before undertaking assessments that count directly in grades. In this regard, there are two critical points. First, it is critical not only that students have opportunities to practice their knowledge, skills, and behaviors, but also that they have opportunities to practice the type of assessment that is to be used summatively before a summative assessment is made. Second, it is also critical that educators use more than one assessment method. This ensures comprehensive and consistent indications of student performance (Rogers and Graham 1997). Travis (1996) supported this viewpoint and suggested that it "is especially true when the educator wants to take varying learning styles and strategies into consideration" (309). This principle is being applied in school districts that are using the "bodies of evidence" concept. The school district of Aurora, Colorado, for example, requires that validation of competency on each of their district standards must involve several assessments, at least one of which must be a performance assessment. Harlen and James (1997) offer a superb analysis of formative and summative assessment and their roles in learning. Below is a valuable set of questions which teachers should think about.

Give students opportunities to practice before undertaking assessments that count directly in grades.

- If students' work is graded on a daily basis, can they relax and really think and learn, or do they have to constantly worry about getting a bad grade?
- Of what value to students is the feedback they receive from practice tests?
- Does an overemphasis on grading increase or decrease the motivation of those most likely to be struggling with the topic or skill?
- When students are just beginning to learn a new skill or topic, do grades on homework or assignments designed to help them explore a topic make some of them fearful and anxious?
- How important is it to help students learn how to assess and improve their work? (McColskey and McMunn 2000, 118)

 # What's the Bottom Line?

What should be included in grades? Scores from summative assessments should be included. What should not be included in grades? Scores from formative assessments should not be included.

What is the practical implication of guideline 4? Teachers should have a page in their grade books for reporting purposes—the formative page, and a page for grading—the summative page.

 # *What's My Thinking Now?*

GUIDELINE 4: Sample student performance—do not include all scores in grades.

Analyze guideline 4 for grading by focusing on three questions:

Why use it?

Why not use it?

Are there points of uncertainty?

After careful thought about these points, answer these two questions:

Would I use guideline 4 now?

Do I agree or disagree with the guideline, or am I unsure at this time?

See the following for one person's reflections on guideline 4.

A Reflection on Guideline 4

WHY USE IT?

- feedback allows students to improve performance
- reduces marking load
- encourages both practice and risk taking
- allows for remedial instruction, intervention, and self-assessment
- encourages competency/mastery
- research supports importance of formative assessment

WHY NOT USE IT?

- some students, if not rewarded by grades, will not work
- fewer marks in grades make grades less reliable
- effect on motivation
- penalizes early success
- students not mature enough to value feedback without marks/grades

POINTS OF UNCERTAINTY

- how to select what goes in a grade and what doesn't
- what balance is there between formative and summative?
- how to include critical employability skills
- can students get over the "does it count" syndrome?
- role/place of quizzes
- students want "pay" to equal grades in order to work

Chapter 5

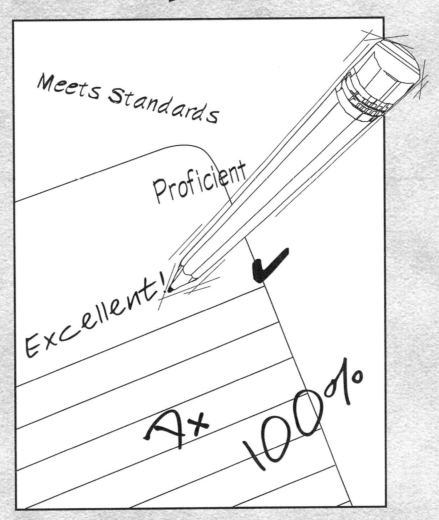

Changing
Grades

If students demonstrate achievement at any time that, in effect, renders past assessment information inaccurate, then you must drop the former assessment from the record and replace it with the new. To do otherwise is to misrepresent that achievement.
— STIGGINS (2001b, 431)

Guideline:

5

Grade in pencil—keep records so they can be updated easily.

THE CASE OF . . .

Anil's Amazing Improvement

Anil enrolled in a grade 9 keyboarding course for one semester. He had never had a computer or a typewriter at home and has had very limited keyboarding opportunities in the schools he attended previously. He chose to take keyboarding because he realized that, in senior high school courses and in college, he would be required to write essays and term papers that teachers would prefer (or require) to be typed. He was, therefore, highly motivated to succeed. He was fortunate also that he had been assigned to Mr. Smith's class. Mr. Smith was an excellent teacher who had great ability in identifying student strengths and weaknesses in keyboarding and in providing appropriate activities to maximize student progress.

As would be expected, Anil did not do very well in the first few weeks. His technique was poor, his speed was slow, and he made many errors—especially as compared with the other students, most of whom had considerable

experience with computers, both at home and in their previous schools. Most of Anil's marks in the first six-week grading period were between 40% and 60%, so on the first report he had a grade of 50%. In the second grading period, Anil improved significantly and most of his marks were between 60% and 80%; his grade for this period was 70%. In the third grading period, it all came together for Anil—the combination of Mr. Smith's excellent teaching and Anil's motivation resulted in marks of 90% to 100% on every project and skill. However, the night before the final exam, Anil's parents told him that they were going to separate. Not surprisingly, he did not do very well on the final exam, receiving a mark of only 60%. When combined with his term work for the third grading period, his grade was 81%!

School policy, however, required that the grades for the three grading periods be averaged; thus, Anil's final grade was only 68%. Anil had clearly mastered keyboarding but, because marks for his early work were included and another assessment opportunity was not provided for the final exam (on which he scored lower than his demonstrated skill) his final grade did not reflect fairly his achievement in keyboarding.

What's the Purpose of the Guideline?

This guideline supports learning by acknowledging that learning is an ongoing process and that what matters is how much learning occurs, not when it occurs. We take courses to learn, and what we did not know at the beginning should not be held against us. We also need to honor individual differences by recognizing that students learn at different rates and do not always perform at their real level on their first attempt, in a set time, or on one method of assessment.

What Are the Key Elements of the Guideline?

The process by which new drivers are accredited in Canada can effectively illustrate the principles involved in this guideline. Driving competence requires both knowledge and skills, and these are usually assessed, respectively, by a selected response test and a performance assessment. The process is multiphased. First, students learn about the rules of the road and other aspects of driving on their own. When they believe they are ready, they present themselves for the written test. If they do not pass the written test, they may study more and take the test again (and again and again, if necessary!). There are costs associated with this—certainly time and usually money— but each test experience is separate. Their efforts on second (or later) tests are not averaged with their previous scores.

What matters is how much learning occurs, not when it occurs.

Second, after passing the written test, aspiring drivers move on to driving lessons. Most struggle at the beginning, but with good instruction and good feedback (formative assessment), they progress. They do not, however, receive marks for each lesson! When their instructor believes they are ready for the driving examination, they present themselves at the test center. (As the instructor has no marks for each student, these cannot be provided to the assessor to average with their performance on the exam.) The student then attempts the driving exam. Many pass on their first attempt, but many (including me) fail on their first attempt. When this happens, most aspiring drivers practice very hard on their deficiencies and, when ready, attempt the exam again. When they present themselves at the test center, the assessor, who does not know—or care—that they failed the first (or previous) time(s), does not average their performances with previous attempts. If student drivers meet the standard on the test this time, they pass and receive their license.

In both the written and performance assessments, the assessor uses the most recent information, and the opportunity exists for more than one attempt at each assessment. It is important to note that the fact that a driver made more than one attempt at either part of the test does not appear on the license!

There are obvious differences between obtaining a driver's license and what happens in schools. Time is the most significant difference: schooling is generally defined by the calendar, whereas obtaining a driver's license is not.

There are, however, many similarities, especially the emphasis on combining knowledge and skills to demonstrate competence. Thus, the principles involved in testing new drivers are applicable, to a considerable extent, in classroom assessment.

Use the More Recent Information

If a kid falls head over heels in love and flunks the first math chapter test (getting 15 out of 100), and gradually over the term comes up to 95 out of 100, the grade the kid gets is going to be a C–. How long is he or she going to pay for that 15? And does the C– really show what the kid knows? (Hart 1996, 60)

. . . the key question is, "What information provides the most accurate description of students' learning at this time?" In nearly all cases the answer is "The most current information." If students demonstrate that past assessment information no longer accurately reflects their learning, that information must be dropped and replaced by the new information. Continuing to rely on past assessment data miscommunicates students' learning. (Guskey 1996, 21)

> **F**or knowledge or skills that are in any way cumulative or repetitive, teachers need to look particularly at the more recent information to determine grades.

These quotes demonstrate very clearly the reasons why teachers should *keep records so they may be updated easily*. The suggestion that teachers should grade in pencil is somewhat symbolic, but it *is* easier to use the more recent information and do the necessary updating of records if the records are entered using a pencil—and, it is suggested, one that has an eraser! What is really important is not the method of recording but the mindset that acknowledges that, for knowledge or skills that are in any way cumulative or repetitive, teachers need to look particularly at the more recent information to determine grades.

Suitability for Different Grade Levels

Another way to say this is that teachers should base grades on the most consistent level of performance, not the whole range of performance. This obviously applies in the previous examples—keyboarding and driving— but it has broad application in elementary schools, where we often see rapid development in student knowledge and skills over the course of the school year. This is especially true in the early grades. Using the more recent information is essential because of the varied and often rapid development of skills and abilities in young learners. Teachers sometimes attach first month and last month writing samples to final report cards; for most early-year students, the differences are immense. When rapid development is taking place, to base grades in any way on first-month work would obviously be wrong.

> *Teachers should base grades on the most consistent level of performance, not the whole range of performance.*

In middle school, high school, and college, basing grades on recent performance applies to some extent in most subjects, but is probably most obvious in modern languages, mathematics, writing, drama, and other courses that emphasize skill development and/or performance. Guskey and Bailey (2001) support this approach as they say what we should look for in the determination of grades is the most consistent level of achievement. However, they suggest that if consistency is lacking, the first thing teachers should use to help determine a grade is the more recent information. At a policy level, this concept has been included in the provincial policy in Ontario where at both the elementary and secondary levels teachers are required to look for evidence of the most consistent achievement. At the secondary level, teachers are also instructed to give special consideration to the more recent evidence of achievement.

Relationship to Improvement Grading

Some may see this guideline as an endorsement for what is often called "improvement grading." It very definitely is not. Advocates of improvement grading, such as MacIver and Reuman (1993/94), support involved mathematical calculation of improvement scores, because they believe that this approach is most effective in motivating students to work hard. Although there may be some truth in this, there are two major problems with improvement grades, particularly if we want the primary purpose of grades to be to communicate student achievement as accurately as possible. First, improvement grades distort achievement by factoring in scores for improvement rather than just achievement. The distortion is particularly severe for students at the top and bottom ends of the achievement scale. Those at the top end find it very difficult to obtain improvement points because they have little room to improve, whereas those at the bottom end may obtain many improvement points, which have the effect of distorting their achievement by communicating that it is much greater than it really is.

Second, it is much better to simply use the more recent information; students then get a full credit for their improvement rather than a score based on

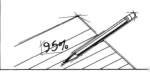

artificial manipulation of numbers. We are able to focus on grading as an exercise in professional judgment, rather than as an exercise in mechanical number crunching.

Improvement is best considered as a reporting variable and not primarily as a grading variable. Grades then are based on the students' most consistent level of achievement, with special consideration for more recent achievement.

REFLECTING ON . . . A SAMPLE GRADING PLAN

Consider the grading plan in Figure 5.1, which has been adapted from a real high school example. After reviewing the plan, ask yourself the following questions:

- ▶ What problems do you see with this grading plan?
- ▶ What changes would you make to the grading plan to make it consistent with guideline 5?

Grading Plan for Grade 9 Keyboarding

Components	First Grading Period %	Second Grading Period %	Third Grading Period %
Skill development (including technique and warm up drills)	40	25	10
Speed and Accuracy	0	10	20
Notebook	10	10	10
Tests and Assignments	30	25	50
Business Habits (including attendance, punctuality, preparedness for class, cooperation)	20	10	10
Exam	0	20	0

The final grade is calculated by averaging the grades from each grading period. A final exam must be taken if a student has not received a grade of 70% in each grading period and/or has not met the school's attendance requirements. If the final exam is taken, it counts for 40% of the final grade with the grade for each grading period counting for 20%.

Figure 5.1

Provide Several Assessment Opportunities

This guideline acknowledges individual differences in many aspects of education, especially in planning teaching/learning strategies, and recognizes that life is full of second chances. The practical application of these principles is that, as much as possible, we must offer students varied assessment opportunities to support learning and encourage student success.

Individual Differences

Students learn at different rates and are able to demonstrate their knowledge and skills in different ways and at different speeds. This is part of our acknowledgment of individual differences, which encompass learning styles and multiple intelligences as well as a more general understanding that students are different in many ways. As we acknowledge differences in learning, it is logical—and critical—that we provide varied opportunities for students to demonstrate their knowledge and skills.

Second Chances

In the real world, very little of consequence depends on a single opportunity for performance. Most performances are practiced several times before they become real—think about writing, theater, and film, to name a few. In each of these fields, and many others, there is a great deal of assessment and redoing before a final product is released. Also, individuals are not evaluated on one piece of writing or one film; judgment of their quality as a performer is made over a body of work. This is also true in sports; individuals get many chances within each game to improve their performance, and teams have multiple opportunities to improve their performance because they play many games over the course of a season. The idea of second chances is taken even further in learning to be a surgeon or a pilot; aspiring surgeons practice on cadavers, while those learning to fly practice for hours in simulators before practicing in a real plane.

As life provides second (and more) chances, so should school. There are many reasons why students do not perform at their best on the day designated by a teacher for a test or performance. These may relate to learning, physical, or emotional factors. The objective of teachers is to identify the most consistent level of performance of students. To do this, teachers need to vary

Offer students varied assessment opportunities to support learning and encourage student success.

assessment in many ways, including the number of opportunities, time available, and the methods used.

Guskey, quoted in the ASCD *Education Yearbook,* puts it this way:

> . . . they have to have a second chance. What happens if a kid doesn't do well
> on this assessment? To me that says just as much about our teaching as it does
> about the skills and talents of that individual. And so for that individual, I
> have to find other ways of approaching [his] learning [and assessment] to help
> [him] learn those things well. (1996, 5)

Assessing the same concepts and skills using different questions and/or tasks can provide a number of opportunities for students to demonstrate achievement. One potential major problem is unreasonable extra work for teachers; to avoid this, teachers may use computers to collect banks of items and tasks. This can be done at the school, district, and/or state level.

> **As** *life provides second (and more) chances, so should school.*

Baron and Boschee (1995) went as far as to say that "students failing to successfully complete all secured tasks (i.e., assessment of individual student's work under controlled conditions) during the course of the academic year should be provided with an opportunity to demonstrate an acceptable level on each unsuccessful task prior to the end of the year" (78). This would obviously be logistically difficult, but it has implications that teachers need to consider for so-called final examinations.

Busick and Stiggins (1997) presented an interesting variation of this idea. They described a school district whose policy required that "incompletes" be given before students failed so that students had extended opportunities to complete missing work. The policy, however, created many problems, which Busick and Stiggins examined in a case study format (103–104). These ideas will be examined in greater depth in chapter 6.

Time

The time available for students on any assessment, especially high stakes summative assessments, needs to be flexible. Very few aspects of knowledge and skill need to be demonstrated in a time-limited manner. In-class tests and formal examinations need to be conducted in a way that allows students considerable flexibility. Teachers recognize that different students process knowledge and skills at different rates—thus, it is important to measure the quality, not the speed, of the performance. Also, when assessments involve on-demand writing, the speed at which individuals write is an important factor. Some students can fill a page in a minute, whereas other students who know and understand just as well may take three or four minutes.

Although there may be logistical difficulties because of a school's timetable or exam timetable, there are many ways to provide flexibility. Teachers can plan in-class tests for significantly less time than the length of the class. One math teacher I know uses this approach in a 76-minute period: 10 minutes to review; 50 minutes to take the test; and 16 minutes for flex time during which students may continue working on the test or do other work.

Another approach can be used if a school has a rotating timetable. Teachers may schedule tests when the class occurs in the period immediately before lunch or in the last period of the day, thus providing automatic flex time. For formal examinations, when there is a schoolwide schedule, exam lengths could be set with a plus or minus factor of, say, one-third. For example, for 90-minute exams, students would have up to 2 hours, whereas for 2-hour exams, students would have an additional 40 minutes available to them. This not only provides some flexibility but also allows an exam schedule with two or three exams per day.

Very few aspects of knowledge and skill need to be demonstrated in a time-limited manner.

Both examples allow exams to be held at 9:00 a.m. and 1:00 p.m. Although it is not a desirable practice, if schools need to have three exams per day, most exams would be 90 minutes with the longer exams scheduled for the last time period. For example, exams would start at 9:00, 11:30, and 2:00 p.m., with any 2-hour exams starting at 2:00 p.m.

For schools on a block schedule, a very educationally appropriate but rather radical approach is to have a four-day exam schedule with one day designated for each period. In this type of schedule, no time limit needs to be set on any exam as each teacher has the whole day to assess students. This type of schedule eliminates common exams, grade 9 math classes, for example, but it also means that teachers have great flexibility with regard to their methods of assessment. These can range from traditional paper-and-pencil exams to individual oral exams or performance assessments. If teachers/schools believe strongly in the need for common exams, modify the above schedule so that the designated-day schedule is used for most subjects in the mornings, with the afternoons being set aside for common exams—or vice versa.

It is very important to emphasize that in all these situations flexible time is provided to allow all students to demonstrate what they know and are able to

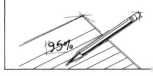

do. Teachers professionally plan tests/exams for the stated time, not for the flexible time. A teacher would plan a 90-minute exam in the belief that most students will be able to comfortably complete the exam in that time. The flex time is not designed as a safety net for teachers who create exams that are too long; it is designed to assist those students who need extra time to show what they know and can do.

Another important point about flexible time is that it must be available to all students, not just to those who have been identified as having special needs in one or more areas.

It is very important to emphasize that flexible time is provided to allow all students to demonstrate what they know and are able to do.

Practical Considerations

Having provided a number of suggestions for how students can be provided with flexible assessments, it is now time for a qualifier. Second or multiple assessment does not mean an endless set of opportunities for students. This would be unrealistic and would place far too great a burden on teachers. As Ebert (1992) said, ". . . second chances do not just appear, nor do they naturally work out without some evidence (of students) using past mistakes to enhance future success. Therefore, reassessment is the opportunity and students learn the responsibility" (32).

There are practical implications from Ebert's remark:

- Any reteaching, review, or reassessment is done at the teacher's convenience.
- Students provide some evidence that they have completed some correctives before they are allowed a reassessment opportunity. Correctives may include personal study/practice, peer tutoring, worksheets, review classes, and so forth.

These views on the responsibility of students and the role of teachers are supported by Stiggins (1997):

> . . . learning requires a collaborative partnership, with both partners fulfilling their part of their bargain. . . . As a teacher you must set limits on your contribution. . . . let's say a student . . . performs poorly on [an] assessment that counts for a grade. As a teacher how do you respond? One option is to say "I told you so" and let it go. Another response is, . . . "I value your learning whenever it occurs. Do you want to practice now and redo the assessment? If you do, I will reevaluate your performance—no penalties. But the reevaluation will need to fit into my schedule." (426)

Correctives and reassessment opportunities can usually be organized somewhat informally, but if teachers want to provide these opportunities with a clear structure, Figure 5.2 suggests a way to do it. Whatever approach teachers use, it is critical that reassessment opportunities be available to *all* students. Although the main purpose of second chance assessment is to help students who have not performed well, in order to be fair and to be seen to be fair, it must be available to all students.

> **S**econd or multiple assessment does not mean an endless set of opportunities for students.

When providing second or multiple assessment opportunities, please do not use the approach recommended by Spiegel (1991), who suggested that students should be allowed "retakes" but that they should not receive "retake grades higher than C" (631). I strongly recommend instead that students should receive whatever mark they earn on the retake, assuming that the assessment used for the retake is a quality assessment and

---

Date: _____
To the parents/guardians of _____

This is to inform you that your child is experiencing difficulties in

_____.

His/her latest test/assessment mark: _____. Teacher: _____

To help your child acquire and improve her/his knowledge and/or skills, a re-teach and review session of 40 minutes is offered _____(day)_____ (time) after school. A re-testing will be offered _____(next day)_____ (time) after school. Please make sure that your child makes good use of this opportunity. It will not be possible to change the time to accommodate everyone's schedule.

If there is a problem concerning your child's progress, please phone _____ (number) to speak to your child's teacher or the department head/chairperson.

Please sign the form to acknowledge that you have been notified about the re-teaching and re-testing opportunity for your child.

Signature of parent/guardian _____ Date: _____

Please return this form to your child's teacher immediately.

Author's Note: This letter focuses on students experiencing difficulties. The re-teach and review sessions and the re-testing opportunity should, however, be available to all students.

Figure 5.2   Adapted from a letter used by the Mathematics Department at Midland Avenue Collegiate Institute, Scarborough, Ontario, Canada.

that it is available to all students who have provided evidence of having completed the necessary correctives. This retake score now represents their real level of achievement and should not be averaged with previous scores or arbitrarily limited in any way.

Guideline 5 is designed to support learning and encourage student success by focusing on the more recent information and by having considerable flexibility in assessment with regard to the number of opportunities, the time, and the methods that students have to demonstrate their knowledge and skills. When acknowledging that students are different, teachers also acknowledge that, in assessment, one size does not fit all.

> *When acknowledging that students are different, teachers acknowledge that, in assessment, one size does not fit all.*

What's the Bottom Line?

Teachers should change grades when new (more recent) information provides a fairer picture of student achievement or when students are given second (or more) chances by having additional opportunities, more time, and varied methods of assessment.

The practical implication of this guideline is that teachers need to keep their records—either on paper or on a computer—in ways that may easily be changed or updated. "Grade in pencil" may not always be literal advice, but it needs to be the mindset that teachers have about recording grades. It means that final grades should never be determined by simply averaging the grades from several grading periods (e.g., adding the grades from terms one through three and then dividing by three).

What's My Thinking Now?

GUIDELINE 5: Grade in pencil—keep records so they can be updated easily.

Analyze guideline 5 for grading by focusing on three questions:

Why use it?

Why not use it?

Are there points of uncertainty?

After careful thought about these points, answer these two questions:

Would I use guideline 5 now?

Do I agree or disagree with the guideline, or am I unsure at this time?

See the following for one person's reflections on guideline 5.

 *A Reflection on Guideline 5*

WHY USE IT?

- success at the end is what counts
- promotes and rewards progress
- learning is not a race
- computer grading programs make it easy to "grade in pencil"
- extent to which learning goal is achieved is more important than when it is achieved

WHY NOT USE IT?

- encourages "slackers" to wait until the last minute
- time constraints make reassessment impractical
- those who do best the first time usually do best later as well
- average of several attempts fairer than best score
- students can manipulate—play the system

POINTS OF UNCERTAINTY

- emphasis on process or product?
- effect on student motivation
- transition into real world—second chances?
- is one student's third attempt a fair comparison with another's first attempt?
- reliability/validity of test items on second or third test

Chapter 6

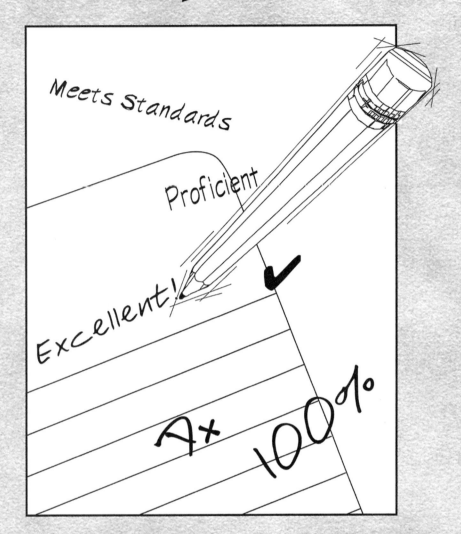

Crunching Numbers

Grades based on averaging have meaning only when averaging repeated measures of similar content. Teachers average marks on fractions, word problems, geometry, and addition with marks for attendance, homework, and notebooks—and call it mathematics. In mathematics we teach that you cannot average apples, oranges, and bananas, but we do it in our grade books!

—CANADY, WORKSHOP, ASSOCIATION FOR SUPERVISION AND CURRICULUM DEVELOPMENT ANNUAL MEETING, APRIL 1993

6
Crunch numbers carefully—if at all.

THE CASE OF . . .

Alexis' Absences

Alexis was a brilliant grade 11 student who received almost perfect marks on every summative assessment (tests, products, demonstrations, etc.) for which she was present—and she usually was present to take major tests/exams and to submit major assignments on the due dates. Alexis, however, missed many classes and often did not hand in required work (homework, first drafts, etc.). She also did not complete her notebook and, because of her absences and shy personality, her participation in class discussions was infrequent. As a result of these circumstances, there were always many zeros in teachers' grade books for Alexis—for missed quizzes, lab reports, small assignments, notebook, attendance, participation, and so forth. Alexis received a D in most subjects, and, because of her lack of success, she was considering dropping out. Alexis' low grades resulted from averaging her many zeros with her 90%+ scores, and clearly did not reflect her achievement. She was penalized over and over again for her poor attendance—which was caused by her single-parent father frequently requiring her to stay at home to look after her younger siblings!

What's the Purpose of the Guideline?

This guideline supports learning and encourages student success by having teachers question the widely accepted practice of simply averaging marks to arrive at final grades. This questioning leads teachers to examine all aspects of number crunching, including weighting and the use of zeros, that are involved in the calculation of grades.

What Are the Key Elements of the Guideline?

Number crunching has been part of teachers' lives from the time grades were introduced. Discussion of each of the grading guidelines focuses on the idea that to have grades with meaning and to have grades that support learning, grading must be an exercise in professional judgment, rather than simply a mechanical, numerical exercise. However, it is realistic to recognize that some teachers see grading as primarily a number-crunching exercise to fulfill the responsibilities imposed on them by their employment. Although such teachers will probably ignore the other guidelines and continue to do what they have always done, this guideline is critical for them because, at the very least, they need to examine their number-crunching practices. For teachers who move toward grading as an exercise in professional judgment and apply one or more of the other guidelines, there will be varying degrees of involvement with number crunching, so this guideline remains important for them as well.

> *The consequence for a student who fails to meet a standard is not a low grade but rather the opportunity—indeed, the requirement—to resubmit his or her work. (Reeves, 2000, 11)*

Mean Versus Median

The average does not have to be the *mean;* teachers should consider using *medians.* Although both are measures of central tendency, a *mean* is the total of the values, divided by the number of values, whereas the *median* is the middle value of the data listed in numerical order. This aspect of guideline 6 asks teachers to consider two dimensions of importance: (1) quantity or quality and (2) all or some evidence.

REFLECTING ON . . . PROBLEMS WITH THE MEAN

Study the information in Figure 6.1. Assume that these are the marks four students have received for ten summative assessments in a school subject—elementary, secondary, or college.

▶ What grade should each student receive?

▶ What additional information would you like to have to help you make this decision?

Note that all students received the same mean scores, but that the median scores for Karen and Jennifer are much higher. In schools using traditional grading schemes, such as the one illustrated in Figure 6.2, all four students would receive a grade of 63%, which would vary from a C to an F depending on the grading scale in use in the school, district, or college.

Issues with the Mean

Assessments in Order	Karen	Alex	Jennifer	Stephen
Assessment #1	0	63	0	0
Assessment #2	0	63	10	0
Assessment #3	0	63	10	62
Assessment #4	90	63	10	62
Assessment #5	90	63	100	63
Assessment #6	90	63	100	63
Assessment #7	90	63	100	90
Assessment #8	90	63	100	90
Assessment #9	90	63	100	100
Assessment #10	90	63	100	100
Total	630	630	630	630
Mean	63%	63%	63%	63%
Median	90%	63%	100%	63%

Figure 6.1

Traditional Grading

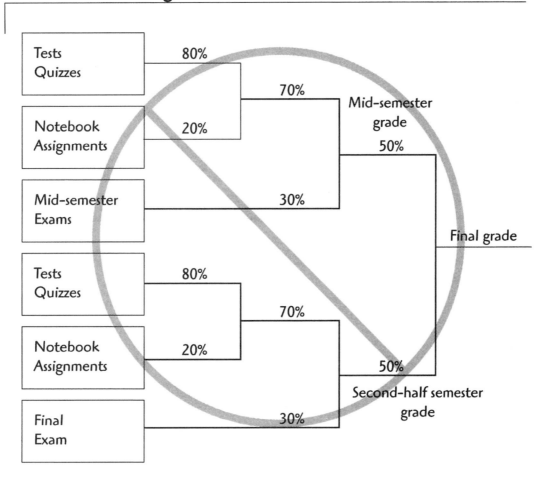

Figure 6.2

The traditional approach emphasizes quantity over quality and completing all work rather than doing some superbly and missing some. It is clear, however that the quality of the work, that is, the achievement of each student, is very different. Karen generally produced high quality work, but for some reason did not submit three of the ten summative assessments. Alex produced consistently mediocre work but submitted all the summative assessments. Jennifer produced superb work on six of the assessments, very poor work on three of the assessments, and did not submit one of the assessments. Stephen's performance was very inconsistent—four assessments were excellent, four were mediocre, and two were not submitted.

In deciding grades for the students in Figure 6.1, consider the following:

Assigning a score of zero to work that is late or missed or neglected does not accurately depict student's learning. Is the teacher certain the student has learned absolutely nothing, or is the zero assigned to punish students for not displaying appropriate responsibility?

A zero has a profound effect when combined with the practice of averaging. Students who receive a single zero have little chance of success because such an extreme score skews the average.

Averaging falls far short of providing an accurate description of what students have learned. For example, students often say, "I have to get a B on the final to pass this course." But does this make sense? If a final examination is truly comprehensive and students' scores accurately reflect what they have learned, should a B level of performance translate to a D for the course grade? If the purpose of grading and reporting is to provide an accurate description of what students have learned, then *averaging must be considered inadequate and inappropriate.* (Guskey 1996, 21)

Guskey's statements clarify the problem with using the mean, the most commonly used measure of central tendency: the mean always lets the bad overtake the good, so that for every low mark earned, a student needs many good marks to return to his or her real level. This is evident in the grades of Karen and Jennifer—most of their work is of a very high quality, but for some reason(s), they either did poorly or did not submit some of the assessments. This problem is compounded when teachers include zeros for behavioral reasons (attendance, tardiness, misconduct, etc).

> **Medians** *"provide more opportunities for success by diminishing the impact of a few stumbles and rewarding hard work."* (Wright 1994, 723)

The Median Alternative

An alternative to using the mean is to use the median. Wright (1994) stated that teachers' marks are ordinal data (numbers on a scale whose intervals are uncertain or inconsistent) and that "the median is the statistically correct measure of central tendency for ordinal data" (724). This is the technical argument for using medians, but an equal or more important argument is the philosophical one. Wright advocates medians and uses them in his college courses because they "provide more opportunities for success by diminishing the impact of a few stumbles and rewarding hard work" (723). Wright noted that all students have days on which they do not produce their best work, and that not every student is good at everything, but neither of these failings

suggests that most of the time students do not produce high-quality work. The use of means emphasizes variability, whereas the use of medians reduces the impact of variability very dramatically.

In order to use medians, teachers must convert all scores to a common scale (ideally, percentages). Then, they calculate a median for all summative assessments used in a course (which, ideally, would not be many more than fifteen) or for each category if different categories are used. Next, they also calculate a median among the categories to arrive at the final grade. (To be consistent with guideline 1, the categories should be learning goals, not assessment methods.) Figure 6.3 is an example of using medians.

It is obvious from the example in Figure 6.3 that the use of the median has the greatest impact when performance is highly variable. Thus, students who perform at a consistently high level or at a consistently low level would see little or no difference in their final grades regardless of which method of central tendency is used.

The problem with the use of medians for many teachers is their fear that it encourages students to play games and manipulate the system to their advantage by making minimal or no effort on some assessments. If this is (or becomes) a problem, it may be necessary to require that students submit/complete a certain percentage of assessments with a required minimal level of performance. It also may be necessary to designate some assessments as

> *The median has the greatest impact when performance is highly variable.*

Computing a Median for One Student

	Learning Goal #1	L.G. #2	L.G. #3	L.G. #4	L.G. #5
Assessment #1	90	100	70	95	60
Assessment #2	90	90	70	90	50
Assessment #3	90	0	70	40	40
Median	90	90	70	90	50
Mean	90	63	70	75	50

Overall Median 90   **Overall Mean 70**

Figure 6.3

essential—this would mean that a mark would be included regardless of whether the assessment was completed and regardless of what method of calculation was used. However, if the median is used in association with the other guidelines, if students have a clear understanding of the supportive success orientation of the grading procedures being used, and if the students are presented with course material and assessments that are interesting and engaging, this should not be a problem.

The main purpose of grades is to communicate achievement. Regardless of which measure of central tendency is used, grades (symbols) need to be supplemented by as much information as possible. If medians are selected, it is particularly important that some form of expanded format reporting be used, so that teachers can provide a clear picture of achievement. For example, for the student in Figure 6.3, it would be very important to be able to report that her achievement on learning goal #5 was weak.

> *Teachers need to devise better ways of dealing with work that is late, missing, or neglected, other than simply assigning zeros.*

It is important to note that guideline 6 suggests only to *consider* using medians. Given that grades should be based on each student's most consistent achievement, teachers should also consider the use of the *mode*—the most frequently occurring number in a series of numbers. They would have to be done by level —4, 3, 2, 1 or A, B, C, D, F. Changing from the use of the mean would be a giant step for many teachers and many communities—for many, the step may be too large. At the very least, however, teachers need to consider the issues involved and devise better ways of dealing with work that is late, missing, or neglected, other than simply assigning zeros.

Weighting Marks

A second aspect of guideline 6 that educators need to consider is weighting components carefully to achieve intent in final grades. The way in which marks are combined generally involves varying the importance or weighting of the different learning goals and/or assessment methods. Chapter 1 suggested that grading plans need to be based primarily on learning goals rather than assessment methods. Regardless of which approach teachers use, it is very important that weighting reflect the intent and emphasis on different learning/assessment in the final grade. For example, in Ontario the subject association for physical and health education recommends that 60–65% of a student's grade should come from the Application category, because that is the focus of PHE courses (see chapter 1).

Use of a Common Scale

Using grade book software (see chapter 10 for more information), it is relatively easy to ensure that the major components (learning goals or assessment methods) receive their intended weights. However, within each component, it is essential that the marks be included on a consistent or common scale. The easiest common scale to use is percentages: convert all marks to a percentage and then use weighting factors to create the final grade. Figure 6.4 presents a comparison of weighting options.

Comparison of Grade-Weighting Alternatives

Scenario	Test	Performance
weight	1	2
point value	40	20
Amanda's scores	10	20
Alan's scores	40	5

Alternative #1

	Amanda	Alan
Apply weighting to raw scores	$\dfrac{(10 \times 1) + (20 \times 2)}{(40 \times 1) + (20 \times 2)} = \dfrac{50}{80} = 60\%$	$\dfrac{(40 \times 1) + (5 \times 2)}{(40 \times 1) + (20 \times 2)} = \dfrac{50}{80} = 60\%$

Alternative #2

Apply weighting to point values (i.e., test, 40 pts; performance, 80 pts)	$\dfrac{10 + 80}{40 + 80} = \dfrac{90}{120} = 75\%$	$\dfrac{40 + 20}{40 + 80} = \dfrac{60}{120} = 50\%$

Alternative #3

Apply weighting using a common scale (percentages)

$$\frac{10}{40} = \frac{25 \times 1}{100 \times 1} \qquad\qquad \frac{40}{40} = \frac{100 \times 1}{100 \times 1}$$

$$\frac{20}{20} = \frac{100 \times 2}{100 \times 2} \qquad\qquad \frac{5}{20} = \frac{25 \times 2}{100 \times 2}$$

$$\frac{25 + 200}{100 + 200} = \frac{225}{300} = 75\% \qquad\qquad \frac{100 + 50}{100 + 200} = \frac{150}{300} = 50\%$$

Figure 6.4

In Figure 6.4, the teacher intended that performance have double the weight of the paper-and-pencil test. Amanda did poorly on the test but achieved a perfect score on the performance assessment; Alan did very poorly on the performance but achieved a perfect score on the test. Examine the results of using three different alternatives for grade weighting. When the weighting factors were applied to the raw scores (alternative 1), both students received the same percentage mark to go in their grade. This clearly was not the teacher's intent; another approach is needed. By applying the weighting to the point values (alternative 2), the teacher ensured that performance was marked on a scale that was double that of the test scale. When the teacher used the common (percentage) scale (alternative 3), each aspect was marked using the same scale (100), and then the weighting factors were applied. Both alternative 2 and alternative 3 achieved the same result—Amanda's final mark was significantly higher than Alan's, which reflected the teacher's intent that performance have double the weight of the test. Although both alternatives achieve the intended weighting, the common scale approach is recommended because, over a one- or two-semester course, it is easier to use than continually balancing the total possible score, that is, weight the score with all the other assessments that count in the final grade.

Review the information in Figure 6.5. For the learning goal in this example, each assessment has a total score of the teacher's choosing, but the students' marks are recorded on a common scale (percentage) and the chosen weighting factors are then applied. In this example, Julia and Derek both receive the same raw score total, but when the raw scores are converted to a common scale, Derek's grade is significantly higher than Julia's. This reflects the fact that he achieved the maximum possible mark on the part of the assessment considered to be more important than the other two parts of the assessment taken together. This is what was intended; the teacher considered the performance to be more important than the two tests combined.

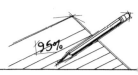

Grading Using a Common Scale

Component	Learning Goal #1											
Assessment Method	Test			Performance			Test					
Weight	1.5			4.0			2.0					
Student	Mark out of 20	Mark as a %	Weighted mark out of 150	Mark out of 50	Mark as a %	Weighted mark out of 400	Mark out of 80	Mark as a %	Weighted mark out of 200	Raw score total 150	Weighted score total 750	Weighted score as a %
Julia	20	100	150	20	40	160	60	75	150	100	460	61.3
Derek	10	50	75	50	100	400	40	50	100	100	575	76.7
Brian	20	100	150	0	0	0	80	100	200	100		
Brittany	0	0	0	50	100	400	50	62.5	125	100		

Figure 6.5

REFLECTING ON . . . WEIGHTING GRADES

Consider the other two students in Figure 6.5. They both received the same raw scores as Julia and Derek. Calculate their weighted score totals and weighted scores as a percentage, then consider the following:

▶ Do their final grades for this learning goal reflect the teacher's intent?

▶ Taking into account the other guidelines in this book, what would you do with Brian and Brittany; that is, what grade would you include for learning goal #1 in your final grade calculation?

The Issue of Variability of Scores

Technically, variability of scores on each assessment also needs to be taken into account; a test with a range of scores from 40% to 80% has a different impact than a performance assessment for which the scores vary from 10% to 100%. It would be ideal if scores were equated through the use of standard scores before being weighted. See Thayer (1991) for a detailed description of these procedures.

Because there is enough in this guideline (let alone the other seven!) for teachers to consider without dealing with these highly technical issues, not much detail is provided here about standardizing scores. As Airasian (1994) suggested, "This is not a major problem with most classroom assessments, which generally are given in the same format to the same group of pupils, cover the topics taught, and are scored in the same way. Under these conditions the spread of scores on different assessments will usually be close enough so that adjustments need not be made" (318). The issue of variability of scores, however, is something that teachers need to be aware of, especially when class rank, scholarships, and awards are being determined.

REFLECTING ON . . . SIMPLE AVERAGING

Consider the situation shown in Figure 6.6.

	Stephen	Megan	Highest Grade in School
English	96%	96%	96%
Chemistry	97%	96%	97%
Biology	96%	100%	100%
Physics	99%	99%	99%
Algebra	92%	92%	94%
Calculus	99%	n/a	99%
Music	n/a	89%	89%

Figure 6.6

Each student stood first or had equal first grades in five subjects, but Stephen was first in calculus with 99% whereas Megan was first in music with 89%. If these grades are simply averaged, Stephen will be ranked first even though Megan had a slightly higher average on the five subjects that they each studied. Is this fair?

The Use of Zeros

Guskey and Bailey (2001) identify the three most questionable grading practices as using simple averages, lowering grades for behavior(s), and the use of zeros. The first was dealt with earlier in this chapter, and the second was dealt with primarily in chapter 3. Now it is time to deal with the issues of the big **0**.

Teachers use zeros when students fail to submit work because teachers feel that if nothing has been submitted, the score should reflect this, and that the zero will lead to more responsible actions in the future. There are, however, a number of serious problems with the use of zeros:

> **T**he issue of variability of scores is something that teachers need to be aware of.

- the effect of such extreme scores, especially when coupled with the practice of averaging;
- the lack of proportionality between 0 and 50–70 as the passing score compared with the much smaller differentials between the other score points in the grading scale;
- the inaccurate communication that results from the use of zeros; and
- the ineffectiveness of zeros as responsibility-creating mechanisms.

Consider the following real example I observed in the spring of 2001. In a high school that issues report cards after 4½ weeks, grades in one subject were based on five scores. One student, whom I shall call Janice, received scores of 90, 0, 82, 72, and 76. The mean score is 64%, and the passing grade in the state is 70%, so Janice received an F. This happened because the extreme score of 0 had a disproportionate impact on the average, and because there is a 70-point differential between the D/F cut point and 0 compared with a 10-point differential between each of the other cut points (D/C, C/B, and B/A). In the interest of mathematical accuracy, the lowest possible score should be no more than the differential between the other cut points (Reeves 2000). If this approach were used, the 0 would become a 60, and Janice's grade would be a C or D (76%).

The inclusion of the zero in the grade for Janice led to a serious miscommunication of her achievement. She clearly was not a failing student as four of her five scores were above or well above the pass/fail level, but because of the one zero and the mean, she received an F. The F in no way communicated the quality of most of her achievement or the fact that one piece of assessment evidence was missing. The teacher expects that the F will cause Janice to make greater effort in the next grading period. Guskey (2000), however,

Completion Contract

Student Name: _____

Course: _____

Missed Work—The following work has not been handed in:

Original Due Date:_____

Reason—Please indicate why the work is late.

Next Steps—What will you now do to get this work completed?

New Date for Submission: _____

Once this new date is negotiated, the student agrees to submit this work on that date or receive a mark of **I** for **Incomplete.** The student and parent acknowledge that Incompletes may lead to the teacher determining that there is insufficient evidence for a grade and that this is the equivalent of a failing grade.

Student Signature: _____
Parent Signature: _____
Teacher Signature: _____

Figure 6.7
Adapted by Ken O'Connor from original work by Jennifer Perkin, Curriculum Consultant, Catholic School Board of Eastern Ontario. Used with permission.

SkyLight Professional Development

disagrees: "No studies support low grades or marks as punishments. Instead of prompting greater effort, low grades more often cause students to withdraw from learning" (25). It is far more appropriate to have Janice take responsibility for her learning and be held accountable for the missing work. Figure 6.7 is a completion contract that may help to prevent some students from using zeros to facilitate work avoidance and failure.

What then should be done about "work not submitted" (which is what late work becomes after a deadline has passed)? If teachers are using a strictly numerical approach to grade determination, the use of the median rather than the mean, and/or the use of a more appropriate point differential (e.g., where if 70 is the pass/fail cut point, 60 is given instead of 0) would help overcome some of the worst effects of traditional approaches. If, however, the missing assessment evidence was a major task essential to valid and reliable assessment of Janice's achievement, or if the teacher takes a more holistic approach to grade determination, then the question that needs to be asked is: Do I have enough evidence to make a valid and reliable judgment of Janice's achievement? If the answer is "yes," the grade should be determined without the missing piece, which is recorded with an I for Incomplete, not zero. The fact that the work was not submitted should be recorded in the work habits/learning skill section and/or in the comment section of a report card. If the answer is "no," then the grade should be recorded as I for Incomplete or Insufficient evidence. This symbol communicates accurately that, while the student's grade could be anywhere from an A to an F, at the point in time when the grade had to be determined there was insufficient evidence to make a fair judgment. If I appears on a progress report, then corrective action can be taken during the next grading period. If the I is on the final report card, it has the same effect as an F, but the student should still have the opportunity to submit the missing achievement by an agreed upon date.

If incompletes are used, there must be mechanisms in place that support students and make it possible for them to complete the missing work.

If Is are used, mechanisms must be in place that support students and make it possible for them to complete the missing work. This means that schools or districts must be prepared to devote human and financial resources to make this possible. Guskey (2000) describes the approach taken at Beachwood Middle School in Ohio where grades are recorded as A, B, C, or I. "Students who receive an I grade are required to do additional work in order to bring their performance up to an acceptable level" (25). This may involve after-school sessions, special Saturday school programs, or summer school.

The use of zeros for work not submitted is a difficult, and often emotional, issue for teachers. The approach suggested here is educative and supportive but "hard" on students because it requires students to provide evidence of achievement of all the major learning goals, not just a passing average. It is also an attempt to acknowledge that although we work in a calendar-driven system, learning is, or should be, time independent.

Including Rubric Scores in Grades

If a teacher uses rubrics instead of scores (out of 10 or 100), another aspect of number crunching needs to be considered: how to include rubric scores in grades. Marzano and Kendall (1996) suggested that teachers should not simply add numbers together over a semester or a year—what they call "the cumulative option"—but that teachers should record scores in a variety of ways and then report a grade for each learning goal.

Review Figure 6.8, which depicts the use of Marzano and Kendall's approach. Assuming that their suggestions are followed, a teacher's grade book might look like Figure 6.8.

Judy's Scores in Grade 5 Social Studies

Based on 4-point Rubric

Learning Goal	Summative Assessment #1	S.A.#2	S.A.#3	S.A.#4	S.A.#5	Total	Weight	Adjusted Total
L.G. 1	3	3	3	3	3	15	2	30
L.G. 2	4	4	4	1	4	17	3	51
L.G. 3	1	2	3	4	4	14	2	28
L.G. 4	3	2	3	2	3	13	1	13
L.G. 5	4	3	4	3	4	18	3	54
L.G. 6	2	2	2	1	2	9	1	9
Total						$86/120$		$185/240$
Percentage						71.7		77.1

Figure 6.8

Regardless of whether an overall grade is determined or whether grades are determined for each learning goal, teachers must decide how to convert nontraditional scores to grades.

Figure 6.8 illustrates a strictly numerical approach. The learning goals can be weighted or based only on total points with no weighting. Judy received a total of thirty scores on five assessments for six learning goals. All were scored on four-point rubrics, so the total possible points are 120. Judy received 86 points, which provides a grade of 72%. (Grades could also be calculated for each learning goal.) If the teacher's judgment leads to the conclusion that weighting is necessary, total weighted points would be used. In Figure 6.8, weights are provided and applied in the last two right-hand columns. As a result, Judy receives a weighted score of 185/240, giving her a final grade of 77%.

This appears to be straightforward and fair, but is it? Twenty of the thirty scores Judy received are 3s or 4s that should be linked to the two highest grades on the scale—As and Bs. In most jurisdictions, Judy's 72% or 77% would be a C, so there is clearly something wrong with the conversion. The problem is the lack of an appropriate relationship between the four-point scale and the grading scale. If Judy had received scores of 3 for every learning goal on every assessment, she would have a grade of 75% (weighted or unweighted), which in most jurisdictions would be a C, but the intent—the second highest category—is clearly that she receive a B. This straightforward calculation "works" if a B is 70–79%, but if a higher grading scale is used, adjustments have to be made. Figure 6.9 provides some possibilities; it is based on the idea that the conversion should be somewhere between the middle and the top of the range.

None of the numerical conversion approaches are entirely satisfactory largely because rubric scoring has an entirely different base than scoring by points. With rubrics, there really is not just a numerical step between each level; there is a qualitative difference between each level, which is described in words and assigned a number simply as a label. Carr (2000) argues that points may be converted to levels but levels should not be converted to points. Carr provides a more detailed discussion (2001, 54–59). For this reason, and because of the difficulties of making appropriate numerical conversion, a much better approach is to use what Arter and McTighe (2001, 80) call a

Rubric Scores to Grades

Letter Grade	%	Rubric Score	Points
A	90–100	4	95–99
B	80–89	3	85–89
C	70–79	2	75–79
D	60–69	1	65–69
F	0–59	0	50

Figure 6.9

"logic rule." For example, most scores at 4 with none below a 2 could be an A, at least half the scores at 3 with some 4s and with no score below a 2 would be a B, and so on. This approach could be applied to determining one overall grade or to determining a grade for each learning goal.

Linda Elman, a testing coordinator in the state of Washington, stated in a letter to the teachers in her district that each method, except for the logic rule, "makes the method seem more scientific than it really is." Her final advice to teachers:

> [O]nce you, as a teacher, arrive at a method of converting rubric scores to a scale that is comparable to other grades, the responsibility is on you to come up with a defensible system for weighting the pieces in the grade book to come up with a final grade for students. This part of the teaching process is part of the professional art of teaching. There is no single right way to do it; however whatever is done needs to reflect evidence of students' level of mastery of the targets of instruction. (Regional Educational Laboratory 1998, Handout A46, H3, p. 5)

For another approach to converting rubric scores to grades, see Linek (1991, 130–131).

 # What's the Bottom Line?

How should teachers crunch numbers? They should crunch numbers very carefully! If at all!

Teachers should consider:

- the effect of various ways of calculating central tendency;
- the effect of extreme marks, especially zeros;
- how scores and/or learning goals should be weighted;
- the effect of mark distribution;
- how to include nontraditional scores (i.e., rubrics) in grades; and
- the possible use of I grades, or Incompletes.

The practical implication of guideline 6 is that teachers need to exercise their professional judgment, not just use mechanical, numerical calculations when assigning grades. The real bottom line is, if guideline 5 is consistently applied, guideline 6 is almost not needed!

What's My Thinking Now?

GUIDELINE 6: Crunch numbers carefully—if at all.

Analyze guideline 6 for grading by focusing on three questions:

Why use it?

Why not use it?

Are there points of uncertainty?

After careful thought about these points, answer these two questions:

Would I use guideline 6 now?

Do I agree or disagree with the guideline, or am I unsure at this time?

See the following for one person's reflections on guideline 6.

 # A Reflection on Guideline 6

WHY USE IT?

- median fairer than mean, allows for a stumble or two
- median reduces impact of low marks, especially zeros
- rewards improvement and progress
- weighting properly reflects importance of learning goal
- weighting properly reflects time spent on learning goal

WHY NOT USE IT?

- encourages students not to do every assignment
- mean usually used by colleges and universities
- teachers don't have time for agreement on weighting
- median too difficult to calculate
- often good reasons for a zero; should count

POINTS OF UNCERTAINTY

- totally new ideas so not sure students would understand
- what do grades mean when different procedures are used?
- what do zeros represent?
- how do you weight learning goals appropriately?
- parent reaction

Chapter 7

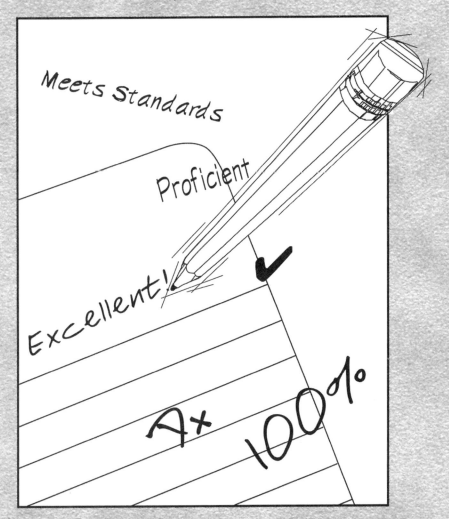

Quality Assessment and Keeping Records

High quality assessment is essential in all assessment contexts . . . All assessments must meet . . . standards. No exceptions can be tolerated because to violate any [standard of quality] is to risk inaccuracy, [thus] placing student academic well-being in jeopardy.

—STIGGINS (2001a, 19–20)

Guideline:

7

Use quality assessment(s) and properly recorded evidence of achievement.

THE CASE OF . . .

Brian's Boosted Grade

Brian was a very good student in academic subjects. He was a high-quality critical thinker with a good memory and writing skills. He did not do well in technical or vocational subjects, because he was all thumbs. He did not enjoy these courses and made little effort to complete quality products. His high school, however, required all freshmen to take one technical or vocational course. Brian chose carpentry because his best friends had chosen it.

Brian's school had a very traditional approach to assessment, with middle and end of semester paper-and-pencil exams. Grades in the carpentry course were based partly on the students' products and partly on the written exams. Brian received failing marks on each of the required products. He received perfect marks on the exams, which asked students to do such things as list safety procedures and describe how to build a birdhouse. At the middle and end of the semester, the carpentry teacher assigned a mark for attitude and participation.

Since Brian knew how to play the game and appeared to be interested and involved, he received a very high mark. His final grade was 74%, which came from the mark breakdown in Figure 7.1.

Products (40%)				Attitude/Participation (20%)		Exams (40%)	
Possible score: 30	70	40	60	20	20	100	100
Brian's score: 11	24	10	27	20	20	100	100
Mean Score:	35%			100%		100%	

Figure 7.1

Brian's teacher neither followed quality assessment principles nor recorded evidence throughout the semester. Brian received an inflated grade—assuming that the main learning goal was the demonstration of carpentry skills.

What's the Purpose of the Guideline?

This guideline supports learning and encourages student success by ensuring that each student's grade comes from quality assessments, the results of which have been recorded accurately and in a timely manner. The issue is that all involved understand the critical dimensions of quality assessment. The other component requires teachers to keep accurate records and not rely on memory.

What Are the Key Elements of the Guideline?

Dimensions of Quality Assessment

Marks and grades are meaningful when—and only when—they are based on quality assessment. Thus, it is essential that teachers know, understand, and apply quality standards when they plan and implement assessment in their classrooms. According to Stiggins (1997, 14–16), there are five quality standards: (1) setting clear and appropriate targets, (2) stating clear purpose(s), (3) matching target to method, (4) selecting appropriate samples for the learning domain, and (5) controlling interference or distortion.

> **M**arks and grades are meaningful when—and only when—they are based on quality assessment.

Setting Clear and Appropriate Targets

The importance of clear and appropriate targets cannot be overstated. If we do not know where we want to go, then we do not need a map to get there; but if we want to know how to get from point A to point B, we need a map. In the classroom, the "map" is provided by standards that have been prescribed or established for each grade or course. In most courses, targets are

- knowledge (what students are to know)—from memory or retrieval from appropriate sources;
- application of knowledge (reasoning and skills)—what students are able to do; and
- values/attitudes—what students are like, that is, how they behave.

In order to meet the standard in this guideline, teachers—and students—must understand what is being assessed and what constitutes quality performance. Suggestions about how this standard can be met are found in chapters 5 and 8.

Stating a Clear Purpose

Clear purpose comes from understanding why the assessment is being conducted and what use will be made of the assessment results by the many potential users—at the classroom level (students, teachers, and parents); at the instructional support level (remedial teachers, school building administrators, central office support personnel); and at the policy level (district administrators, school board trustees, state/provincial department personnel). All these users have different needs, but as Stiggins (1997) said, "There is no single assessment capable of meeting all these different needs. Thus, the developer of any assessment must start with a clear sense of whose needs the assessment will meet" (16). At the classroom level, which is the focus of this book, this quality standard means that the teacher needs a very clear understanding of purpose, that is, whether for diagnosis or for formative or summative assessment, and whether and how the results will be included in student grades. Detailed consideration of these issues is found in chapter 4.

Matching Method with Target

Matching method with target requires that the assessor choose a method of assessment that is capable of effectively and efficiently providing the needed information. If knowledge of vocabulary in French is the target, then a selected response test is an appropriate choice; but if the target is the student's ability to speak French, then a performance assessment is needed. Meeting this standard is made easier by the fact that there are many different assessment methods available for use. They may be classified as paper-and-pencil tests, performance assessment, and personal communication (see Figure Intro.5 on page 14). Matching assessments with targets, which may be part or all of specified learning goals, requires that teachers know and understand targets and learning goals, know and understand various methods of assessment, and put the methods and targets/learning goals together.

Reflecting on . . . Assessment Methodology

Decide which assessment methods match with which learning goals in Figure 7.2. Place a check mark (√) in boxes where there is a match and a cross (x) in those boxes where there is no match. Use an asterisk (*) to indicate the

Matching Assessment and Learning Goals

Types of Learning Goals / Assessment Methods	Paper-and-Pencil Tests *(selected response)*	Performance Assessment *(constructed response, product, performance, process)*	Personal Communication *(conversation, observation)*
Knowledge			
Application of Knowledge *(Skills, Products, Performances)*			
Reasoning			

Figure 7.2

best matches for knowledge, application of knowledge, and reasoning. You may want to add a few words to explain your understanding of appropriate matches. When you have completed this exercise, compare your responses with the choices shown in Figure 7.3.

Figure 7.3 may serve as a guide for teachers. Matching method with target requires choices that will give an accurate picture of student achievement, while taking into account the human, material, and time resources available in the classroom.

Another interesting approach to matching assessments with targets can be found in Marzano's book *Transforming Classroom Grading* (2000, 87). Matching also requires that assessments do what they are intended to do in another way.

Matching Assessment and Learning Goals

Types of Learning Goals / Assessment Methods	Paper-and-Pencil Tests *(selected response)*	Performance Assessment *(constructed response, product, performance, process)*	Personal Communication *(conversation, observation)*
Knowledge	* ✓	✓	✓
Application of Knowledge *(Skills, Reasoning, Products)*	X	* ✓	✓
Values/Attitudes *(Affects/Behavior)*	✓	✓	✓

Figure 7.3

Test Specification Chart

Content / Type of Thinking	Concept #1	Concept #2	Concept #3	Concept #4	Total
Recall	2 (5)*	2 (5)	2 (5)	2 (5)	8 (20)
Comparison	1 (5)		1 (5)		2 (10)
Inference		1 (10)		1 (10)	2 (20)
Analysis		1 (10)	1 (10)		2 (20)
Evaluation	1 (15)			1 (15)	2 (30)

*The first figure is the number of items; (the number in the parentheses) is the percentage value of the test.

Figure 7.4

Figure 7.4 suggests that reasoning questions can tap five types of thinking skills, ranging from recall to evaluation. If test or exam questions are aimed at comparison, inference, analysis, and/or evaluation and are really matched to these skills, then the questions must present situations that are new to students, so that they can apply their knowledge. The emphasis needs to be put on "knowledge in use" not "knowledge about." Teachers often think that they ask students higher-level thinking skill questions, but if, for example, a comparison of two battles has been taught in class, a question asking students to compare the two battles is a recall question.

> *The emphasis needs to be put on "knowledge in use" not "knowledge about."*

Selecting Appropriate Samples for the Learning Domain

Sample selection is necessary because, in all assessment situations, only part of the learning domain can be chosen and because there are practical time and length considerations. Returning to the French example introduced on page 165, in a vocabulary test, a representative sample of the words a student is supposed to know is used, whereas in a speaking ability performance, students speak long enough for teachers to make an accurate assessment of their ability.

Careful planning is the key to sample selection for all assessment methods. All require that teachers think carefully about what will be included so that valid inferences can be made about student achievement. For example, for paper-and-pencil tests, teachers may use some form of test specification chart in which they check that each thinking skill and all the content is sampled. Planning of this type should lead to teachers being able to draw confident conclusions about student achievement.

Controlling Interference and Distortion

Interference or distortion from all sources must be controlled as much as possible in all assessment situations.

Interference or distortion from all sources must be controlled as much as possible in all assessment situations. Stiggins (1997) says teachers need to "design, develop, and use assessments in ways that permit us to control for all sources of bias and distortion that can cause our results to misrepresent real student achievement" (16). How often have we heard teachers say things like "Dexter's grade doesn't represent what he knows and can do because he doesn't test well"? If Stiggins' advice is followed, the teacher will adjust for Dexter's test problems, possibly by providing him with an alternative method or more time to demonstrate his real achievement.

Bias or distortion can occur in a number of circumstances:

1. With all methods of assessments for all students (e.g., physical conditions—noise, lighting, seating; motivation; assessment anxiety; poorly worded directions or questions)
2. With all methods of assessments for some students (e.g., emotional or physical health; reading/language ability; test-taking skill)
3. With specific methods of assessment (e.g., multiple choice—more than one correct response; performance assessment, including essay questions—criteria inappropriate or lacking)

(Further detail on sources of bias can be found in Stiggins and Knight, 1997, 56, and in Stiggins, 2001a, 22.)

The most common source of distortion in the assessment of student achievement is time—or the lack of it—because most assessments are time limited. Students who know and can achieve the learning goal(s) but who work slowly and need a lot of time to demonstrate their achievement have their achievement misrepresented when they are forced to rush their work or when

they are unable to complete an assessment activity. There are some skills that do need to be demonstrated in a timed manner, for example, words per minute in keyboarding, but for most other knowledge and skills, the critical dimension is—or should be—quality, not speed.

Many students who achieve at high levels need considerable time to reflect and analyze before they are able to produce quality work. Other students are simply methodical and slow in their approach, and some simply write slowly. Teachers need to take these personal differences into account and be flexible with time limits. This problem is usually most obvious in tests and exams. Teachers may help students by always testing in the period before a break and by providing some flexibility in the time allowed for students to complete examinations.

The most common source of distortion in the assessment of student achievement is time—or the lack of it.

The complexity of this issue and the problem of trying to give students challenging tasks on exams is described beautifully by Manon (1995):

> . . . trying to crowd together several important tasks into one fretful hour makes no sense at all. . . . That our students ever complete a finished product on a timed mathematics test is indeed quite remarkable. Asking them to do their best work under such constraints is neither productive nor fair. Even the most accomplished of mathematicians would not wait until an hour before publication to begin work on *someone else's* hard problem. (140)

In the same article, Manon acknowledged that a difficult question he had put on an exam "should rightly have been posed as an extended exploration" (139). He realized that "the students had not been given adequate time or resources to complete the problem" and that "discovery on demand is a highly risky business" (140).

If teachers know that student marks and grades are not a true reflection of their achievement, it is almost certainly because one or more of the quality standards has been breached. In such situations, teachers must remember that grading is (or should be) an exercise in professional judgment, not just a mechanical, numerical exercise. Stiggins (2001a) suggests that schools should have an assessment policy that establishes "standards of sound assessment practice" which holds "all teachers accountable for meeting those standards" (25). He acknowledges that "although sound assessment policies do not ensure sound practices, they can contribute by reaffirming a commitment to quality" (25). An example of such a policy can be found in Appendix 3.

Keeping Records

The second part of guideline 7 requires teachers to keep careful and timely records of student achievement. The key point here is that records must be kept somewhere—on paper or on a computer—not just held in a teacher's head.

Records need to be as individualized as possible.

There are, of course, myriad ways for teachers to keep appropriate records. Records need to be as individualized as possible, so the best approach is to have a separate page for each student (see Figures 1.2, 1.3, and 1.4). It is important that the records are organized by learning goals, not methods of assessment. This desirable approach was discussed in chapter 1.

This is manageable when teachers have a homeroom or core group, but it is very difficult for teachers in a rotary system, who will probably see one hundred to two hundred students each day. In these situations, teachers need to adapt the individual student sheets or forms to whole class use. This sheet can accommodate many students, and records can be kept for a number of learning goals. Chapter 9 addresses forms for whole class use (see Figure 9.4b on page 193).

Figure 7.5 summarizes the variety of assessment methods available and suggests a variety of recording approaches. Use of these assessment methods and recording approaches will provide teachers with a rich variety of achievement information—a student profile—on which to base grading decisions. Terwilliger (1989) suggested that all data collected for the purpose of judging student achievement should be expressed in quantitative form, but this is probably necessary only for summative assessments and in the later years of high school and in college. Depending on grade level and subject, teachers decide which of the recording approaches are practical and appropriate for them and their students.

Assessment Methods

Assessment Method	Strategy	Recording Approaches
Personal Communication	Observation Conversation	· ✓ or x (done or not done) · Rubric Score · Letter or Number Mark (x/10, %, A, B)
Performance Assessment	Product Performance Process	· Symbol (G—good; S—satisfactory, · NI—needs improvement) · Anecdotal Comment
Paper-and-Pencil Tests	Constructed Response Selected Response	Score: Number or Proportion Correct

Figure 7.5

 # What's the Bottom Line?

Quality assessment and accurate written or electronic record keeping are essential if grades are to reflect real student achievement. There are practical implications of guideline 7:

- Teachers need to be aware of and apply the five standards of quality assessment.
- Schools/districts should have assessment policies that affirm a commitment to quality assessment.
- Teachers need to keep records on paper or on the computer—not in their heads.

 ## *What's My Thinking Now?*

GUIDELINE 7: Use quality assessment(s) and properly recorded evidence of achievement.

Analyze guideline 7 for grading by focusing on three questions:

Why use it?

Why not use it?

Are there points of uncertainty?

After careful thought about these points, answer these two questions:
Would I use guideline 1 now?

Do I agree or disagree with the guideline, or am I unsure at this time?

See the following for one person's reflections on guideline 7.

 A Reflection on Guideline 7

WHY USE IT?

- · professional responsibility
- · inspires greater confidence from students, parents
- · provides real measure of achievement
- · fair to learners
- · ensures varied and appropriate assessment

WHY NOT USE IT?

- · amount of paper needed to record everything
- · amount of time needed to record everything
- · time needed to ensure quality is too great
- · lack of available quality assessments
- · tracking learning goals much more difficult than recording marks

POINTS OF UNCERTAINTY

- · subjective nature of some assessments
- · who determines validity and reliability?
- · level of assessment literacy
- · who determines quality?
- · political agenda

Chapter 8

Communicating with Students About Grades

We must constantly remind ourselves that the ultimate purpose of education is to have students become self-evaluating. If students graduate from our schools still dependent on others to tell them when they are adequate, good, or excellent, then we have missed the whole point of what education is about.

—COSTA AND KALLICK (1992, 280)

Guideline:

8

Discuss and involve students in assessment, including grading, throughout the teaching/learning process.

THE CASE OF . . .

Huang's Lunchtime Surprise

It was early November, fall sports had just finished, and it was almost time for midsemester exams and reports. The junior boys' volleyball team was having a pizza lunch to celebrate their season; they had won only one game, but most of the team were first-year players and had greatly improved over the course of the season. In addition to their skill development and their improved understanding of game strategy, they had also developed a very strong team spirit. Thus, the time and effort they put in was fun and worthwhile, even if their team record did not suggest a successful season. About fifteen minutes into the luncheon, the coach noted that Huang, their best defensive player who had never missed a practice or a game, was absent. He asked about this and was told that Huang and several other students had stayed behind in English class to discuss their

grades with Ms. Hector. A few minutes later, Huang arrived at the luncheon; it was obvious that he was upset as he joined in the celebration half-heartedly.

At the end of the luncheon, the coach asked Huang to stay and talk. Huang explained that his first quarter English grade, which would be a significant portion of his final grade, was much lower than he expected. Ms. Hector had included a number of scores that Huang and other students thought were not going to be included. Most of these were for what they thought were practice activities in the first three weeks of classes.

Whether or not these scores should have been included relates to other grading guidelines (see chapters 4 and 5). The issue here is that Huang and other students did not know what was included in grade calculations for their English class. This was in contrast to the assessment approach used on the volleyball team. For the team, the coach had stressed that the measure of the season would not be their win/loss record but their growth in skills and strategy and their enjoyment of practices, games, and the team experience. Throughout the season, he gave feedback to individuals and the team on their progress and growth in these areas; their league matches and the final luncheon were the summative assessment!

What's the Purpose of the Guideline?

This guideline requires that the assessment practices, including how grades will be determined, are discussed with students at the beginning of instruction in each class. When students know how they will be assessed, and especially when they have been involved in assessment decisions, the likelihood of student success is increased greatly.

What Are the Key Elements of the Guideline?

From nursery school to graduate school, teachers strive for student growth and progress on stated learning goals. Application of this guideline is obviously very different at different ages. What is important is the principle that students will be involved and know how and why they are being assessed.

Student Involvement in Assessment

Several factors are involved in this discussion of student involvement and assessment, including:

- the balance between student involvement and teacher decision making;
- age appropriateness;
- the amount of detail provided students about assessment; and
- what is meant by the beginning of instruction.

Student Involvement and Teacher Decision Making

Giving students real opportunities for meaningful input into decisions about the how and what of classroom assessment, including grading, does not mean that students take over the teacher's professional responsibility to decide about assessment. Several decisions can be discussed with students. One is how they will demonstrate their competence on the learning goals of a course. Armstrong (1994) provided an example of this by designing a form for students to indicate the type of performance assessment they would like to use to show their knowledge and skills. Armstrong provided a list of possible assessment activities from which students might choose, but students also were allowed to add their own suggestions to the list. Teachers could adapt this form to match the learning goals and provide a customized form for each of the major groupings of learning goals/standards.

A second type of decision in which students could be involved concerns how to mark or score each assessment.

> **W**hen students know how they will be assessed, and especially when they have been involved in assessment decisions, the likelihood of student success is increased greatly.

Teachers can set criteria for their students. Teachers can set criteria with their students. Students can set or negotiate their own criteria. [There are] many ways to involve students in setting criteria. . . . when students take part in developing criteria, they are much more likely to understand what is expected of them, "buy in," and then accomplish the task successfully. (Gregory, Cameron, and Davies 1997, 7)

Criteria development may involve a marking scheme, a checklist, or a fully developed rubric. Grade 9 students, in collaboration with their teachers, developed the rubric shown in Figure 8.1. The students brainstormed the characteristics of an oral presentation; the teachers provided the categories; the students classified the characteristics; and the teachers provided the

Oral Presentation Criteria—Independent Research Project

Topic: _____   Name: _____

A. Content
- complete information
- details
- interesting/exciting
- visual aid(s)

Needed more   Kept interest   Wanted more

B. Organization
- intro., body, conclusion
- stayed on topic
- emphasized main points
- asked question(s) at end

Did not make   Part made   Made sense
sense   sense

C. Delivery
- spoke clearly
- talked loudly enough
- talked at a normal pace

Unclear,   Was difficult to   Clear, loud
inaudible   hear at times

D. Nonverbal
- eye contact
- body posture
- hand gestures
- energetic/enthusiastic

Out of touch   Some "touch"   In "touch"

E. Length
- 5–7 minutes

3 minutes   4 minutes   5 minutes

Figure 8.1   Adapted with permission, © 1995 from Toronto District School Board, Ontario, Canada.

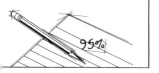

measurement scale (which is not very good!). The total class time to develop this rubric was about twenty-five minutes. Time well spent, both in principle and in practice, because in the class in which it was first used, twenty-two of twenty-three students performed in the top half of the scale. Even more significant was that all twenty-three students said they enjoyed doing the oral presentation, when previously it had been something that they hated doing.

Sperling (1993) provides a third example of decision making that involves students in their own assessment. She described how the students in Gail Hughes's grade 4 classroom in Ann Arbor, Michigan, developed their understanding of what good writing is by scoring writing samples and then developing a written list of criteria. Students were helped in this with scored writing samples from their teacher. Sperling called this "collaborative assessment" and although she acknowledged that it required a great deal of work by teachers, she concluded that "the results far outweigh the effort. Because criteria are clearly spelled out, students can take the responsibility to evaluate their own work. They compare their self-assessment with the teacher's assessment, set goals for future work, and initiate corrective action to improve their own work" (75). Kohn said this involvement in determining criteria and then judging their work using these criteria "achieves several things at once: it gives students more control of their education, it makes evaluation feel less punitive, and it provides an important learning experience in itself" (1993a, 13).

> **B**ecause criteria are clearly spelled out, students can take the responsibility to evaluate their own work. (Sperling 1993, 75).

A fourth way to involve students in assessment decisions is by discussing how teachers will determine grades. Teachers may review some of the difficult issues, such as what ingredients they will include (e.g., how cooperative learning will be assessed), which activities will be marked for grades and which will not, and how performance over a semester, term, or year will be dealt with, especially if work shows marked improvement. Students may also contribute to the decision about how teachers will determine grades, that is, helping to determine the weighting factors and the use of means or medians.

In these four types of decisions, it is important to note that teachers provide opportunities for students to discuss how assessments will be chosen, scored, and combined, but that the decision about each issue rests with the teachers. This is how it needs to be—teachers apply their professional judgment and balance student suggestions with policy regulations.

Age Appropriateness

The amount and nature of an assessment discussion with students will obviously vary with their age. It is, however, important that students are involved with assessment at an early age. This will help them to develop an assessment vocabulary and also their ability to self-assess. Students who have such opportunities in the primary grades will likely develop a sophisticated understanding of assessment in high school.

Students' ages will influence the way in which teachers share information with them. When most students in a class can read, it is not sufficient to simply tell students how they will be assessed; it is appropriate to provide assessment information in writing—to students and parents.

Amount of Detail

Students must be able to manage and understand the details about assessment of a whole course or an individual assessment. Information, especially about how teachers will determine grades, needs to be clear and concise. Ideally, teachers use methods that are not complicated to determine grades.

Throughout the Learning Process

Students should be involved in discussion about assessment throughout the learning process beginning during the first week of class. Teachers generally preview course content and learning goals in the first day or two of each term; at about the same time teachers should also inform students about assessment, especially about the nature of final or culminating assessment(s) because this gives students an understanding of essential questions embedded in the course. Timing is critical so that students see that assessment is integral, not just an add-on to learning. In addition to the "big picture" described earlier—how assessment will be used for the course as a whole, it is equally important that students are provided with this view throughout the learning process—what we could call the "small picture," i.e., how assessment of each unit will be done and what summative assessments will be used.

> **T**iming is critical so that students see that assessment is integral, not just an add–on, to learning.

Ideally, teachers discuss assessment with students and provide a written assessment plan, including grading for each course, but these assessment plans are not carved in stone. If teachers believe a change is needed, they are flexible and make the change. It would be ideal to discuss the proposed

change with students; at the very least, students must be informed of any change. This principle applies also to marking schemes or rubrics used to score assessments—if it becomes obvious during the scoring process that there is something wrong with the scoring approach, then the teacher changes the rubric. The teacher informs students about the why and what of the change, and the amended scoring approach is, of course, applied to the work of all students.

Test the Teaching, Don't Teach the Test

It almost goes without saying that when it comes to tests and exams, students must know what will be included. This knowledge covers the content of the test/exam as well as the types of questions and how the test/exam will be marked.

Interference or distortion from all sources must be controlled as much as possible in all assessment situations.

Tests and other assessments should not surprise students. They should be aware of (the learning goals) . . . and understand what they will be asked to do to provide evidence of their learning. This does not mean that teachers should "teach to the test" (at least in the traditional meaning of this phrase); it means that teachers must "test the teaching" in a way which is fair and reasonable for their students. (Schafer 1997, 545)

 # What's the Bottom Line?

Student involvement in developing assessment approaches and student understanding about how teachers will assess their academic achievement, including how teachers will determine grades, is critical to support learning and encourage student success. Assessment is not something that is done **to** students separate and apart from instruction; assessment must be—and must be seen to be—something that is done **with** students as an integral part of the learning process.

 # *What's My Thinking Now?*

GUIDELINE 8: Discuss and involve students in assessment, including grading, throughout the teaching/learning process.

Analyze guideline 8 for grading by focusing on three questions:

Why use it?

Why not use it?

Are there points of uncertainty?

After careful thought about these points, answer these two questions:

Would I use guideline 8 now?

Do I agree or disagree with the guideline, or am I unsure at this time?

See the following for one person's reflections on guideline 8.

A Reflection on Guideline 8

WHY USE IT?

- expectations are clear to all
- students learn better
- student and parent buy-in is greater
- no secrets or mystery to grading
- stops any game playing, favoritism

WHY NOT USE IT?

- student understanding of assessment is too limited
- puts teacher in a straitjacket—too restrictive
- sets up false idea that life is fair
- does not allow sufficiently for individual differences in students
- teacher should be in control

POINTS OF UNCERTAINTY

- degree of student involvement
- variation with student age/grade level
- amount of time needed to do this effectively
- amount of teacher collaboration needed
- appeal mechanism

SkyLight Professional Development

Chapter 9

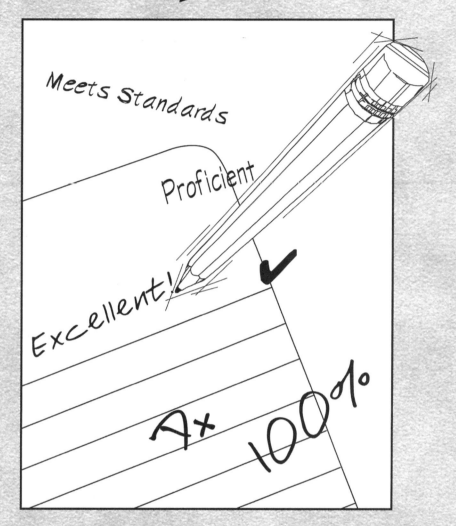

Putting It All Together

Data should inform, not determine, decisions.
—CONSULTANT, THE HAY GROUP, INTERNATIONAL MANAGEMENT CONSULTANTS

> *In order to have grades that have real, not just symbolic, meaning, and enable us to focus on learning, not grades, grading must be seen not just as a numerical, mechanical exercise, but as an exercise in professional judgment.*

The quote that opens this chapter was what led me to add this chapter to the book. It was said by a consultant for the Hay Group, a large international management consultancy, who was sitting next to me on a flight from Philadelphia to Toronto in late January, 2001. He was describing the most difficult aspect of his job, namely convincing his clients of the truth of this statement. We talked about this for a while, and then it struck me that this is exactly the message I have been trying to get across about grades. In order to have grades that have real, not just symbolic, meaning, and in order to enable us to focus on learning, not grades, grading must be seen not just as a numerical, mechanical exercise, but as an exercise in professional judgment. In other words, we must use the evidence we collect—numbers or words, separate or combined—to determine grades in such a way that any measures of central tendency (mean, median, or mode) are just part of the evidence, not the determinant of the grade.

There are five basic approaches to determining grades (see Figure 9.1). The first approach is traditional grading: there is no basis for grades other than a letter/percentage relationship, the weighting is based on assessment methods, and the only calculation considered is the mean. The other approaches utilize the organizing structure of standards as the basis for grades. The second approach represents the minimum movement into standards-based grading and uses the mean as the method of calculating the central tendency. The third approach suggests an alternative numerical calculation—the median. (Note that the mode is another possibility.) The fourth approach acknowledges that evidence is now being collected in various formats (x/10, %, checklists, level scores), but these multiple measures are converted to percentages and calculations are used as in either approach 2 or 3. Approach 5 centers on guideline 5 and focuses on the most consistent and more recent achievement and emphasizes professional judgment—based on a body of evidence and the performance standards. In order to put this approach into operation, educators must

Approaches to Determining Grades

Basis for Grades	Weighting Base	Grade Determination
Approach 1. Numerical grading scale (e.g., A=80–100%)	Assessment methods (e.g., tests–50%, projects–50%)	Mean/Average
Approach 2. Description of grades (i.e., in words)	Learning goals organized in categories (e.g., strands, standards, benchmarks)	Mean/Average
Approach 3. Description of grades	Learning goals organized in categories	Median/Mode
Approach 4. Description of grades	Learning goals organized in categories	Multiple measures converted to %, then mean, median, or mode
Approach 5. Description of grades	Learning goals organized in categories	Multiple measures · no conversion/calculation · most consistent with consideration for more recent · professional judgment supported by body of evidence

Approach 1.	Traditional
Approaches 2–5.	Moving from traditional to holistic—based on learning goals (whatever they are called: "standards," "outcomes," "expectations," etc.) in categories.

Figure 9.1

acknowledge that they really cannot distinguish 101 levels of achievement and that it is more realistic to use somewhere between five and sixteen levels (see Figure 9.2). Whatever the number of levels that teachers utilize, each level must be linked to clear descriptions of the performance standards represented by that level.

The grade book page in Figure 9.3 (for two students with essentially the same achievement) illustrates how teachers can implement the philosophy and guidelines described in this book. It is important to note that for the grading period there are only nine summative assessments included (guideline 4), and that the organizing structure for the page is strands from the standards

Grading Levels

Letter Grade	Level	5-Level Scale %	10-Level Scale %	16-Level Scale %
A	4	90–100	100 97 93	100 98 95 92
B	3	80–89	87 83	88 85 82
C	2	70–79	77 73	78 75 72
D	1	60–69	67 63	68 65 62
F	0	<60	<60	55 50 45

Figure 9.2

(guideline 2). In this example I have chosen to use the proposed Pennsylvania geography standards, largely because there are only four strands! This approach will work, however, for up to about ten categories. For each of the nine assessments, teachers record scores in the strands in which the standard or benchmark is found or classified. For example, assessment A included only standards from basic literacy and physical characteristics, while assessment I included standards from all four strands. Each of the strands has been weighted equally so that 25% of the grade comes from each strand, but this may vary with the subject and grade level. Having recorded the data in this way, teachers can use the approaches listed in Figure 9.1 to determine grades.

Traditional grading (approach 1) is not represented in Figure 9.3 because the data is organized by strands. Teachers whose comfort zone would be with approaches 2 or 3 would record evidence as shown for Kathy and then calculate respectively the mean or the median for each strand. Hopefully, this is what would be reported because it is more valuable information than a composite grade. It shows that Kathy's strength is human characteristics and that her weak area is basic literacy. Note though that her recent achievement in

Determining Percentage Grades for First Grading Period

Assessments Included in Grade Determination

Unit 1	Unit 2	Unit 3
A Perf. task i	D Test	G Perf. task v
B Perf. task ii	E Perf. task iii	H Test
C Test	F Perf. task iv	I Perf. task vi

Strands		BL	PC	HC	I
Weighting		25%	25%	25%	25%
Kathy	A	65	75		
	B	55		75	78
	C	65	79	79	
	D	85	90	95	
	E	90		90	90
	F	85	100		85
	G	95		95	82
	H	82	90	100	
	I	88	95	95	88
Total		710	529	629	423
Mean		71	88	90	85
Median		85	90	95	85

PENNSYLVANIA GEOGRAPHY STANDARDS
BL   Basic Literacy
PC   Physical Characteristics
HC   Human Characteristics
I   Interactions

REPORT CARD GRADE

85

84
88

Nancy	A	6/10	7/10		
	B	5/10		7/10	7/10
	C	65%	79%	79%	
	D	3	4	4	
	E	90%		90%	90%
	F	3	4		3
	G	4		4	3
	H	82%	90%	100%	
	I	3	4	4	3
Summary					

GRADING SCALE
A   90–100%   4
B   80–89%   3
C   70–79%   2
D   60–69%   1
F   <60%   0

REPORT CARD GRADE

Figure 9.3

this strand is much better than it was at the beginning of the grading period. It is recognized, however, that in many, probably most, jurisdictions teachers will be required to determine an overall grade.

REFLECTING ON . . . NANCY'S GRADE

▶ What overall level would you decide for Nancy?

▶ If you were using the 16-level scale (see Figure 9.2), what grade would Nancy receive for each strand and as an overall grade?

The evidence of Nancy's achievement has been recorded in a variety of formats using multiple measures so that teachers using this type of data would need to use approaches 4 or 5. Approach 4 involves converting level scores to percentages, either always at mid range (e.g., 85%) or as low, middle, and high scores for each level (e.g., 82, 85, 88). Grades would then be calculated using the mean or median. Approach 5 acknowledges that such conversion is really inappropriate (see chapter 6) and requires the teacher do no mathematical conversion or calculation. In this approach, teachers must have a clear sense of the levels, hopefully because the district or state/province has clear descriptors of the levels as their performance standards. They then use their professional judgment to decide what level is appropriate for each student. This decision should be based on looking for the most consistent level of achievement with special consideration for more recent achievement evidence. This is relatively easy if only one of five letter grades is required. If percentage grades are required, teachers must decide first the level of achievement for each student, and then whether the student's achievement is high or low (ten-level scale) within that level (see Figure 9.2).

It is important to note that in both the ten- and sixteen-level scales 100% is possible. Also remember that it is preferable to provide grades for each strand than to provide an overall grade.

I realize that approach 5 will make some teachers very nervous, but I would urge them to recognize that *there are no right grades, only justifiable grades!* Thus, when we have a body of evidence and clearly stated performance standards, it is appropriate that teachers use the professional judgment that they have been trained and paid to use to determine grades.

If you are still nervous, think about a comparison with doctors. Let's imagine that you have a health problem and that over a period of time you consult with your doctor. The doctor will almost certainly order some tests and will have "scores" for blood pressure, temperature, cholesterol levels, etc. (which by the way they never average!) and a number of observations recorded in words. At some point the doctor will look at this body of evidence and recommend a course of action to you. Especially if that action is fairly drastic—major surgery or medication with serious side effects—you will question your doctor about the reasons for the recommended action. The doctor will defend the recommendation, linking the body of evidence to his or her medical knowledge. Hopefully he or she will do this without being defensive, and you and the doctor will reach agreement on what is to happen. I believe that this is basically the situation teachers are in or should be in with regard to determining grades. We put the body of evidence together with our professional knowledge and the performance standards to determine a grade. We are then prepared to defend our decision if necessary. As with the doctor, we should do this without being defensive. Herein lies one of the basic problems: teachers have tended to be very defensive about their assessment and evaluation decisions. It is time that we get past this defensiveness. As competent, confident professional assessors, we must be prepared to defend our judgment. This will be relatively easy if we have collected quality evidence, if we have a clear sense of the performance standards, and if we are consistently applying a set of principles and procedures such as the guidelines presented in this book.

Grade Books and Checklists

Figure 9.3 (and Figures 1.2, 1.3, and 1.4 on pages 53, 54, and 56, respectively), are examples of an individual approach to tracking achievement evidence that may not be practical for middle and high school teachers. Figure 9.4 is a grade book page that can be used for a whole class; Figure 9.4 provides an example using the same strands as Figure 9.3 but different data; Figure 9.4b is a blank grade book page that may be used as a blackline master. Checklists are useful to track progress toward "putting it all together." Figures 9.5 and 9.6 should help. Figure 9.5 focuses on grading practices and suggests guidelines as action steps. Figure 9.6 would be more useful for a school or district committee that is preparing changes in grading policy and procedures.

Grade Book for Use with the Pennsylvania Geography Standards

Students	Basic Literacy												Physical Characteristics						Human Characteristics						Interaction				Summary
	1	3	4	6	7	9	10	11	12	13	14	15	2	3	4	5	8	9	1	2	4	6	7	8	2	5	8	9	
Alan	1	1	2	3	3	3	6/10	7/10	13/20	13/20	14/20	14/20	2	1	3	3	3	3	2	3	1	2	3	3	2	5	8	9	BPH/ LCC
Bronwyn	3	4	3	4	4	4	9/10	10/10	19/20	20/20	20/20	20/20	4	3	4	4	4	4	4	4	4	4	4	4	2	3	3	4	
Chris	1	2	1	2	1	1	5/10	4/10	11/20	10/20	10/20	10/20	1	2	1	2	1	1	1	1		1	2	1	1	2	1	1	
Donna	1	2	1	2	2	2	6/10	6/10	12/20	14/20	14/20	14/20	1	2	1	2	2	2	1	1	1	2	2	2	1	2	2	2	

Assessment #1   20/9   PA
Assessment #2   26/9   PA
Assessment #3   4/10   T

Assessment #4   6/10   PC
Assessment #5   11/10   PA
Assessment #6   15/10   T

Assessment #7   19/10   PC
Assessment #8   28/10   PA
Assessment #9   3/11   T

PC – Personal Communication
T – Test
PA – Performance Assessment

Figure 9.4

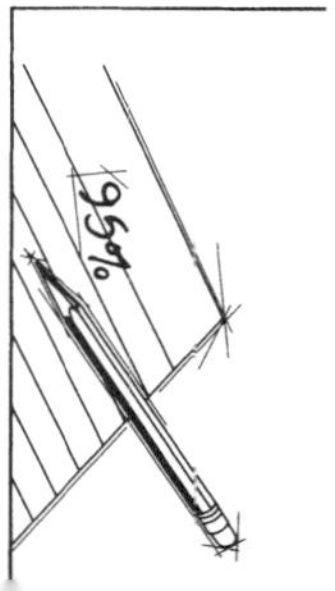

Grade Book Page

Students																										Summary

Assessment #1 —/—
Assessment #2 —/—
Assessment #3 —/—

Assessment #4 —/—
Assessment #5 —/—
Assessment #6 —/—

Assessment #7 —/—
Assessment #8 —/—
Assessment #9 —/—

PC – Personal Communication
T – Test
PA – Performance Assessment

Figure 9.4b

Determining Report Card Grades Checklist

❏ Assessment covers all strands or categories of knowledge and skills in the standards.

❏ A variety of methods are used to reliably and fairly assess student achievement.

❏ Assessments which "count" are summative and represent learning at the "end" of units or periods of time after students have had a chance to practice and take risks . . . with learning and strategies.

❏ Students know which assessments "count" in determining their report card grade.

❏ Assessments are scored in a variety of ways appropriate to the method used.

❏ Grades are based on *individual* achievement of learning goals separated from behaviors/learning skills.

❏ Assessment strategies and report card grades are determined by classroom teachers working collaboratively.

❏ Grades are based on learning goals, NOT assessment methods.

❏ The student's more recent, most consistent level of performance guides the teacher's judgement in determining the grade.

❏ Simple arithmetic averages that give equal weighting to a student's earlier performances are not used.

❏ In addition to summary information on student achievement, "portfolios" of students' work are available as evidence of achievement.

❏ Clear descriptors of performance standards guide judgement in determining the grade.

Figure 9.5

SkyLight Professional Development

Grading Issues Checklist

Purpose(s)
- ❏ clearly established
- ❏ clearly stated

Grading Method
- ❏ Standards-based with criterion-referenced descriptors (# levels?)
- ❏ Letter grades—5 levels (descriptors?)
- ❏ Plus/Minus letter grades—13+ levels (descriptors?)
- ❏ Percentage grades—101 levels (descriptors?)
- ❏ Pass/Fail—2 levels (descriptors?)
- ❏ Mastery—2 levels (descriptors?)

Subject grades
- ❏ one per subject
- ❏ several per subject by strand or benchmark

Grade Determination
- ❏ achievement only
- ❏ individual achievement
- ❏ achievement for grading period
- ❏ from summative assessment only
- ❏ consistent level of achievement
- ❏ consideration for more recent
- ❏ student involvement and understanding
- ❏ use of penalties, deductions, zeros, extra credit
- ❏ number crunching informs, does not determine decision
- ❏ evidence from quality assessment
- ❏ clearly linked to grading scale descriptors
- ❏ age appropriate

Quality Assessment
- ❏ Clear criteria
- ❏ Shared understanding of criteria
- ❏ Clear purpose(s)—diagnostic, formative, summative
- ❏ Appropriate target/method match
- ❏ Appropriate sampling
- ❏ Eliminate bias and distortion

Tracking Achievement
- ❏ Appropriate forms
- ❏ Use of technology

Figure 9.6

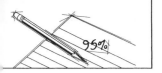

Conclusion

I hope that ultimately all teachers will use approach 5, but this would clearly be a giant step for many teachers. For many, it would be too big a step to take at this time, so I hope that teachers will see this set of approaches as a series of steps through which (individually and collectively) they can move as they implement standards-based curricula. If they do this, they will be bringing principle and practice together in ways that honor the professionalism of teachers and make their grades fair and honest summaries of student achievement.

Chapter 10

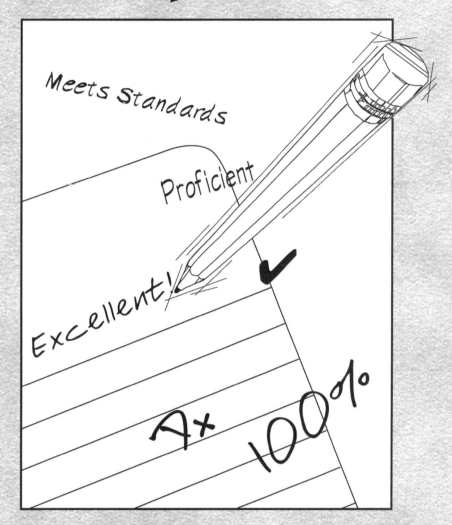

More Grading Issues

Teachers can't rewrite the regulations that govern (grading) but (they) can look at them and think how best to work within them on behalf of student learning.

—Davies (2000, 73)

There are many grading issues that have not been dealt with or are only touched upon in the detailed consideration of the grading guidelines. This chapter examines six issues: grading systems, grading exceptional students, computer grading programs, calculating grade point averages (GPAs), legal issues, and grading policies. Discussion focuses on raising the issues, providing some direction, and identifying references that have more detailed analyses.

Grading Systems

There are a large number of grading systems in use in schools in North America. Some school districts use checklists or rating scales, especially when grading younger students. Some districts and colleges use pass/fail systems. The most common system is the use of letter grades, usually on a five-point scale (A, B, C, D, F). Closely related are grading systems with numerical scores, usually percentages. There is a great debate about which of these systems is better—that is, the system that has clear meaning and encourages learning.

Checklists or Rating Scales

Many critics of grading favor the use of checklists or rating scales because they provide real, rather than symbolic, information. An advantage is that they focus on individual achievement rather than on comparison between students.

Pass/Fail Systems

Some educators prefer the use of pass/fail or credit/no credit systems. They believe that all that is necessary or desirable is to identify whether students have reached the minimum level of achievement necessary to obtain credit and/or to move to the next level.

The very difficult issue that must be resolved with both checklist and pass/fail systems is what constitutes the necessary minimum level of achievement. One would hope and expect that it would be rather different, for example, for a surgeon or a pilot than for a grade 9 visual arts student.

Letter Grades

Symbol systems using letters or numbers are the most commonly used grading systems. Letter grades may have three to five points on the scale. Three-point scales (e.g., Excellent, Satisfactory, Needs Improvement) are used most commonly for grades 1, 2, and 3.

Four-point scales are usually designed without a failing grade. Variations include (1) A, B, C, and Pass and (2) HP (High Pass), P (Pass), LP (Low Pass), and I (Incomplete). Those in favor of four-point scales suggest that they improve student attitudes toward learning by producing less competition and less cheating, while developing more creativity and increased student self-esteem. Critics of four-point scales contend that they are unrealistic and that they are really five-point scales without the fifth point added.

Five-point scales—A, B, C, D, F— are the most commonly used scales in the United States. Most school districts establish numerical equivalents for letter grades (most commonly, A = 90% to 100%, B = 80% to 89%, C = 70% to 79%, D = 60% to 69%, and F = less than 60%, but see also introduction, case study 6 on pages 33 and 34). Some, have detailed descriptors for the characteristics of each letter grade—for an example, see the policy of the Cupertino, California, Elementary School District as cited in Robinson and Craver (1989, 113). As was indicated in the introduction, opinions differ considerably about the value of this type of grading system.

> *Many critics of grading favor the use of checklists or rating scales because they provide real rather than symbolic information.*

Numerical Scores

A similar debate occurs around the use of numerical scores. Many school districts, especially those in Canada, report grades as percentages, (e.g., 73%).

Precision: Real or Imagined?

Impreciseness is the main point of those who argue for letter grades rather than percentage grades; they believe that dividing student achievement into a limited number of categories is all that we can ever hope to do with any pretense of real meaning. According to this argument, using a 101-point scale gives a false sense of precision and, therefore, detracts from the main purpose of grades—meaningful communication of student achievement.

This argument has a great deal of merit, especially for elementary and middle schools, where grades are not involved in high stakes decisions, except pass/fail. However, where grades are involved in high stakes decisions—that is, where they influence decisions about students' educational future—such as college entrance, graduate school acceptance, and employment opportunities, numbers may be preferable to letters because there are more scale points available.

Figure 10.1 dramatically illustrates this problem. With letter grades, arbitrary cutoffs must be set; so, whether one is calculating a grade for a subject (right side) or for an overall grade average (left side), students who score just below the cutoff point are seriously disadvantaged relative to those whose scores are right on the cutoff point. In Figure 10.1, Jacqueline scored only 1% higher on each summative assessment and in each subject than Jack, but her English grade and her grade average were As, whereas Jack received Bs. This is obviously an extreme example, but it illustrates very clearly that the use of letter grades with percentage equivalents gives an advantage to some students while disadvantaging others. Many critics contend this is not acceptable when students' futures are at stake. Maybe a compromise is necessary with fewer points than the legal fictions of the percentage scale and more points than the traditional five-point scale.

The use of letter grades with percentage equivalents gives an advantage to some students while disadvantaging others.

If all the guidelines and principles described in chapters 1–8 are applied, then letter grades based on teachers' professional judgments using a detailed descriptive scale (see Figure 2.5 on page 75 and Robinson and Craver 1989, 113) will produce the best grades. But if teachers crunch numbers to arrive at grades, especially in high school and college, then percentage grades are probably fairer, and therefore better, than letter grades.

Letter Versus Percentage Grades

Subject	Jack		Jacqueline		English
	%	Letter	%	Letter	
English	89	B	90	A	Summative Assessment #1
Mathematics	89	B	90	A	Summative Assessment #2
Social Studies	89	B	90	A	Summative Assessment #3
Science	89	B	90	A	Summative Assessment #4
Computer Studies	89	B	90	A	Summative Assessment #5
Music	89	B	90	A	Summative Assessment #6
Total	534		540		
Mean	89	B	90	A	

Figure 10.1

Grading Exceptional Students

This is one of the most difficult grading issues for teachers, especially in school districts that have explicit or implicit norm-referenced approaches to grading. It is preferable *not* to grade specially challenged students using letter or numerical grades. Checklists or rating scales that focus on improvement or learning gain are more appropriate. However, if district policy or parental expectations require traditional grades, teachers should remember that each of the grading guidelines is relevant to this issue and should pay primary attention to guidelines 1 and 2 for exceptional students.

Applying Guideline 1

Grading should always be related to learning goals. If these have been modified to meet the needs/abilities of exceptional students, then grading should be based on the modified goals, not those that apply to regular students. Reporting of grades based on modified learning goals should clearly indicate that such modification has been made and ideally should indicate what the modifications are.

Applying Guideline 2

Grading should always be based on criterion-referenced standards, not norms. In a gifted class, if all student results meet the predetermined standard, then all should receive As. If some students' performances are also well above that standard, this becomes a reporting variable, but it is not a grading variable. The bottom line here is that being the weakest student in a high-achieving group should not disadvantage a student, nor should any student be advantaged by being the strongest student in a low-achieving group.

It is preferable not to grade specially challenged students using letter or numerical grades.

For identified special education students, whether they are mainstreamed or not, the grades they receive should be based on the extent to which they meet the modified predetermined standards. If they meet these standards, then they should get As, and, as noted, reporting should clearly indicate that the standards have been changed from those that apply to nonidentified students.

The grades obtained by identified exceptional students that are based on modified learning goals/standards should never be used to compare exceptional students with other students. However, there is some evidence (Selby and Murphy 1992, 97) that identified exceptional students do not value modified grades. Therefore, teachers might consider reporting two grades for these students—the grade on the adapted goals and the grade that (probably) would have been reported if the grades/standards had not been adapted.

Applying Other Guidelines

Teachers grading exceptional students may also consider other criteria:
- individual achievement (guideline 3)
- summative assessments (guideline 4)
- the more recent information (guideline 5)
- the teacher's professional judgment, not just number crunching (guideline 6).

If teachers follow all of these practices, exceptional students will receive grades that are meaningful and that support their learning. The key is that grades are based on public learning goals/standards and reflect real achievement, not some vague perception of their effort and their achievement relative to their ability.

Legal Considerations for Exceptional Students

The practices just described constitute what I believe is the educative approach to grading and reporting for exceptional students. This is reflected in the check boxes for IEP, ESL, and ESD in the Ontario Provincial Report Cards (Figures 11.3 and 11.4 in chapter 11), but because this is considered discrimination in the United States no such identification can be used. This interpretation is based on Letter to Runkel, 26 IDELR 387 written by David Dunbar (1996), Chief Regional Attorney for the Office for Civil Rights Education, September 30, 1996, to Robert Runkel, State Director of Special Education for the State of Montana. The Office for Civil Rights "is the enforcement branch of the Department of Education assigned to investigate violations of civil rights statutes, including 504 of the Rehabilitation Act of 1973 . . . Title VI of the Civil Rights Act of 1964, and Title IX of Education Amendments of 1972" (Richards and Martin 1999, 1).

Runkel had written to the OCR to find out what criteria apply to a variety of aspects of grading for students with disabilities. The letter covers a wide range of issues including class rank, honor roll, graduation, and the issuance of diplomas. From a grading and reporting point of view, the key considerations seem to be that the only identification of exceptionality can be something like an asterisk which indicates modified curriculum but there can be no "notations on permanent transcripts (that) designate instructional delivery modification," (Richards and Martin 1999, 13) whether they be special education or ESL.

This legal requirement obviously creates a dilemma for educators since educators want communication to be fair and to honestly indicate the level at which each student is being assessed. The law, and its interpretation, must be followed; therefore, teachers must exercise great care. There is apparently little case law to help, but there are many legal opinions on the subject on the Internet.

Computer Grading Programs

Stiggins (1997) said, "It troubles me deeply that so many 1990s teachers still maintain grade records the way teachers did at the turn of the century" (442).

Why Use a Grading Program?

If teachers follow the guidelines discussed in this book, record keeping is a complex endeavor because:

1. Grades need to be related to learning goals (guideline 1).
2. Grades need to be related to clear descriptors of performance standards (guideline 2).
3. Teachers need to separate achievement data from other information, such as effort and participation (guideline 3).
4. Teachers need to separate formative assessments from summative assessments (guideline 4).
5. More recent information takes the place of older information, and teachers need to record second—or more—chance assessment scores (guideline 5).
6. Numerical calculations involve more than the mean, and educators need to apply weighting factors consistently (guideline 6).

Unless teachers rely completely on the more recent information and their professional judgment, this complexity means that most teachers will do at least some number crunching. Whether number crunching is done manually or by using a calculator, it takes a great deal of time.

This wasted time may be reduced by using one of a variety of available grading software packages to more efficiently enter, calculate, store, retrieve, and summarize grading data. If teachers are very competent computer users, they may develop their own systems using spreadsheet programs. Figure 10.2 lists some software that was available in 2001. Inclusion on this list is not intended as endorsement of any product, but is simply information for teachers who may wish to investigate one or more of these products.

For a comprehensive listing of grading software with tips for making choices, visit <http://education-world.com/a_tech/tech031/shtml>.

A Sampling of Computer Grading Programs

GradeQuick	Jackson Software	www.jacksonsoftware.com
Grade Machine	Misty City Software	www.mistycity.com
MarkBook 01	Asylum Software	www.markbook.com

Note: This list is not intended as an endorsement.

Figure 10.2

Potential Problems

There is one major potential problem with computer grading programs that teachers need to be aware of—grading programs vary considerably in what they can and cannot do. Before deciding on a particular program, the teacher must check that the program has the flexibility to determine grades the way he wants. The teacher must be able to control the program; the program should not control how the grades are determined. In order to follow guidelines 3, 4, and 5, the grading program must allow a nil value or no mark for data the teacher wants on file but does not want included in the grade (e.g., formative assessment scores such as quizzes and first drafts).

The teacher must be able to control the program; the program should not control how the grades are determined.

Another problem that teachers must be aware of is "garbage in, garbage out"—or put less colorfully, if incorrect information is entered into the computer, incorrect grades will be calculated. Teachers must check for errors in the same manner that they check manually calculated grades.

As long as these potential shortcomings are avoided, teachers are encouraged to use computer grading programs to save time and as a support to their professional judgment. They are excellent tools for manipulating data, and the varied reports that can be printed provide valuable information to students and teachers. An example of the variety of such information from the MarkBook program is shown in Figure 10.3.

HOW TO GRADE FOR LEARNING

Example of a Report from MarkBook

V. Smart
416-555-0575 X123

SNC2D0D - 00/01 STUDENT REPORT Science 10	O'Watt, Meg (146481 - 2N1 - 15y 6.6m)	4-
	Type: [ALL] Avg. Age: 15y 9.8m Absent: 4	Wt. Mode 2001 01 30
	Category: [ALL]	Late: 0 Page: 1 of 1

CATEGORY ANALYSIS	Number of Entries	% of SNC	Student Mark %
Appl'ns	13	25.0	70
Commun	11	25.0	77
KnowUnd	14	25.0	69
ThinkInq	10	25.0	56

INCOMPLETE ENTRIES These entries have Zero!	Date	Type	Category	% of SNC
20. 3.2 Biogeography Note	09 28	1	KnowUnd	1.6
29. Self-Evaluation for Sep.	10 08	1	Appl'ns	1.6
37. Lab Single & Dble. Displ.	11 06	2	ThinkInq	2.0
40. Household Products Lab	11 26	2	ThinkInq	2.0
45. Reaction Time Lab	11 21	3	Appl'ns	1.6

TRENDS

This graph shows student performance for all entries.

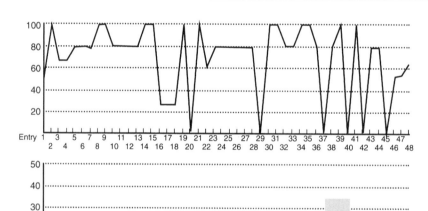

LEVELS ANALYSIS (WEIGHTED)

Achievement at each level is indicated in this graph. The tallest bar is the Mode.

The vertical scale is Percent.

Bracketed number is that level's lower limit (%).

Please sign and return the form below. Thank you.

....

Ding Dong High - SNC2D0D - 00/01 - Science 10 - V. Smart - 2001 01 30

O'Watt, Meg: 4-

With 5 incomplete (Zero!) entries.

(Signature of Parent or Guardian)

Figure 10.3

Beyond Grading Calculations

Also, teachers should be aware that software is available for a number of other assessment functions. These include collecting classroom observation records (e.g., Learner Profile), creating portfolios of student work (e.g., Grady Profile), and developing classroom assessments, primarily in mathematics (e.g., Objective Tracker). Again, the programs listed are not being endorsed but are offered as examples.

Calculating Grade Point Averages

Grade Point Averages (GPAs) are traditionally used by many schools to determine standing on the honor roll and class rank and, in some places, eligibility for cocurricular activities. Also, many colleges use GPAs as all or part of acceptance decisions. Thus, they are very important for students and parents. How they are calculated is a matter of concern for school board members, administrators, and teachers.

Mathematical Calculation Systems

The Four-Point Scale

Traditionally, grade point averages have been calculated over the four years of high school on the following basis: A = 4 points; B = 3; C = 2; D = 1; and F = 0.

Weighted Scales

Some school districts use other approaches to calculating GPAs. Gilman and Swan (1989) identified seven different systems, all of which included sliding scales for A, A–, B+, B, B-, and so on. They say that "the most common system . . . is to assign different weights to some courses" (92–93). Weighting is applied to more difficult courses such as calculus and honors and advanced placement classes, so that for these courses a higher value is assigned to grades, for example, A = 5.2; A– = 4.77; B+ = 4.33; B = 3.9, and so on.

Problems With GPA Systems

Weighting is done to overcome one of the most serious criticisms of GPAs, which is that unweighted systems encourage students to take easy courses to inflate their GPAs. Weighted GPAs are intended to encourage students to take the more difficult courses without penalizing them when they receive lower grades. In the earlier example, a student would get more points for a B+ on a weighted course than for an A on an unweighted course.

One of the major problems with weighted systems is that they cause problems between teachers who are teaching courses that are weighted and those who are teaching unweighted courses. Partly for this reason and partly because of community attachment to existing systems, it is often very difficult to change how GPAs are calculated. As an example, Ashenfelter described a two-year struggle in High School District 214, Illinois, in his wonderfully titled article "Our Schools Grappled with Grade Point Politics and Lost," which can be found in the January 1990 edition of *The Executive Educator*.

The Effect of Using GPAs

Even more basic than concern for the mathematical system used to calculate GPAs is the need for schools, school communities, and colleges to examine the whole GPA process and its effects. The first question educators need to consider is what is the effect of the use of GPAs? Clearly, the main effect is to turn the whole high school experience into a four-year competition that emphasizes points rather than learning. This is obviously inconsistent with the philosophy expressed in this book—and the mission statements and goals of many school districts. Because very few colleges disadvantage students in admission decisions if they do not have class rank or GPA information, the necessity for this mathematical, noneducational process needs to be seriously debated.

What is the effect of the use of GPAs? The main effect is to turn the whole high school experience into a four-year competition that emphasizes points rather than learning.

If, however, after debating the issue of whether to calculate GPAs, a school district decides in favor of GPAs, then a second question arises—over how many years should a GPA be calculated? Students change quite dramatically over their high school years; very frequently, underachieving freshmen become high-achieving seniors. Why should their first-year performance be held against them at the end of high school? Guideline 5 states that for grading decisions, we should use the more recent information. The same principle applies to GPA calculation—if GPAs are

used, calculate them only on an annual basis and never cumulatively. For college admission, the only GPA that should count is that of the senior year. Furthermore, schools should refuse to provide class rank data to anyone outside the school because it has no validity outside of the individual school.

Other Legal Issues

The principle that the US courts applied is that lowering grades as a disciplinary matter is illegal because it causes academic achievement to be misrepresented.

Teachers, especially in the United States, need to be aware that grading is, or can become, a legal minefield. Obviously, if this is a major personal concern, a lawyer should be consulted, but here are a few general comments on two aspects of grading that have attracted legal attention—lowering grades for nonacademic misconduct and due process, or the lack of it. Some of the legal issues involved in special education were discussed earlier in this chapter.

Lowering Grades for Nonacademic Misconduct

Hobbs (1992) reported on several cases in which school officials were ordered to reinstate students' grades, which had been lowered because of students' absences, some of which were due to suspension. In these cases, the principle that the courts applied is that lowering grades as a disciplinary matter is illegal because it causes academic achievement to be misrepresented.

Due Process

Hobbs (1992) noted, however, that "the courts do not always decide for the plaintiff in challenges to academic practices or policies that deal with student grades" (205). The key issue appears to be due process—if school officials have notified students of their rights and responsibilities, and if there is an appeal process within the school or school district, then the courts are much more likely to rule in favor of the school. If, on the other hand, actions taken by teachers or schools are seen as being arbitrary, capricious, or in bad faith, then the courts are willing to intervene and rule in favor of students who have been denied due process.

It appears that the legality of grades is established when academic and nonacademic factors are kept separate and when students are accorded due process. All the grading guidelines have a part to play in ensuring that grades can stand up to scrutiny by the courts. In particular, following guidelines 3 and 8 should help teachers protect themselves against legal challenges to their grading practices.

Grading Policy

District or school policies need to be in place so that teachers know what procedures to follow in their classrooms. Also, as indicated in the previous section, the existence of clearly stated grading policies helps protect educators from legal challenges to their grading practices.

The problem with most school and/or district policies is that they usually do little more than establish what grades are—for example, A is 93% to 100%, B is 88% to 92%, and so on—but give very little guidance to teachers on what is to be included in grades and how they are to be determined. This produces a lack of consistency between and within schools. When policies provide detail, it is usually a litany of rules for lowering grades in extremely punitive ways.

What is needed are grading policies and procedures that provide the basis for a reasonable level of consistency between and within schools and that provide specific guidance for teachers at the classroom/grade book level. Any such policies also support learning and encourage student success. These are the purposes for which the guidelines described in this book have been developed. The guidelines can be translated into policy language. A sample grading policy based on the guidelines is provided in appendix 3.

Chapter 11

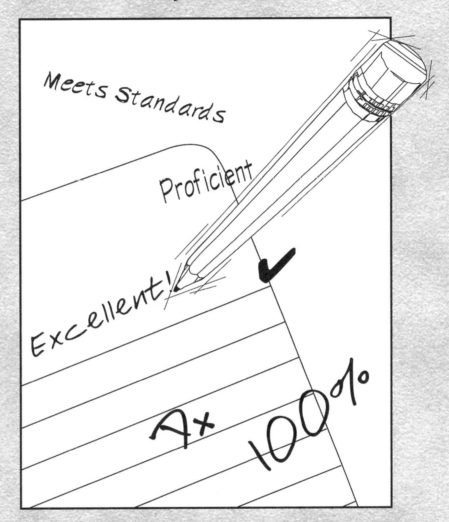

Communicating Student Achievement to Others

Teachers must make thoughtful changes to their systems for reporting student learning and progress to parents and others. Just as assessment practices need to be authentic, so do reporting practices.

—BAILEY AND GUSKEY (2001, 100)

T he primary purpose of grades is to communicate meaningful information to students, parents, teachers, potential employers, colleges, and other individuals and institutions concerning the achievement status of students. Although grades will be meaningful and will support learning if they are developed following the guidelines described in this book, much more is needed to communicate effectively with all those who need quality information about student achievement. Whether they are letters or numbers, grades are merely symbols; in order to provide real information, they should be seen as only a part—probably a very small part— of our communication system.

> **G**rades are merely symbols; in order to provide real information, they should be seen as only a part— probably a very small part—of our communication system.

All of the methods listed in Figure 11.1 have a place in effective communication systems. The most effective communication, however, takes place when several methods are used. The specific strategies listed are taken from a list of seventeen tools for comprehensive reporting systems provided by Guskey and Bailey (2001, 176). The key to an effective communication system is being clear about the purpose of the system and each of its parts.

Report Cards

Traditionally, report cards, especially for secondary schools, have been little more than a list of grades and brief comments about student progress and behavior. Because comments were severely limited in length, they were frequently of little value. Comments such as "a pleasure to teach" or "try for honors next term" do little to provide understanding of student achievement or directions for the future.

The Communication System

Grades	Report Cards (limited information, usually grades and brief comments)	Informal Communications (infrequent, usually criticism/warning)	Parent/ Teacher Interviews (no student present)	Report Cards (expanded format)	Informal Communication (frequent and ongoing, usually positive)	Student-Involved Conferencing	Student-Led Conferencing
	Standardized Assessment Reports, Weekly/ Monthly Progress Reports	Phone Calls, Notes, Letters	School Open Houses	School Web Pages	Phone Calls, Notes, Letters, Projects, Assignments, Homework, and Homework Hotlines	Portfolios Exhibitions	Porfolios Exhibitions

Figure 11.1

Expanded Format Reporting

For report cards to provide effective communication, they need to have an expanded format in which teachers can give information on student achievement of specific learning goals and of general learning skills or work habits. In addition, other reporting opportunities are provided by expanded format reports, including

- sharing student achievement on cross-curricular or exit learning goals
- reflecting by students on their own strengths, weaknesses, and goals
- acknowledging actions that need to be taken by partners in learning—students, parents, and teachers
- giving teachers the opportunity to write an anecdotal summary comment on each student
- meeting legal requirements, such as attendance, tardies, promotion status, and signatures

What is provided must not overwhelm parents. What is expected must not overwhelm teachers.

Expanded format report cards provide a great deal of information, but what is provided must not overwhelm parents. Two sides of 8 1/2" x 14" paper is a sufficient size; parents do not need, want, or benefit from a small book! Equally important is that what is expected must not overwhelm teachers; the reporting workload must not require so much time that teachers are virtually unable to teach in the week(s) just before report card time. Also, the number of formal reports per year must be reasonable; two or three expanded format report cards are sufficient as long as other means of communication, described later, are also used.

Several examples illustrate the features of expanded format report cards. While none of these report cards is perfect, they all have some key strengths as well as some weaknesses. It is hoped that as schools and districts move to expanded format reporting, these samples will be helpful.

Figure 11.2-1 is a sample of an expanded format report card from a school district in Wisconsin that was piloted by several teachers at each grade

Expanded Format Report Card

Student _____

> **Achievement Key:** This symbol indicates how the student is performing in relationship to a standard.
> Bg—Beginning: Is at the initial stage of understanding concept/skill
> Dv—Developing: Uses and understands concept/skill with support
> Sc—Secure: Independently uses and understands concept/skill
> Ex—Exceeds grade level expectations
> X—Not assessed at this time

LANGUAGE ARTS

Reading	Q1	Q2	Q3	Q4
Level*				
Comprehension strategies				
Vocabulary development				
Decoding strategies				
Oral reading				

Writing	Q1	Q2	Q3	Q4
Process (pre-writing,, first draft, editing, revising, publishing)				
Style				
Mechanics				
Grammar				
Spelling/application				
Penmanship				

Research/Inquiry	Q1	Q2	Q3	Q4
References				
Organization				

Oral Communication	Q1	Q2	Q3	Q4
Listening				
Speaking				

*Generally students in the following grades fall within these reading levels:
R—Kindergarten = Readiness
PP—Beginning 1st Grade = Pre Primer 1, 2, 3
P—Middle 1st Grade = Primer
1—End of 1st Grade = 1st Reader
2.1 or 2.2 = 2nd Grade
3.1 or 3.2 = 3rd grade
4 = 4th grade or 4+ = above 4th grade

Figure 11.2-1   From Shorewood School District, 2001, Shorewood, Used with permission

MATHEMATICS

	Q1	Q2	Q3	Q4
Number relationships				
Computation				
Measurement				
Geometry				
Algebra/Patterns				
Data Analysis				
Probability				
Problem-solving/Communicating				

Initiative, Social and Work Skills Key:
This symbol represents the student's effort to improve.
3—Consistent 2—Inconsistent
1—Minimal

Initiative/Effort	Q1	Q2	Q3	Q4
Independent Reading				
Language Arts				
Mathematics				
Science				
Social Studies				

SCIENCE

	Q1	Q2	Q3	Q4
Physical Sciences				
Earth and Space Sciences				
Life and Environmental Sciences				
Science Processes (Connections, nature of science, inquiry, applications, social and personal perspectives)				

• Grade includes science lab work

SOCIAL SKILLS

	Q1	Q2	Q3	Q4
Shows respect for: Adults				
Peers				
Property				
Follows rules				
Accepts responsibility for own actions				
Cooperates and compromises				
Develops successful peer relationships				
Uses self-discipline				
Resolves conflict peacefully				

SOCIAL STUDIES

	Q1	Q2	Q3	Q4
Geography				
History				
Political Science				
Economics				
Behavioral Sciences				

WORK/STUDY SKILLS

	Q1	Q2	Q3	Q4
Uses time wisely				
Asks for help when needed				
Works independently				
Stays on task				
Produces quality work				
Completes and returns homework assignments on time				
Organizes work and belongings				
Uses technology effectively				

Attendance	Q1	Q2	Q3	Q4
Days Absent				
Times Tardy				

✓ Indicates student progress is affected by absences or tardiness

---

Figure 11.2-1 continued   From Shorewood School District, 2001, Shorewood, WI. Used with permission.

level in the 2000-01 school year. A revised version was used for all students in 2001–02. To support this report, parents were provided with curriculum guides specific for each grade level. All the factors reported are taken directly from the state standards. Note that teachers do not use traditional letter grades; there is a four-point scale, but it is developmental, rating achievement as beginning, developing, secure, and exceeding grade level expectation. (Note: The highest-level title and descriptor was problematic and probably will be revised in the final version of the report card.) The right-hand column separates the initiative/effort, social, and work/study skills from achievement. It provides a very comprehensive picture of the nonachievement factors, which parents like to know about. There are twenty-two separate pieces of information here, which may be too many for some schools/districts.

Figure 11.2-2 is the report teachers use for art, music, and physical education for grades 1–6, using the same scale as the other subjects for grades 1–4. (Letter grades were still used for grades 5 and 6.) Figure 11.2-2 makes a very important statement about the importance of these subjects, which often get little space on report cards (and sadly decreasing amounts of time in school programs). The expanded format report card also has room for a specific individual comment on each of these subjects. It is emphasized that this report card is presented not as a model, but rather as an example that demonstrates some of the desirable characteristics of expanded format reporting.

Figure 11.3 is the elementary report card used in all public elementary schools in the Province of Ontario. It is an expanded format report, but it is only standards-based for English, second language, and mathematics. For each of these subjects, the strands from the curriculum expectations are listed with grades for each strand and no overall grade. Figure 11.3-1 is page one of the grade 1–6 report card, which provides letter grades. Figure 11.3-2 is page one of the grade 7–8 report card, which provides percentage grades. Figure 11.3-3 is page two of both report cards. The subjects on page two receive only an overall grade. An important feature of both reports is the expanded comment section with the heading Strengths/Weaknesses/Next Steps that provides clear focus for teacher comments. Another important feature of page two is the separation of learning skills from achievement; nine learning skills are evaluated on a four-point scale: excellent, good, satisfactory, and needs improvement.

Expanded Format Report Card

Student _____

Homeroom Teacher _____

ART

Teacher:	Q1	Q2	Q3	Q4
Demonstrates an understanding of concepts				
Craftsmanship/manipulation of materials				
Creative exploration and analysis of work				
Initiative/Effort				
Personal/Social behavior				

GENERAL/VOCAL MUSIC

Teacher:	Q1	Q2	Q3	Q4
Singing				
Perceptive listening				
Reading and writing notes				
Creative expression				
Initiative/Effort				
Personal/Social behavior				

PHYSICAL EDUCATION

Teacher:	Q1	Q2	Q3	Q4
Skills development				
Understands/applies movement concepts				
Initiative/Effort				
Personal/Social behavior				

Achievement Key: This symbol indicates how the student is performing in relationship to a standard.
Bg—Beginning: Is at the initial stage of understanding concept/skill
Dv—Developing: Uses and understands concept/skill with support
Sc—Secure: Independently uses and understands concept/skill
Ex—Exceeds grade level expectations
X—Not assessed at this time

Initiative and Personal/Social Behavior Key:
This symbol represents the student's effort to improve.
3—Consistent   2—Inconsistent   1—Minimal

Figure 11.2–2   From Shorewood School District, 2001, Shorewood, WI. Used with permission.

Page 1 of the Grade 1–6 Report Card

⑦ Ontario   **PROVINCIAL REPORT CARD**   Date:

Student:		Days Absent:	Total Days Absent:
Grade: Teacher:		Times Late:	Total Times Late:

Board: Address:	School: Address: Principal: Telephone:

Promotion Status:	○ Progressing well towards promotion ○ Progressing with some difficulty towards promotion ○ Promotion at risk	**Grade in September:**

Letter Grades	Achievement of the Provincial Curriculum Expectations
A- to A+	The student has demonstrated the required knowledge and skills. Achievement exceeds the provincial standard. (Level 4)
B- to B+	The student has demonstrated most of the required knowledge and skills. Achievement meets the provincial standard. (Level 3)
C- to C+	The student has demonstrated some of the required knowledge and skills. Achievement approaches the provincial standard. (Level 2)
D- to D+	The student has demonstrated some of the required knowledge and skills in limited ways. Achievement falls much below the provincial standard. (Level 1)
R	The student has not demonstrated the required knowledge and skills. Extensive remediation is required.

IEP - Individual Education Plan that addresses special learning needs   ESL- English as a Second Language   ESD - English Skills Development

Subjects	Report 1	Report 2	Report 3	Strengths/Weaknesses/Next Steps
English ☐ ESL ☐ ESD ☐ Not applicable ☐ IEP				
Reading				
Writing				
Oral and Visual Communication				
Second Language ☐ French ☐ Native ☐ Not Applicable ☐ Core ☐ Extended ☐ Immersion ☐ IEP				
Oral Communication				
Reading				
Writing				
Mathematics ☐ ESL ☐ ESD ☐ French ☐ IEP				
Number Sense and Numeration				
Measurement				
Geometry and Spatial Sense				
Patterning and Algebra				
Data Management and Probability				

Grades 1-6   Page 1 of 3

Figure 11.3-1   © Queen's Printer for Ontario, 2002. Reproduced with permission.

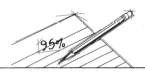

Page 1 of the Grade 7–8 Report Card

⑦ Ontario — PROVINCIAL REPORT CARD — Date:

Student:	Days Absent:	Total Days Absent:
Grade:	Teacher:	Times Late:	Total Times Late:

Board:
Address:

School:
Address:

Principal: | Telephone :

Promotion Status:
- ○ Progressing well towards promotion
- ○ Progressing with some difficulty towards promotion
- ○ Promotion at risk

Grade in September: _____

% Marks	Achievement of the Provincial Curriculum Expectations
80 - 100	The student has demonstrated the required knowledge and skills. Achievement exceeds the provincial standard. (Level 4)
70 - 79	The student has demonstrated most of the required knowledge and skills. Achievement meets the provincial standard. (Level 3)
60 - 69	The student has demonstrated some of the required knowledge and skills. Achievement approaches the provincial standard. (Level 2)
50 - 59	The student has demonstrated some of the required knowledge and skills in limited ways. Achievement falls much below the provincial standard. (Level 1)
Below 50	The student has not demonstrated the required knowledge and skills. Extensive remediation is required.

IEP - Individual Education Plan that addresses special learning needs   ESL- English as a Second Language   ESD - English Skills Development

Subjects	Report 1 Mark / Grade Average	Report 2 Mark / Grade Average	Report 3 Mark / Grade Average	Strengths/Weaknesses/Next Steps
English ☐ ESL ☐ ESD ☐ Not Applicable ☐ IEP				
Reading				
Writing				
Oral and Visual Communication				
Second Language ☐ French ☐ Native ☐ IEP ☐ Core ☐ Immersion ☐ Extended ☐ Not Applicable				
Oral Communication				
Reading				
Writing				
Mathematics ☐ ESL ☐ ESD ☐ French ☐ IEP				
Number Sense and Numeration				
Measurement				
Geometry and Spatial Sense				
Patterning and Algebra				
Data Management and Probability				

Grades 7-8 Page 1 of 3

Figure 11.3-2   © Queen's Printer for Ontario, 2002. Reproduced with permission.

Page 2 of Both Report Cards

Student: _____   Grade: _____

Subjects	Report 1	Report 2	Report 3	Strengths/Weaknesses/Next Steps
Science and Technology ☐ ESL ☐ ESD ☐ French ☐ IEP				Life Systems, Matter / Materials, Energy / Control, Structures / Mechanisms, Earth / Space Systems
Social Studies ☐ ESL ☐ ESD ☐ French ☐ IEP				
Health and Physical Education ☐ ESL ☐ ESD ☐ French ☐ IEP				
The Arts Music ☐ ESL ☐ IEP ☐ ESD ☐ French				
Visual Arts ☐ IEP				
Drama and Dance ☐ IEP				
☐ ESL ☐ ESD ☐ IEP				
☐ ESL ☐ ESD ☐ IEP				

| Learning Skills | E - Excellent | G - Good | S - Satisfactory | N - Needs Improvement |

Independent work			Use of information			Class participation			
Initiative			Cooperation with others			Problem solving			
Homework completion			Conflict resolution			Goal setting to improve work			

Strengths/Weaknesses/Next Steps

To Parents or Guardians and Students: This copy of the report card should be retained for reference. The original or an exact copy has been placed in the student's Ontario Student Record (OSR) folder and will be retained for five years after the student leaves school.

Teacher's Signature _____   Principal's Signature _____

Grades 1-6   Page 2 of 3

Figure 11.3-3   © Queen's Printer for Ontario, 2002. Reproduced with permission.

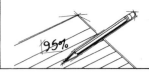

Figure 11.4 is the Ontario Provincial Report Card for grades 9–12, which was used for the first time in the 1999–2000 school year. Figure 11.4-1 is the first page of the report for use in semestered schools where the students typically take four subjects for about eighteen weeks. There is also a version for nonsemestered schools. The report card requires percentage grades for achievement and provides (inappropriately) the median percentage grade for each course in a school. The format of this report card is not a standards-based, but provincial policy requires teachers to use the categories from the achievement charts as reference points for assessment (see Figure 2.6 on page 76), so teachers must follow guidelines 1 and 2 if they are using this report card properly. The most positive features of this report are the expanded comments section with the clear focus and the five learning skills, which are evaluated for each subject. Figure 11.4-2 is used with the first report in semestered schools and the first and second (of three) reports in nonsemestered schools. It is an interesting attempt to involve students in communicating about their achievement and to obtain response from parents.

Informal Communications

Brief meetings in the school, phone calls, postcards, and quick notes are all informal communications that teachers use. Although informal, they are part of the communication system. If communication is seen as a system, even informal communications are planned, at least to some extent. Planning involves the availability of postcards or quick notes so that it is easy for teachers to send informal written communications home. If using printed cards or notes that have a set format, teachers have only to fill in the blanks and the communication is ready to go.

Another aspect of planning for schools is seeking to ensure that each parent receives at least one positive informal communication each term.

Although schools have always seen it as their duty to inform parents when students misbehave or are frequently tardy or absent, it is important that informal communication also be used for positive feedback. This is another aspect of planning for schools—seeking to ensure that each parent receives at least one positive informal communication each term. For this to happen, teachers need to keep brief records of their use of informal communications. Informal communication and the associated record keeping must not be a major burden for teachers; as with other methods of communication,

Page 1 of Report Card for Grades 9–12

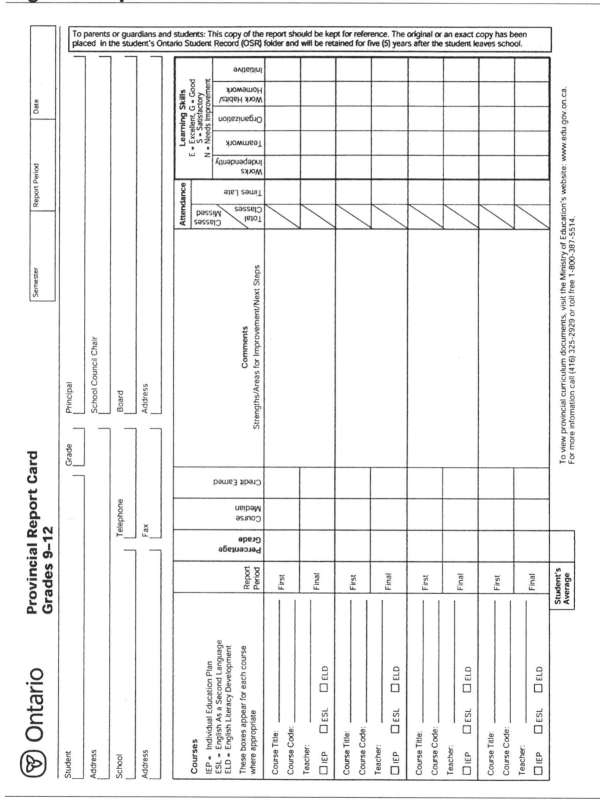

Figure 11.4-1

© Queen's Printer for Ontario, 2002. Reproduced with permission.

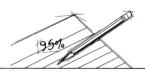

Report Card Response Form

⊗ Ontario   **Provincial Report Card, Grades 9–12**

Response Form

Report Period	Date

Student 's Name	Grade

Address

School   Telephone

Principal   Teacher

Student's Comments
To be completed by the student in consultation with the teacher as part of the student's annual education plan.

1. Goals

2. Achievement

3. Action Plan

4. Community Involvement

Student's Signature   Date   Teacher's Signature   Date

Parent/Guardian's Comments
To be completed by the parent/guardian, signed, and returned to the school

Parent/Guardian's Signature   Date

(School information regarding opportunities for parent-teacher communication)

To view provincial curriculum documents, visit the Ministry of Education and Training's website: www.edu.gov.on.ca
For more infomation call (416) 325-2929 or toll free 1-800 387-5514

Figure 11.4-2   © Queen's Printer for Ontario, 2002. Reproduced with permission.

planning is needed to ensure that teacher workload is reasonable. In addition, teachers need flexibility in choosing a method that is most comfortable for them—some prefer to make phone calls, others prefer to write.

Student-Involved Conferencing

Another part of a communication system involves planned meetings between parents, teachers and, increasingly, students. Traditionally, these meetings have been parent-teacher interviews with no student participation. Much valuable information can be exchanged in such interviews, and although sometimes privacy is necessary, almost always parents, teachers, or both discuss the interview with students afterwards. How much better for the student to be present and participate in the conference rather than receive secondhand, and inevitably somewhat distorted, accounts of what occurred. This leads to the concept of student-involved conferencing.

The continuum shown in Figure 11.5 demonstrates that student-involved conferencing may vary from the student merely being present as a listener but not really participating through increasing student participation to conferences that are truly led by students. Schools and teachers may start at the point on the continuum that is comfortable for them and their community. There is a huge variety of possible formats, and it is hoped that teachers will move quickly toward increasing levels of student involvement.

Schools and teachers may start at the point on the continuum that is comfortable for them and their community.

In one possible format, students share work samples that demonstrate their growth and their best work with their parent(s). Students identify for their parent(s) the strengths and weaknesses of the shared samples and what they could do to improve on a similar task in the future. Work samples may come from an organized portfolio assessment system, but it is not essential to have student portfolios to institute student-involved conferencing. Teachers can simply state the number of pieces of work that students are to share, some designated by the teacher and some chosen by the students. This approach applies particularly to interviews for middle and high school students (see Figure 11.6), where parents have many teachers to see and teachers have very limited amounts of time with each student and his or her parent(s). Gregory, Cameron, and Davies (2001) offer additional guidance for developing student conferencing.

Student Involvement Continuum

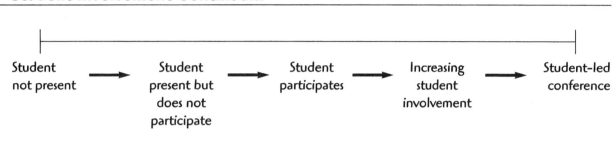

Figure 11.5

Parent's Night Interview—Science

Dear _____,

I look forward to meeting you on Thursday, _____ at _____ p.m. in Room _____.
Your daughter/son is welcome to attend, too.

Before you come to see me, please find time to sit down with your daughter/son and ask her/him
to show you the following from her/his SCIENCE NOTEBOOK:

1. Two pieces of work that she/he is particularly pleased with
2. One piece of work that she/he could have done better on
3. The self-tracking sheet outlining progress on the essential performance criteria
4. The self- and teacher evaluation of her/his participation in the learning process

Please discuss these pieces of work with her/him. I suggest you make several positive comments
and outline one or two steps for improvement if necessary. Please bring this sheet with you on
parents' night.

Positive comments:

Steps for improvement:

Questions arising from your discussion:

Many thanks,

_____

Figure 11.6 Adapted by permission from Hilary Gerrard, former Head of Science, Thornlea, S.S.
York Region District School Board, Ontario, Canada.

Students may lead conferences in the absence or presence of teachers. One of the most practical formats is to have a number of conferences occurring at the same time—the number largely determined by the size of the available room. Students lead each conference by taking their parent(s) through each work sample and inviting their reactions to the work and the student's description and explanation. The teacher deals with any problems that arise and spends a relatively short period of time with each student and parent(s). For example, conferences may be set for forty-five minutes, with four to eight different student-parent groups meeting simultaneously. The teacher rotates among the groups, giving about five minutes to each, a mix of what Davies, Cameron, Politano, and Gregory (1992) call two-way and three-way conferences.

As with other parts of the communication system, student-involved conferencing requires a great deal of preparation and planning. Students have to be trained for whatever type of involvement they are to have, and parents need to be informed about how conferencing will be conducted and what is expected of them. Millar, Heffler, and Meriwether (1995) provided a detailed, generic, four-month calendar that includes all the steps teachers need to prepare a class for student-involved conferencing.

Student-involved conferencing has many benefits for students, parents, and teachers.

Student-involved conferencing has many benefits for students, parents, and teachers. Students hone their self-assessment abilities and develop their understanding and vocabulary about learning and assessment. They also learn in a very powerful way that they are responsible for their own learning.

Parents are able to see their children as learners and gain a much richer understanding of their children's growth and progress than is provided by report cards. Often, in fact, where student-involved conferencing is used, report cards play a very small part in the conference because the real information is in the shared work samples. Parents who do not speak the language used in the school benefit greatly from this approach because the student can conduct the conference in the parents' language.

Teachers benefit from student-involved conferencing by improved communication with and between students, parents, and teachers, which develops a better understanding of their students' strengths and weaknesses and, thus, promotes dealing with them more effectively. Another major benefit for teachers (and schools) is that attendance by parents at student-involved conferences is almost always much better than at traditional parent interviews.

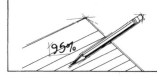

It is hard to think of any major problems with student-involved conferencing apart from logistical and time issues. It is obviously much easier to organize conferences for a self-contained grade 2 class than it is for a grade 8 class or a high school on a rotary timetable, but, as indicated earlier, there are ways to adapt this approach for all grade levels. For example, universities have been using a version of student-involved conferencing (without parents) for centuries. They do this by having students attend lectures in large groups, but then organizing students into small tutorial groups where students meet with a leader (often a graduate student) to examine their understanding of the concepts and problems presented by the professor in the lecture.

One small problem with student-involved conferencing is that teachers lose some of the control they normally have with parent/teacher interviews. As with other aspects of communication, teachers should search to find a comfort zone in which they honor the principle (in this case, student involvement) to the extent that it is comfortable for them. Some teachers want to begin with the type of conference in which the students are just present, whereas others are happy to jump right in to student-led conferencing. The important thing is that teachers involve students, and over time, move further to the right of the continuum (see Figure 11.5 on page 225). At all times, parents should be offered the opportunity for a parent-teacher interview in place of, or in addition to, a student-involved conference.

Summary

Schools and teachers have a responsibility to communicate effectively with parents and others who are interested in the progress of students. Traditionally, report cards with letter or percentage grades and brief comments have been the main vehicles for communication. This has led to cult-like status for grades, but grades are only part of the communication system. In addition to these symbols (or, where acceptable, in place of these symbols), teachers can provide parents with real information by using expanded format reporting, informal communications, and student-involved conferencing. School districts, schools, and teachers must plan their communication system carefully and train students, parents, and teachers to participate effectively in the system. Prime considerations in developing such systems are effective and clear communication, clear purpose(s), and reasonable workloads for teachers.

This is not a situation where more is always better. Careful choices need to be made that are within the comfort zone of both teachers and the community and that move everyone involved toward more effective communication. Great strides have been made in this area by elementary schools; it is now time that expanded format reporting and student-involved conferencing become a regular part of middle and high school communication systems. The checklist provided as Figure 11.7 is intended to help schools/districts check where they are and where they want to go as they revise their report cards.

Reporting Issues Checklist

COMMUNICATION SYSTEM

❑ Informal ──────────▶ __ Conversations
__ Notes/postcards
__ Phone calls
__ E-mail

❑ Interim reports
❑ Report cards (quarterly)
❑ Parent teacher interviews
❑ Student involvement ──▶ __ Present
__ Participate
__ Lead

GENERAL CONSIDERATIONS (FOR STAKEHOLDER DISCUSSIONS)

❑ Fair   ❑ Credible
❑ Honest   ❑ Feasible
❑ Useful   ❑ User friendly

REPORT CARD
Purpose
❑ Clearly established
❑ Clearly stated

Amount/Type of Information
❑ Multiple grades   ❑ Achievement   ❑ Learning skills   ❑ Other
❑ Subject grades ──────▶ __ One per subject
__ Several per subject by strands or benchmarks

❑ Comments
❑ Attendance and tardies
❑ Clarity of layout

Learning/Skills/Behaviors
❑ Appropriate   ❑ Number
❑ Scale   ❑ Criteria/descripters

Comments
❑ Focus
❑ Teacher generated
❑ Computer "bank"

Use of Technology

Figure 11.7

Chapter 12

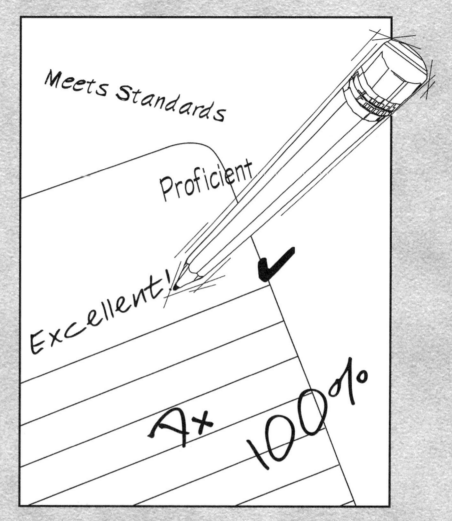

The Way Ahead

The time has come to de-emphasize traditional grades and to demystify the entire grading process. We need to focus instead on the process of learning and the progress of the individual student.

—KAY BURKE

his may seem an odd quote to start the final chapter of a book on grading, but it does summarize the intent and message of this book. Let us look at this by discussing each of the main ideas.

De-Emphasizing Traditional Grades

Traditional grades have both too little and too much meaning. They have too little meaning because there are so many things mixed in them, in such idiosyncratic ways by different teachers, that their meaning is very unclear. They have too much meaning because of the cult-like status accorded them and because of their importance in high stakes educational decisions. Traditional grades may be de-emphasized (1) by using new approaches to grading that give grades clear meaning and (2) by giving to students, parents, and interested others information about learning that is much better than grades.

New Approach to Grading

The grading guidelines described and analyzed in this book produce grades with meaning, that is, grades that are based on individual achievement data (guideline 3), that use more recent information (guideline 5), that are derived from summative assessments (guideline 4), and that are based on opportunities for reassessment (guideline 5). These grades are directly related to learning goals (guideline 1) and result from appropriate number crunching, if necessary (guideline 6). They are derived from quality assessments (guideline 7), that are based on public, criterion-referenced standards (guideline 2) and have been thoroughly discussed with and understood by students (guideline 8).

The grading guidelines described in this book produce grades with meaning.

As a result of all these characteristics, this new approach to grading supports learning and encourages student success. This contrasts markedly with traditional grades, which have little to do with learning

Standards-Based Grading Contrasted with Traditional Grading

Guideline	Standards-Based	Traditional
1	Directly related to standards	Usually related to assessment methods
2	Criterion-referenced standards	Often norm-referenced or a mix of criterion and norm referenced
	Public criteria/targets	Criteria unclear or assumed to be known
3a	Achievement only	Uncertain mix of achievement, attitude, effort, and behavior
3b	Individual	Often includes group marks
4	From summative assessments only	From formative and summative assessments
5	More recent information only	Everything marked included
	Reassessment without penalty	Multiple assessments recorded as average, not best
6	Limited and careful "number crunching"	Many formulas and calculations
	Use of median/mode	Always use means ("average")
7	Derived from quality assessments	Huge variation in assessment quality
	Data carefully recorded	Often only stored in teachers' heads
8	All aspects discussed with, and understood by, students	Teacher decides and announces

Figure 12.1

because they are competitive, punitive, and encourage game playing by students and teachers alike. Traditional grades encourage grade grubbing, not learning, and are often used just as control measures. Grading with the guidelines de-emphasizes grade grubbing and control and differs from traditional grades in the ways shown above in Figure 12.1.

Information About Learning That Is Much Better Than Grades

Portfolios, expanded format reporting, effective informal communication, and student-involved conferencing each provide better information than grades. Grades are—and can never be anything more than—symbols that summarize achievement. These other methods of communication provide real information about student learning far more effectively than grades because each contains a wealth of information and provides an effective method to communicate the information.

Educators (and the media) have a responsibility to educate parents and the community about the place of grades in the communication system. In the past, this frequently has not been done well. An unfortunate example of this is provided by the Province of Ontario, which introduced a standard Provincial Report Card for grades 1–8 beginning in the 1997–1998 school year (see Figure 11.3-1 on page 218). Although many school districts in Ontario (including the author's) did not previously provide grades on report cards given to students in grades 1–6, the new Provincial Report Card required the use of letter grades for grades 1–6 and percentage grades for grades 7–8. These grades were required not for clearly justified educational reasons, but because, according to the politicians, "this is what parents said they wanted." It is hoped that elementary educators in Ontario—and elsewhere—will be able to prevent a fixation on grades in the early years by providing parents with other methods of communication, ones that give a fuller picture of their children as learners. As was noted in chapter 11, this report card also has many strengths.

> *Grading has been the preserve of individual teachers operating in the isolation of their own classrooms with minimal direction.*

A hopeful sign at the other end of the educational spectrum is that many colleges and universities are increasingly requiring information in addition to or in place of grades for decisions about admission of first-year students. They recognize that to make good selection decisions, they need more information than is provided by grades, GPA, and/or class rank. Many postsecondary institutions are using supplementary information forms that give students the opportunity to present a complete picture of themselves.

Demystifying the Entire Grading Process

For the most part, grading has been the preserve of individual teachers operating in the isolation of their own classrooms with minimal direction from school or district policies and minimal guidance from administrators. The grading guidelines presented in this book demystify the process:

1. Guideline 8 requires that students be part of the process that establishes grading procedures. If they are not part of the process, at the very least, they must be well informed about assessment and grading procedures.
2. If these guidelines are adopted, it is expected that they will be given policy status at both the school and district level. This means that grading procedures are no longer a mystery, and teachers can be held accountable for the procedures they follow. A grading policy based on the guidelines is provided in appendix 3.

In many ways, grading has also been a mystery for teachers because there is so little discussion about grading in education courses, staff development and conference workshops, or staff rooms. Teachers have basically done what was done to them as students or relied on individual help from a more experienced colleague. These grading guidelines demystify the process for teachers because they provide a clear, practical process for teachers to follow in their classrooms—and in their grade books.

> *Teachers have basically done what was done to them as students or relied on individual help from a more experienced colleague.*

Focusing on the Process of Learning

Although grades always ultimately focus on the results of learning, use of the grading guidelines, expanded format reporting, and the other methods of communication advocated in this book honors the process of learning far more than traditional grading. Guidelines 4 and 5, in particular, acknowledge learning as a process:

1. They require that formative assessment provide reporting, not grading, information.
2. They emphasize that summative assessment is the only proper source of information for grades.
3. They emphasize the more recent information rather than early information or first attempts.
4. They provide two or more assessment opportunities.

Seeing grades as only part of the communication system and emphasizing other methods of communication that provide more detailed information also moves the focus more to the process of learning.

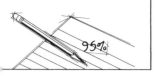

Focusing on the Progress of the Individual Student

There are many ways in which the guidelines focus on the individual student. First and foremost, guideline 3 emphasizes individual achievement. Although it is critically important that teachers use cooperative learning structures in their classrooms, it is even more important that any marks that students receive from cooperative learning activities (either process or product) be based on each individual's contribution, not the achievement, or lack of achievement, of others. Group grades are inappropriate and should not be used because they are so unfair and because they contribute in a significant and unfortunate way to giving cooperative learning a bad reputation.

The guidelines also acknowledge students as individuals and enable individuals to progress, because each student's learning styles, multiple intelligences profile, and/or needs are taken into account. Guideline 5 acknowledges that students learn at different rates and need varying amounts of time to be able to adequately demonstrate their knowledge and skills. Guideline 6 suggests using medians rather than means, which allows students to have a few stumbles without the poorer performances detracting from their normal level of achievement. Guideline 2 leads to each individual student having the opportunity to succeed at the highest level. Criterion-referenced standards foster learning that is not competitive and the standards also prevent success from being artificially rationed by a mathematical formula. Guideline 7 requires that teachers record assessment data accurately and consistently—producing quality information to students and parents about the progress of each individual student. Guideline 8 gives every individual the best opportunities to progress because it requires that students be involved in, and clearly understand, how assessment and grading will be carried out.

Finally, this information is provided in ways that can contribute to the growth of individuals. Because grades are seen as only part of the communication system, other methods of communication that give rich information about the strengths and weaknesses of each student are used. This rich information enables students to be effective self-assessors and assists them, their parents, and their teachers to set goals and to identify needed actions to reach those goals.

Summary

Using the grading guidelines and the communication methods described in this book is a new—or at least a different—approach to grading and reporting. The guidelines and methods go a long way toward providing the student-involved assessment advocated by Stiggins (2001b) and the honesty and fairness in grading and reporting that Wiggins (1996) has been advocating for many years. They also clearly acknowledge that grading and reporting must be directly related to learning goals and standards, which have become such a large part of education (Marzano and Kendall 1996). This approach to grading and communication does what Burke advocated—"de-emphasize traditional grades," "demystify the entire grading process," and "focus on the process of learning and the progress of the individual student." All of these desirable characteristics occur because (1) the prime purpose of grades is recognized as communication, not competition, and (2) determining student grades is based on a pedagogy that views the teacher's role as supporting learning and encouraging student success.

> **T**he prime purpose of grades is recognized as communication, not competition.

Recommendations

Although the focus of this book is grading, it is important to acknowledge that there are many things more important than grading in education, especially quality instruction and assessment. Teachers must take many steps to implement the grading guidelines advocated in this book. They require a philosophy and a whole assessment approach that include the following six action steps (only one of which is grading itself!):

1. Use a variety of assessment methods that meet the needs of all students.
2. Match assessment methods with learning goals. Generally, this will require more use of performance assessment and clearer identification of formative assessment.

3. With student involvement (where appropriate), develop clear criteria (rubrics) and provide models (exemplars or anchor papers) illustrating the levels of performance. Base marking on these criteria and levels.

4. Provide reteaching and reassessment opportunities.

5. Encourage assessments by self and peers—this could include the use of portfolios, response journals, and student-involved conferencing.

6. Base grades on only the most consistent, summative, individual achievement data. When appropriate, also give consideration to more recent achievement (Midwood, O'Connor, and Simpson 1993).

 What's My Thinking Now?

Having now reached this point in the book (and, it is hoped, having read all of it!), readers are in a position to consider two things—how the ideas presented will influence their own practices and what the links are between the grading guidelines. With this in mind, two final activities are provided.

Activity 1: This activity asks teachers to examine their own grading practices and consider changes that will benefit their students. Readers are encouraged to answer the questions and share the results with a colleague.
1. Which grading practices were reinforced by the book?
2. What revisions to my grading practices do I need to make?
3. What points of uncertainty still exist?
4. What actions do I want to take now?

Activity 2: This activity begins a web of the grading guidelines; readers are encouraged to complete the web by identifying the links between the grading guidelines and the links to the ideas and issues discussed in chapters 9, 10, and 11.

Glossary

The glossary is an explanation of the way terms are used in this book. It is based on many sources, but the major source is the glossary developed by the Evaluation Policy Committee of the Scarborough Board of Education, Ontario, Canada.

achievement. The demonstration of student performance measured against established criteria (performance standards).

assessment. Gathering and interpreting information about student achievement (group or individual) using a variety of tools and techniques. It is the act of describing student performance, primarily for the purpose of enhancing learning. As part of assessment, teachers provide students with feedback that guides their efforts toward improved achievement.

content standards. What students are expected to know and be able to do.

criteria. Characteristics or dimensions of student performance.

criterion-referenced. Assessment of students' success in meeting stated objectives, learning goals, expectations, or criteria. (See also *norm-referenced* and *self-referenced*.)

diagnostic. Assessment usually carried out prior to instruction that is designed to determine a student's attitude, skills, or knowledge in order to identify specific student needs. (See also *formative* and *summative*.)

evaluation. Making judgments about the quality of student achievement over a period of time, primarily for the purpose of communicating student achievement.

formative. Assessment designed to provide direction for improvement and/or adjustment to a program for individual students or for a whole class (e.g., quizzes, initial drafts/attempts, homework [usually], and questions during instruction). (See also *diagnostic* and *summative*.)

grade. The number or letter reported at the end of a period of time as a summary statement of student performance. (See also *mark*.)

learning goal. An observable result demonstrated by a student's knowledge, skills, or behavior; a generic term.

mark. The "score" (number or letter) given on any single test or performance. (See also *grade*.)

norm-referenced. Assessment/evaluation in relation to other students within a class or across classes/schools or a segment of the population. (See also *criterion-referenced* and *self-referenced*.)

performance standards. How well students are expected to demonstrate knowledge and skill.

reliability. The consistency with which an assessment strategy measures whatever it is meant to measure. (See also *validity*.)

rubric. A set of guidelines for assessment that states the characteristics and/or the dimensions being assessed with clear performance criteria and a rating scale.

self-referenced. Assessment designed to compare an individual's performance with his or her previous performance. (See also *criterion-referenced* and *norm-referenced*.)

standard. Statement that describes what and/or how well students are expected to understand and perform.

summative. Assessment designed to provide information about a student's achievement at the end of a period of instruction (e.g., tests, exams, final drafts/attempts, assignments, projects, performances). (See also *diagnostic* and *formative*.)

validity. The degree to which an assessment strategy measures what it is intended to measure. (See also *reliability*.)

Guidelines for Grading in Standards-Based Systems

to Support Learning and to Encourage Student Success

1. Relate grading procedures to learning goals (i.e., standards).

   a. Use learning goals (standards or some clustering of standards [e.g., strands] as basis for grade determination).

   b. Use assessment methods as the subset NOT the set.

2. Use criterion-referenced performance standards as reference points to determine grades.

   a. The meaning of grades (letters or numbers) should come from clear descriptions of performance standards.

   b. If they hit the goal, they get the grade! (i.e., NO bell curve!)

3. Limit the valued attributes included in grades to individual achievement.

   a. Grades should be based on achievement (i.e., demonstration of the knowledge and skill components of the standards). Effort, participation, attitude, and other behaviors should be reported separately.

   b. Grades should be based on *individual* achievement.

4. Sample student performance—do not include all scores in grades.

   a. Provide feedback on formative performance—use words, rubrics, or checklists.

   b. Include information only from varied summative assessments in grades.

5. Grade in pencil—keep records so they can be updated easily.

   a. Use the most consistent level of achievement with special consideration for the more recent information.

   b. Provide several assessment opportunities (varying in method and number).

6. **Crunch numbers carefully—if at all.**
   a. Avoid using the mean; consider using the median or mode.
   b. Weight components to achieve intent in final grades.

7. **Use quality assessment(s) and properly recorded evidence of achievement.**
   a. Meet standards for quality assessment (e.g., clear targets, clear purpose, appropriate target-method match, appropriate sampling, and avoidance of bias and distortion).
   b. Record and maintain evidence of achievement (e.g., portfolios, conferences, tracking sheets, etc.).

8. **Discuss and involve students in assessment, including grading, throughout the teaching/learning process.**

A Proposed Grading Policy

If the ideas and guidelines presented in this book were to be included in a school or district grading policy, the wording should be similar to the following. (The number of each section parallels the grading guidelines.)

1. Grading procedures shall be related directly to stated learning goals.
2. Criterion-referenced standards shall be used to distribute grades and marks.
3. a. Individual achievement of stated learning goals shall be the only basis for grades.
   b. Effort, participation, attitude, and other behaviors shall not be included in grades but shall be reported separately unless they are a stated part of a learning goal.
   c. Late work shall be handled as follows:
      (1) Teachers may set due dates and deadlines for all marked work that will be part of a student grade.
      (2) Work handed in late if penalized shall not exceed 2% per day to a maximum of 10%.
      (3) Teachers may exempt students from penalties.
      (4) Care should be taken to ensure that penalties (if used) do not distort achievement or motivation.
   d. Absences shall be handled as follows:
      (1) Students shall not be penalized only for absence.
      (2) Absent students shall be given make-up opportunities for all missed summative assessments (marked work that will be part of student grades) without penalty.
   e. Incomplete work shall be handled as follows:
      (1) Work that is not submitted will be identified as I (incomplete). Zeros will not be used.
      (2) Students are expected to complete all required work and will be given opportunities to do so.
      (3) In determining grades, teachers must decide whether they have sufficient evidence of achievement. If not, the grade recorded shall be an I for Insufficient Evidence/Incomplete. Where credits are involved, an I means no credit until the missing work is completed and the grade is updated.

4. a. Teachers shall mark and/or provide feedback on formative assessment.

b. Marks from formative assessment shall not be included in grades.

c. Marks from summative assessments only shall be included in grades.

5. a. Where repetitive measures are made of the same or similar knowledge, skills, or behaviors, the more recent mark or marks shall replace the previous marks for grade determination.

b. Second chance (or more) assessment opportunities shall be made available to students; students shall receive the highest, most consistent mark, not an average mark for any such multiple opportunities.

6. a. Grades shall be determined to ensure that the grade each student receives is a fair reflection of his or her performance.

b. Consideration shall be given to the use of statistical measures other than the mean for grade calculations; for example, consider using median or mode.

c. Grades shall be weighted carefully to ensure the intended importance is given to each learning goal and to each assessment.

7. a. Teachers shall use quality assessment instruments. "Each assessment must meet five standards of quality. It must arise from a clearly articulated set of achievement expectations, serve an instructionally relevant purpose, rely on a proper method, sample student achievement in an appropriate manner, and control for all relevant sources of bias and distortion that can lead to inaccurate assessment. All assessments must be reviewed and adjusted as needed to meet these standards." (Stiggins 2001a, 25).

b. Teachers shall properly record evidence of student achievement on an ongoing basis.

8. a. Teachers shall discuss assessment with students, in an age appropriate manner, at the beginning of instruction. Where feasible, students shall be involved in decisions about methods of assessment and scoring scales.

b. Teachers shall provide to students and parents a written overview of assessment, including grading, in clear, easily understandable language during the first week of classes in each course or grade.

c. Teachers shall provide students with a written overview in clear, easily understandable language, indicating how each summative assessment throughout the course will be evaluated before each such assessment is administered.

Bibliography

Airasian, P. W. 1994. *Classroom assessment*. 2d. ed. New York: McGraw Hill.

Anderson, K. E., and F. C. Wendel. 1988. Pain relief: Make consistency the cornerstone of your policy on grading. *The American School Board Journal*, October, 36–37.

Armstrong, T. 1994. *Multiple intelligences in the classroom*. Alexandria, VA: Association for Supervision and Curriculum Development.

Arter, J., and J. McTighe. 2001. *Scoring rubrics in the classroom*. Thousand Oaks, CA: Corwin.

Arter, J., and R. Stiggins. 1991. *Assessment policy: Workshop notes*. Portland, OR: NorthWest Regional Educational Laboratory.

Ashenfelter, J. W. 1990. Our schools grappled with grade point politics and lost. *The Executive Educator*, January, 21–23.

Bailey, J. M., and T. R. Guskey. 2001. *Implementing student-led conferences*. Thousand Oaks, CA: Corwin.

Bailey, J., and J. McTighe. 1996. Reporting achievement at the secondary level: What and how. *In Communicating student learning: ASCD yearbook 1996*, edited by T. R. Guskey. Alexandria, VA: Association for Supervision and Curriculum Development.

Baron, M. A., and F. Boschee. 1995. *Authentic assessment: The key to unlocking student success*. Lancaster, PA: Technomic.

Bellanca, J. 1992. How to grade (if you must). In *If minds matter: A foreword to the future*, Vol. 2, edited by A. L. Costa, J. Bellanca, and R. Fogarty. Palatine, IL: Skylight Publishing.

Benevino, M., and D. Snodgrass. 1998. *Collaborative learning in middle and secondary schools: Applications and assessments*. Larchmont, NY: Eye on Education.

———. 1998. "Revisiting cooperative learning. . . and making it work: Success with cooperative learning on the secondary level." *NASSP Bulletin* 82(597): 67.

Bissinger, H. G. 1990. *Friday night lights*. Harper Perenial.

Black, P., and D. Wiliam. 1998. Inside the black box. *Kappan*, October, 139–148.

Bonstingl, J. J. 1992. *Schools of quality: An introduction to total quality management in education*. Alexandria, VA: Association for Supervision and Curriculum Development.

Brewer, W. R., and B. Kallick. 1996. Technology's promise for reporting student learning. In *Communicating student learning: The ASCD yearbook 1996*, edited by T. Guskey. Alexandria, VA: Association for Supervision and Curriculum Development.

Brookhart, S. M. 1994. Teacher's grading: Theory and practice. *Applied Measurement in Education* 7(4): 279–301.

Burke, K. 1999. *How to assess authentic learning*. Arlington Heights, IL: SkyLight Training and Publishing Inc.

———— 1993. *The mindful school: How to assess authentic learning*. Palatine, IL: IRI/Skylight Publishing.

Burke, K., R. Fogarty, and S. Belgrad. 2002. *The portfolio connection: Student work linked to standards*. Arlington Heights, IL: Skylight Training and Publishing Inc.

Busick, K. 2000. Grading and standards-based assessment. In *Grading and reporting student progress in an age of standards*, pp. 71–86, edited by E. Trumbull and B. Farr. Norwood, MA: Christopher Gordon.

Busick, K. U., and R. J. Stiggins. 1997. *Making connections: Case studies for student-centered classroom assessment*. Portland, OR: Assessment Training Institute.

Canady, R. L., and P. R. Hotchkiss. 1989. It's a good score: Just a bad grade. *Phi Delta Kappan*, September, 68–71.

Carr, J. 2000. Technical issues of grading methods. In *Grading and reporting student progress in an age of standards*, pp. 45–70, edited by E. Trumbull and B. Farr. Norwood, MA: Christopher Gordon.

Carr, J. and B. Farr. 2000. Taking steps toward standards-based report cards. In *Grading and reporting student progress in an age of standards*, pp. 185–208, edited by E. Trumbull and B. Farr. Norwood, MA: Christopher Gordon.

Chapman, C. 1993. *If the shoe fits . . .: How to develop multiple intelligences in the classroom*. Palatine, IL: IRI/Skylight Publishing.

Cizek, G. J. 1996a. Grades: The final frontier in assessment reform. *NASSP Bulletin*, December, 103–110.

————. 1996b. Setting passing scores. *Educational Measurement: Issues and Practices*, Summer, 20–31.

Cohen, S. B. 1983. Assigning report card grades to the mainstreamed child. *Teaching Exceptional Children*, Winter, 86–89.

Conklin, T. 2001. Testing for learning. *The Trillium, Ontario ASCD Newsletter*, March, 3–4.

Costa, A. L., and B. Kallick. 1992. Reassessing assessment. In *If minds matter: A foreword to the future*, Vol. 2, edited by A. L. Costa, J. Bellanca, and R. Fogarty. Palatine, IL: IRI/Skylight Publishing.

Costello, C., and B. McKillop. 2000. Dealing with lates and absences. *Orbit*, 30: 4, 43–46.

Culp, L., and V. Malone. 1992. Peer scores for group work. *Science Scope*, March, 35, 36, 59.

Danielson, C. 1997. *A collection of performance tasks and rubrics: Upper elementary school mathematics*. Larchmount, NY: Eye on Education.

Darling-Hammond, L., R. Ancess, and B. Falk. 1995. *Authentic assessment in action*. New York: Teachers College Press.

Davies, A. 2000. *Making classroom assessment work*. Merville, BC, Canada: Connections Publishing.

Davies, A., C. Cameron, C. Politano, and K. Gregory. 1992. *Together is better: Collaborative assessment, evaluation and reporting*. Winnipeg, MB, Canada: Peguis Publishing.

Dunbar, D. 1996. *Letter to Runkel, 26IEDLR387*. Office of Civil Rights.

Earl, L., and J. B. Cousins. 1995. *Classroom assessment: Changing the face, facing the change.* Toronto, ON, Canada: Ontario Public School Teachers Federation.

Ebert, C. 1992. So when can I take the retest? *Quality Outcomes-Driven Education,* December, 32–34.

Engelberg, R. A., and E. D. Evans. 1986. Perceptions and attitudes about school grading practices among intellectually gifted, learning disabled and normal elementary school pupils. *Journal of Special Education,* Spring, 91–101.

Farr, B. 2000. Grading practices: An overview of the issues. In *Grading and reporting student progress in an age of standards,* pp. 1–21, edited by E. Trumbull and B. Farr, Norwood, MA: Christopher Gordon.

Fogarty, R., and J. Bellanca. 1987. *Patterns for thinking: Patterns for transfer.* Palatine, IL: IRI/Skylight Publishing.

Frary, R. J., L. M. Gross, and L. J. Weber. 1992. Testing and grading practices and opinions in the nineties: 1890's or 1990's. Paper presented at the Annual Meeting of the National Council on Measurement in Education, April 21– 23, at San Francisco, CA.

Frisbie, D. A., and K. K. Waltman. 1992. Developing a personal grading plan. *Educational Issues: Measurement and Practice,* Fall, 35–42.

Gardner, H. 1983. *Frames of mind: The theory of multiple intelligences.* New York: HarperCollins.

Gathercoal, F. 1997. *Judicious discipline,* 4th ed. San Francisco: Caddo Gap Press.

Gilman, D. A., and E. Swan. 1989. Solving G.P.A. and class rank problems. *NASSP Bulletin,* March, 91–97.

Glasser, W. 1990. *The quality school.* New York: Harper Perennial.

Grading performance assessments. 1996. *ASCD Education Update,* December 4–5.

Gregory, K., C. Cameron and A. Davies. 2001. *Knowing what counts: Conferencing and reporting.* Merville, BC, Canada: Connections Publishing.

———. 1997. *Knowing what counts: Setting and using criteria.* Merville, BC, Canada: Connections Publishing.

Gronlund, N. E., and R. L. Linn. 1990. *Measurement and evaluation in teaching.* 6th ed. New York: Macmillan.

Guskey, T. R. 2000. Grading policies that work against standards . . . and how to fix them. *NASSP Bulletin,* December, 20–29.

———. 1996. Reporting on student learning: Lessons from the past—prescriptions for the future. In *Communicating student learning: The ASCD yearbook 1996,* edited by T. R. Guskey. Alexandria, VA: Association for Supervision and Curriculum Development.

———. 1994. Making the grade: What benefits students? *Educational Leadership,* October, 14–20.

———. 1993. ASCD Update. September, 7.

Guskey, T. R. and J. M. Bailey. 2001. *Developing grading and reporting systems for student learning,* Thousand Oaks, CA: Corwin Press.

Haladyna, T. M. 1999. *A complete guide to student grading.* Boston: Allyn and Bacon.

Hargis, C. H. 1990. *Grades and grading practices: Obstacles to improving education and to helping at-risk students.* Springfield, IL: Charles C. Thomas.

Harlen, W., and M. James. 1997. Assessment and learning: Differences and relationships between formative and summative assessments. *Assessment in Education: Principles, Policy and Practices*, November, 365–379.

Hart, G. 1996. Grades: Both a cause and result of fear. *Middle School Journal*, March, 59–60.

Hensley, L. D., R. Aten, T. A. Baumgartner, W. B. East, L. T. Lambert, and J. L. Stillwell. 1989. A survey of grading practices in public school physical education. *Journal of Research and Development in Education* 22(4): 37–42.

Hills, J. R. 1991. Apathy concerning grading and testing. *Phi Delta Kappan*, March, 540–545.

Hobbs, G. J. 1992. The legality of reducing student grades as a disciplinary measure. *The Clearing House*, March/April, 204–205.

———. 1989. The issuance of student grades and the courts. Paper presented to the Annual Meeting of the Eastern Educational Research Association, February 22–25, at Savannah, GA.

Jensen, E. 1998. *Teaching with the brain in mind*. Alexandria, VA: Association for Supervision and Curriculum Development.

Johnson, B. 1996. *The performance assessment handbook*. Vol. 1, Portfolios and socratic seminars. Princeton, NJ: Eye on Education.

Juarez, T. 1996. Why any grades at all, Father? *Phi Delta Kappan*, January, 374–377.

———. 1990. Revitalizing teacher planning—Grade eggs, not learners. *Holistic Education Review*, Winter, 36–39

Kagan, S. 1995. Group grades miss the mark. *Educational Leadership*, 52(8): 68–71.

———. 1994. Cooperative learning. San Clemente, CA: Kagan Cooperative Learning.

Kain, D. L. 1996. Looking beneath the surface: Teacher collaboration through the lens of grading practices. *Teachers College Record*, Summer, 569–587.

Kasnic, M. 1995. Expanding reporting options through technology. In *Report card on report cards: Alternatives to consider*, edited by T. Azwell and E. Schmar. Portsmouth, NH: Heinemann.

Keefe, J. W. 1984. Assessing and reporting student progress. In *Instructional leadership handbook*, edited by J. W. Keefe and J. M. Jenkins. Reston, VA: National Asssociation of Secondary School Principals.

Kirschenbaum, H., R. Napier, and S. B. Simon. 1971. *Wad-ja-get?: The grading game in American education*. New York: Hart Publishing.

Kohn, A. 1994. Grading: The issue is not how but why. *Educational Leadership*, October, 38–41.

———. 1993a. Choices for children: Why and how to let students decide. *Phi Delta Kappan*, September, 9–19.

———. 1993b. *Punished by rewards: The trouble with gold stars, incentive plans, A's, praise and other bribes*. New York: Houghton Mifflin.

———. 1991. Group grade grubbing vs. cooperative learning. *Educational Leadership*, February, 83–87.

Linek, W. M. 1991. Grading and evaluation techniques for whole language teachers. *Language Arts,* February, 125–132.

MacIver, D. J., and D. A. Reuman. 1993/94. Giving their best—Grading and recognition practices that motivate students to work hard. *American Educator*, Winter, 24–31.

Madgic, R. F. 1988. The point system of grading; A critical appraisal. *NASSP Bulletin*, April, 29–34.

Mahon, R. L. 1996. A grading system for composition papers. *The Clearing House*, May/June, 280–282.

Malehorn, H. 1994. Ten measures better than grading. *The Clearing House*, July/August, 323–324.

Manitoba Education and Training. 1997. Reporting on student progress and achievement. Winnipeg, MB, Canada: Manitoba Ministry of Education and Training.

Manon, J. R. 1995. The mathematics test: A new role for an old friend. *Mathematics Teacher*, February, 138–141.

Marzano, R. 2000a. *Transforming classroom grading*. Alexandria, VA: Association for Supervsion and Curriulum Development.

Marzano, R., and J. S. Kendall. 1996. A comprehensive guide to designing standards-based districts, schools, and classrooms. Aurora, CO.: MidContinent Regional Education Laboratory/Association for Supervision and Curriculum Development.

Matanin, M., and D. Tannehill. 1994. Assessment and grading in physical education. *Journal of Teaching in Physical Education* 13: 395–401.

McColskey, W. and N. McMunn. 2000. Strategies for dealing with high-stakes tests. *Kappan*, October, 115–120

McTighe, J. 1996/97. What happens between assessments. *Educational Leadership*, December/January, 6–12.

McTighe, J., and S. Ferrara. 1995. Assessing learning in the classroom. *Journal of Quality Learning*, December, 11–27.

Mengeling, M. A. 1996. Computer software for classroom assessment. Portland, OR: Assessment Training Institute.

Midwood, D., K. O'Connor, and M. Simpson. 1993. *Assess for success*. Toronto, ON, Canada: Ontario Secondary Teachers Federation.

Millar Grant, J., B. Heffler, and K. Meriwether. 1995. *Student-led conferences*. Markham, ON, Canada: Pembroke.

Munk, D. D., and W. D. Bursuck. 1997/98. Can grades be helpful and fair? *Educational Leadership*, December/January, 44–47.

National Association of Secondary School Principals. 1996. *Breaking ranks: Changing an American institution*. Reston, VA: National Association of Secondary School Principals.

National Council of Teachers of English. 2000. Teacher Talk—How do you handle late work. *Classroom Note Plus*, January, 18–21.

Nemecek, P. M. 1994. Constructing weighted grading systems. *The Clearing House*, July/August, 325–326.

Nottingham, M. 1988. Grading practices—Watching out for land mines. *NASSP Bulletin*, April, 24–28.

O'Connor, K. 1995. Guidelines for grading that support learning and student success. *NASSP Bulletin*, May, 91–101.

Olson, L. 1995. Cards on the table. *Education Week*, June 14.

Ontario Institute for Studies in Education of the University of Toronto. 2000. Classroom assessment issue. *Orbit*, 30:4.

Phillips, S. E. 1997. Standards and grading for disabled students. *National Council on Measurement in Education Quarterly Newsletter*, May, 2.

Pomperaug Regional School District 15. 1996. *A teacher's guide to performance-based learning and assessment*. Alexandria, VA: Association for Supervision and Curriculum Development.

Popham, W. J. 2000. Assessing master of wish-list content standards. *NASSP Bulletin*, December 30–36.

Pratt, D. 1980. *Curriculum design and development*. New York: Harcourt Brace Jovanovich.

Queen's Printer for Ontario. 2002. Achievement card (grades 9–10) and provincial report cards (grades 1–12). Toronto, ON: Ministry of Education.

Reedy, R. 1995. Formative and summative assessment: A possible alternative to the grading-reporting dilemma. *NASSP Bulletin*, October, 47–51.

Reeves. D.B. 2001. Standards make a difference: The influence of standards on classroom assessment. *NASSP Bulletin*, January 5–12.

_____. 2000. Standards are not enough: Essential transformations for school success. *NASSP Bulletin*, December, 5–19.

_____. 1996/8. *Making standards work*. Denver, CO: Center for Performance Assessment.

Regional Educational Laboratories. 1998. *Improving classroom assessment—A toolkit for professional developers—Toolkit 98*. Washington, DC: U.S. Department of Education, Office of Educational Research and Improvement.

Richards, D. M. and J. Martin. 1999. *Understanding and working with the Office of Civil Rights*. Austin, TX.

Robinson, G. E., and J. E. Craver. 1989. *Assessing and grading student achievement*. Arlington, VA: Educational Research Service.

Rogers, S., and S. Graham. 1997. *The high performance toolbox*. Evergreen, Col.: Peak Learning Systems.

Rojewski, J. W., R. R. Pollard, and G. D. Meers. 1991. Grading mainstreamed special needs students: Determining practices and attitudes of secondary vocational educators using a qualitative approach. *Remedial and Special Education*, January/February, 7–15, 28.

Schafer, W. D. 1997. Classroom assessment. In *Handbook of academic learning*, edited by G. D. Phye. San Diego, CA: Academic Press.

Schmoker, M. 2000. Standards versus sentimentality: Reckoning—successfully—with the most promising movement in modern education. *NASSP Bulletin*, December, 49–60.

Seeley, M. 1994. The mismatch between assessment and grading. *Educational Leadership*, October, 4–6.

Selby, D., and S. Murphy. 1992. Graded or degraded: Perceptions of letter grading for mainstreamed learning disabled students. *British Columbia Journal of Special Education* 16(1): 92–104.

Sheeran, T. J. 1994. Measuring and evaluating student learning in cooperative settings: Practices, options and alternatives. *Social Science Record*, Spring, 20–24.

Spady, W. G. 1991. Shifting the grading paradigm that pervades education. *Outcomes*, Spring, 39–45.

———. 1987. On grades, grading and school reform. *Outcomes*, Winter, 7–12.

Sperling, D. 1993. What's worth an "A"? Setting standards together. *Educational Leadership*, February, 73–75.

Spiegel, C. 1991. Grading schemes that reward students. *The Mathematics Teacher*, November, 631.

Stiggins, R. J. 2001a. The principal's role in assessment. *NASSP Bulletin*, January, 13–26.

———. 2001b. *Student-involved classroom assessment*, 3rd ed. Upper Saddle River, NJ: Merrill Prentice Hall.

———. 1999. Assessment, student confidence, and school success. *Kappan*, November, 191–198.

———. 1997. *Student-centered classroom assessment*. 2d ed. Upper Saddle River, NJ: Merrill/Prentice Hall.

Stiggins, R. J., D. A. Frisbie, and P. A. Griswold. 1989. Inside high school grading practices: Building a research agenda. *Educational Measurement: Issues and Practices*, Summer, 5–13.

Stiggins, R. J., and T. Knight. 1997. *But are they really learning?* Portland, OR: Assessment Training Institute.

Stigler and Stevenson. 1991. How Asian educators polish each lesson to perfection. *American Educator*, Spring, 44.

Terwilliger, J. S. 1989. Classroom standard setting and grading practices. *Educational Measurement: Issues and Practices*, Summer, 15–19.

Toronto District School Board. 1995. Assessments. Toronto, ON: Toronto District School Board.

Thayer, J. D. 1991. Use of observed, true and scale variability in combining student scores in grading. Paper presented at the Annual Meeting of the National Council on Measurement on Education, April 4–6, at Chicago, IL.

Travis, J. 1996. Meaningful assessment. *The Clearing House*, May/June, 308–312.

Trumbull, E. and B. Farr, eds. 2000. *Grading and reporting student progress in an age of standards.* Norwood, MA: Christopher Gordon.

Vockell, E. L., and D. Kopenec. 1989. Record keeping without tears: Electronic gradebook programs. *The Clearing House*, April, 355–359.

Whitton, L., and K. Mowrer. 1995. Making the grade: Assessing mainstreamed students in regular classes. *The High School Magazine*, June, 18–20.

Wiggins, G. 1996. Honesty and fairness: Toward better grades and reporting. In *Communicating student learning: The ASCD yearbook 1996*, edited by T. R. Guskey. Arlington, VA: Association for Supervision and Curriculum Development.

Wiggins, G., and J. McTighe. 1998. *Understanding by design*. Alexandria, VA: Association for Supervision and Curriculum Development.

Willis, S. 1993. Are letter grades obsolete? *ASCD Update*, September, 1, 4, 8.

Wright, R. G. 1994. Success for all: The median is the key. *Phi Delta Kappan*, May, 723–725.

ADDITIONAL RESOURCES

Print Resources

Aker, D. 1995. *Hitting the mark: Assessment tools for teachers.* Markham, ON, Canada: Pembroke.

Allison, E., and S. J. Friedman. 1995. Reforming report cards. *The Executive Educator,* January, 38–39.

Arnold, C. B., S. H. Reynolds, C. D. Stellern, D. Bohannon, K. Harmon, L. Hill, C. Mamantov, and S. Reed. 1992. Grading. *The Mathematics Teacher,* September, 442–443.

Arter, J. and K. Busick. 2001. *Practice with student-involved classroom assessment.* Portland, OR: Assessment Training Institute.

Assessment Reform Group. 1999. *Assessment for learning: Beyond the black box.* Cambridge, UK: Cambridge University School of Education.

Azwell, T., and E. Schmar, eds. 1995. *Report card on report cards: Alternatives to consider.* Portsmouth, NH: Heinemann.

Bateman, C. F. 1988. Goldy's coffee. *Phi Delta Kappan,* November, 252–254.

Beckerman, L. 1996. Worth their while. *Executive Educator,* July, 31, 32, 39.

Berliner, D., and U. Casanova. 1998. Are grades undermining motivation? *Instructor,* October, 18–19.

Blackmore, L., and C. Politano. 1992–93. Half a dozen ways to make reporting powerful and painless. *Prime Areas* 35(3): 2.

Blynt, R. A. 1992. The sticking place: Another look at grades and grading. *English Journal,* October, 66–71.

Brandt, R. 1995. Punished by rewards: A conversation with Alfie Kohn. *Educational Leadership,* September, 252–254.

British Columbia Ministry of Education. 1994. *Guidelines for student reporting for the kindergarten to grade 12 education plan.* Victoria, BC, Canada: Province of British Columbia, Ministry of Education.

Buckley, G. 1995. First steps: Redesigning elementary report cards. In *Report card on report cards: Alternatives to consider,* edited by T. Azwell and E. Schmar. Portsmouth, NH: Heinemann.

Bursh, P., and M. Neill. 1996. Principles to guide student assessment. *Thrust for Educational Achievement,* May/June, 16–19.

Bursuck, W., E. A. Polloway, L. Plante, M. H. Epstein, M. Jayanthi, and J. McConeghy. 1996. Report card grading and adaptations: A national survey of classroom practices. *Exceptional Children,* February, 301–318.

Carr, J. F. and D. E. Harris. 2001. *Succeeding with standards: Linking curriculum, assessment and action planning.* Alexandria, VA: Association for Supervision and Curriculum Development.

Cizek, G. J., R. E. Rachor, and S. Fitzgerald. 1995. Further investigation of teachers' assessment practices. Paper presented at the Annual Meeting of the American Educational Research Association, April 18–22 at San Francisco, CA.

Clarridge, P. B., and E. M. Whitaker. 1994. Implementing a new elementary progress report. *Educational Leadership,* October, 7–9.

Collins, C. 1994. Grading practices that increase teacher effectiveness. *The Clearing House,* December, 167–169.

Cordero, P. 1998. Designing and evaluating student work. *Thrust for Educational Leadership,* January, 19–21.

Curren, R. R. 1995. Coercion and the ethics of grading and testing. *Educational Theory*, Fall, 425–449.

Davies, A. 2001. Involving students in communicating about their learning. *NASSP Bulletin*, December, 11–14.

Doran, R., F. Chan, and P. Tamir. 1998. *Science educators' guide to assessment.* Arlington, VA: National Science Teachers Association.

Foundation for Critical Thinking. 1996. *Critical thinking workshop handbook.* Santa Rosa, CA: Foundation for Critical Thinking.

Friedman, S. J., and M. Manley. 1998. Grading teachers' grading policies. *NASSP Bulletin*, April, 77–78.

———. 1992. Improving high school grading practices: "Experts" vs. "practitioners." *NASSP Bulletin*, May, 100–104.

Gaustad, J. 1996. *Assessment and evaluation in the multi-age classroom.* Eugene, OR: Oregon School Study Council.

Gentile, J. R., and N. C. Murnyack. 1989. How shall students be graded in discipline-based art education? *Art Education*, November, 33–41.

Goodrich, H. 1996/97. Understanding rubrics. *Educational Leadership*, December/January, 14–17.

Gregory, K., C. Cameron, and A. Davies. 2000. *Knowing what counts: Self-assessment and goal-setting.* Merville, BC, Canada: Connections Publishing.

Gribbin, A. 1992. Making exceptions when grading and the perils it poses. *Journalism Educator*, Winter, 73–76.

Haley, B. 1988. Does an A really equal learning? *NASSP Bulletin*, April, 35–41.

Herman, J. L., P. R. Aschbacher, and L. Winters. 1992. *A practical guide to alternative assessment.* Alexandria, VA: Association for Supervision and Curriculum Development.

Johnson, B. 1996. *The performance assessment handbook.* Vol. 2, Performances and exhibitions. Princeton, NJ: Eye on Education.

Jones, L. H., Jr. 1995. Recipe for assessment: How Arty cooked his goose while grading art. *Art Education*, March, 12–17.

Jongsmaa, K. S. 1991. Rethinking grading practices. *The Reading Teacher*, December, 318–320.

Juarez, T. 1994. Mastery grading to serve student learning in the middle grades. *Middle School Journal*, September, 37–41.

Kagan, S. 1996. Avoiding the group grades trap. *Learning*, January/February, 56–58.

Kenney, E., and S. Perry. 1994. Talking with parents about performance-based report cards. *Educational Leadership*, October, 24–27.

Kulm, G. 1994. *Mathematics assessment—What works in the classroom.* San Francisco: Jossey-Bass.

Laska, J. A., and T. Juarez, eds. 1992. *Grading and marking in American schools.* Springfield, IL: Charles C. Thomas.

Lawton, V. 1994. Stressed-out students play numbers game. *Toronto Star*, April 23.

Lohman, D. F. 1993. Learning and the nature of educational measurement. *NASSP Bulletin*, October, 41–53.

Loyd, B. H., and D. E. Loyd. 1997. Kindergarten through grade 12 standards: A philosophy of grading. In *Handbook of academic learning, construction of knowledge*, edited by G. D. Phye. San Diego, CA: Academic Press.

Marzano, R.J. 2000b. Introduction to special section. Implementing standards in schools. Updating the standards movement. *NASSP Bulletin*, December. 11–14.

Marzano, R., D. Pickering, and J. McTighe. 1993. *Assessing student outcomes: Performance assessment using the dimensions of learning model.* Alexandria, VA: Association for Supervision and Curriculum Development.

Marzano, R.J., D.J. Pickering, and J.E. Pollock. 2001. *Classroom instruction that works.* Alexandria, VA: Association for Supervision and Curriculum Development.

Mazzarella, D. 1997. When everyone gets an A, grades are meaningless. *USA Today*, March 25.

McMillan, J. H. 2001. Secondary teachers' classroom assessment and grading practices. *Educational Measurement: Issues and Practice*, Spring, 20–32.

Mehring, T., C. Parks, K. Walter, and A. Banikowski. 1991. Report cards: What do they mean during the elementary school years? *Reading Improvement*, Fall, 162–168.

Nava, F. J. G., and B. A. Loyd. 1992. An investigation of achievement and nonachievement criteria in elementary and secondary school grading. Paper presented at the Annual Meeting of the American Educational Research Association, April 20–24, in San Francisco, CA.

Noam, G., moderator. 1996. Assessment at the crossroads: A conversation. *Harvard Educational Review* 66(3): 631–657.

Nott, R. L., C. Reeve, and R. Reeve. 1992. Scoring rubrics: An assessment option. *Science Scope*, March, 44–45.

O'Connor, K. 1996. Grading—Myth, mystery or magic. *Research Speaks to Teachers*, April.

Ohlhausen, M. M., R. R. Powell, and B. S. Reitz. 1994. Parents' views of traditional and alternative report cards. *The School Community Journal*, Spring/Summer, 81–97.

O'Neil, J. 1994. Making assessment meaningful. *ASCD Update*, August, 1, 4, 5.

Ornstein, A. C. 1989. The nature of grading. *The Clearing House*, April, 365–369.

Rogers, E. 1994. Meeting student needs through the levels program and grade weighting. *The Clearing House*, July/August, 327–330.

Ryan, J. M., and J. R. Miyasaka. 1995. Current practices in testing and assessment: What is driving the changes? *NASSP Bulletin*, October, 1–10.

Selleri, P., F. Carugati, and E. Scappini. 1995. What marks should I give? *European Journal of Psychology in Education* 10(1): 25–40.

Shedlin, A., Jr. 1988. How about a national report card month. *Principal*, May, 34.

Sizer, T. 1996. *Horace's hope: What works for the American high school.* New York: Houghton Mifflin.

Stallings-Roberts, V. 1992. Subjective grading. *The Mathematics Teacher*, November, 677–679.

Stiggins, R. J. 1990. *Developing sound grading practices (Classroom Assessment Training).* Portland, OR: Northwest Regional Educational Laboratory.

Thomas, W. C. 1996. Grading—Why are school policies necessary? What are the issues? *NASSP Bulletin*, February, 23–26.

Tomlinson, C. A. 2001. Standards and the art of teaching: Crafting high quality classrooms. *NASSP Bulletin*, February, 38–47

Trotter, A. 1990. What to do if you're worried about how students are graded. *The Executive Educator*, January, 24–25.

Walvoord, B. E. and V. J. Anderson. 1998. *Effective grading*. San Francisco: Jossey Bass.

Wiggins, G. 1994. Toward better report cards. *Educational Leadership*, October, 28–37.

———. 1991. Standards, not standardization: Evoking quality student work. *Educational Leadership*, February, 18–25.

Wilson, L. 1994. What gets graded is what gets valued. *The Mathematics Teacher*, September, 412–414.

Wilson, R. J. 1996. *Assessing students in classrooms and schools*. Scarborough, ON, Canada: Allyn & Bacon.

———. 1994. Back to basics: A revisionist model of classroom-based assessment. Invited Presidential address to the Annual Meeting of the Canadian Educational Researchers Association, June, at Calgary, AB, Canada.

———. 1992. Evaluation of student achievement: Perception vs. reality. *Canadian School Executive*, April, 13–16.

Wood, A. 1994. An unintended impact of one grading practice. *Urban Education*, July, 188–201.

Wright, R. G. 1989. Don't be a mean teacher. *Science Teacher*, January, 38–41.

Zeidner, M. 1992. Key facets of classroom grading: A comparison of teacher and student perspectives. *Contemporary Educational Psychology*, July, 224–243.

Videos

Davies, A., and R. Stiggins. 1996. *Student-involved conferences*. Portland, OR: Assessment Training Institute.

North Central Regional Educational Laboratory. 1991. *Schools that work: The research advantage*, Vol. 4. Oak Brook, IL: North Central Regional Educational Laboratory.

Stiggins, R. 1996a. *Maximizing achievement in paper and pencil assessments*. Portland, OR: Assessment Training Institute.

———. 1996b. *Assessing reasoning in the classroom*. Portland, OR: Assessment Training Institute.

———. 1995. *Creating sound classroom assessments*. Portland, OR: Assessment Training Institute.

Victoria Learning Society. 1992. *Observation: Finding the inner eye*. Victoria, BC, Canada: Victoria Learning Society.

Wiggins, G. 1991. *Standards not standardization*, Vols. 1– 4. Geneseo, NY: Center on Learning, Assessment, and School Structure.

Association for Supervision and Curriculum Development Audiotapes

Guskey, T. R. 1996. *New news on grading, reporting and communicating student learning*. ASCD catalog number 96 3216.

Kohn, A. 1995. *From degrading to de-grading: Basic questions about assessment and learning*. ASCD catalog number 95 128.

Rogers, S. 1992. *Tackling the complex grading issues related to outcomes-based restructuring*. ASCD catalog number 92 6817.

Internet Resources

Note: An annotated list of alternative assessment web sites can be found in "Finding Alternative Assessment Resources on the Web," by P. Butts, *Technology Connection,* December, 1997, 10–13.

Assessment Training Institute
http://www.assessmentinst.com/

ERIC Clearinghouse on Assessment and Evaluation
http://ericae.net/

Kathy Schrock's Guide for Educators
http://www.school.discovery.com/schrockguide/

Michigan Electronic Library
http://mel.lib.mi.us/education/edu-assess.html

Midcontinent Regional Educational Laboratory
http://www.mcrel.org/

National Center for Research on Evaluation, Standards, and Student Testing
http://www.cse.ucla.edu/

National Council on Measurement in Education
http://www.ncme.org

North Central Regional Educational Laboratory
http://www.ncrel.org/

Northwest Regional Educational Laboratory
http://www.nwrel.org/

Office for Civil Rights, US Department of Education
http://www.ed.gov/offices/OCR/

re: Learning by Design (Grant Wiggins)
http://www.relearning.org

South Eastern Regional Vision for Education (SERVE)
http://www.serve.org/

Index

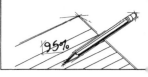

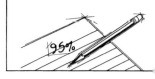

SkyLight Professional Development

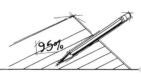